The Irish Drama of Europe
from Yeats to Beckett

The Irish Drama
of Europe
from Yeats to Beckett

KATHARINE WORTH

THE ATHLONE PRESS *of the University of London*
1978

Published by
THE ATHLONE PRESS
UNIVERSITY OF LONDON
at 4 Gower Street London WCI

Distributed by
Tiptree Book Services Ltd
Tiptree, Essex

USA and Canada
Humanities Press Inc
New Jersey

© *Katharine Worth* 1978

British Library Cataloguing in Publication Data
    Worth, Katharine Joyce
        The Irish drama of Europe from Yeats to Beckett.
        1. English drama – Irish authors – History and
        criticism   2. English drama – 20th century –
        History and criticism
        I. Title
        822'.9'1209   PR8789
    ISBN 0 485 11180 2

Printed in Great Britain by
WESTERN PRINTING SERVICES LTD
Bristol

For George

Acknowledgements

My grateful thanks to the Athlone Press for encouraging this book and to the many friends and colleagues who have taken an interest in it, among them especially: the late T. R. Henn; fellow Yeatsians, Barbara Hardy, Joan Grundy, Warwick Gould, Richard Cave; and Dr Lionel Butler, Principal of Royal Holloway College, who has generously supported the student productions on which I have drawn for illustrations. Thanks above all to my husband for his patient help with typing and many details of preparation.

K.W.

Dates of Plays

Where it seemed appropriate to the discussion I have included dates of first production: otherwise dates in brackets after titles refer to publication (except in Chapter 8, where dates of ballets refer to production). Dates of Maeterlinck's plays refer to the original French texts.

For Yeats's plays publication dates are as in *Collected Plays*. For full details of production dates of his plays see:

Jeffares, A. N. and A. S. Knowland, *A Commentary on the Collected Plays of W. B. Yeats*, 1975

Alspach, R. K. (ed.), *Variorum Edition of the Plays of W. B. Yeats*, 1966

Contents

Introduction

This book offers a European perspective on the Irish drama, bringing Yeats, Synge and Beckett, Wilde and O'Casey under the same light with Maeterlinck and, above all, showing how Yeats's evolution of a modern technique of total theatre and his use of it to construct a 'drama of the interior' makes him one of the great masters of twentieth-century theatre.

To appreciate the central role Yeats has in the modern theatre, to capture the right tone for Synge or O'Casey, we need to move away from the narrower perspective implied in the phrase 'The Irish Dramatic Movement' which has prevailed for a long time now, inviting a somewhat misleading approach to this drama. Of course it was the right term at one time. It was natural in 1939 for that most perceptive critic of Irish drama, Una Ellis-Fermor, to call her influential book on the subject *The Irish Dramatic Movement*;[1] but already, when she revised it just before her death in 1954, she was beginning to look further afield and ask tentatively what future there might be for Yeats's theatre. It did not seem too promising, to judge from the state of things at the Abbey Theatre, where realism was still in the ascendant; perhaps 'The Irish Dramatic Movement' might have to be remembered as a glorious bonfire that had burnt itself out, leaving only a very small fire to be coaxed from its embers. Una Ellis-Fermor could not quite bring herself to take that view: even with her sights fixed on the Abbey she thought she detected signs that Yeats's theatre was not in its final phase, that a movement towards imaginative fantasy could be discerned. But the evidence was scanty: she had to conclude, 'It is too early to prophesy whether this will bring back a new poetic movement or whether it represents only the last phase of that which began fifty-four years ago'.

It is a pleasure for me, as her pupil, to be able to confirm her intuition that Yeats's theatre was not only alive but generating new life. The evidence does not come from the Abbey; it seems still to be working through the phase of Ibsen-inspired realism which every theatre in Europe apparently has to experience; even Yeats could not short-circuit that influence, though he did his best. No, the evidence comes

[1] U. Ellis-Fermor, *The Irish Dramatic Movement* (1939, rev. edn. 1954).

from the quarter where Yeats looked from the start, the European theatre centred in Paris. In that very year, 1954, when Una Ellis-Fermor asked herself whether there were not new stirrings of life in the Irish drama, the answer was at hand, for it was then that *Waiting for Godot* first appeared in English,[2] translated by Beckett from the French text which had been performed in Paris the year before; here was the first of that prodigious flood of self-translations in which Beckett seemed to proclaim and glory in the Irish/French nature of his drama. Twenty years later we can see this clearly, see that *Waiting for Godot* is in the same line of country as *At the Hawk's Well* and *The Well of the Saints,* that Beckett's many affinities with his Irish predecessors, especially with Yeats, are growing stronger, if anything, with time. The most recent plays, *Not I, That Time, Footfalls,* are complete Yeatsian 'movements', ghost plays, as Beckett tells us more and more emphatically with every play; in *Footfalls* there is a spectral walking over a narrow strip of the past, and the latest play for television, *Ghost Trio,* calls up Beethoven at *his* most ethereal or ghostly.

In those last twenty years since *Waiting for Godot* first appeared, the entire European theatre has experienced the revolution which Yeats carried through single-handed in Dublin in the first two decades of the century. We have become accustomed to the ideas of Artaud and Grotowski, read Peter Brook on the 'empty space' and followed his explorations in theatre of cruelty, in ritual and improvisation. We have seen the symbolist doctrine of the concrete establish itself, seen the diaphanous imaginings of that arch-prophet, Apollinaire, realised in exquisite patterns of colour, light and sound on the stage of the Aldwych Theatre in one of those World Theatre seasons which have also familiarised us with the techniques of Japanese Nō and much of the important avant garde theatre of Europe. We have become used to a bare, open stage, direct addresses to the audience, invitations to collaborate with the actors. We have seen the ideas of Gordon Craig, long thought of (except by Yeats) as an inspired but ineffectual dreamer, realised in many types of experiment with masks and marionettes, notably Tadeusz Kantor's strange, hypnotic representation of life as a death class, where adult people carry round with them their puppet alter ego. And all the time we see the frontiers of drama and ballet, drama and opera dissolving in works like Lindsay Kemp's

[2] The English version, *Waiting for Godot*, was first published in 1954 in New York. *En attendant Godot* was performed first at the Théâtre de Babylone, Paris, 5 January 1953.

balletic adaptation of Genet, *Flowers*, and the Bond/Henze *We Come to the River*, which the collaborators describe as 'Actions with Music'. Now we can look again at Yeats and see how amazingly he anticipated all that is most original in the European theatre. 'Everyone here is as convinced as I am that I have invented a new form in this mixture of dance, speech and music', he wrote to Olivia Shakespear in 1929;[3] understatement indeed, for his remarkable achievement in conjuring out of nothing the forms the theatre at large would not see for almost fifty years. He grasped with a thoroughness which is astounding in a master of words, that words were not enough for the theatrical task he had set himself, the exploration of the 'interior'. 'A deep of the mind can only be approached through what is most human, most delicate.' It was a paradox to delight his contradictious heart that, to achieve this delicacy, a technique of intense physicality was needed. All the resources of the theatre—scene, colour, music, dance and movement—had to be brought into play: only a synthesis of the arts, supporting and high-lighting the words, drawing attention to their value by allowing spaces between them, stretches of silence, unanswered questions, could hope to render anything like the complexity of the mind's processes, its intuitions and fine shades of feeling, the whole undertow of the stream of consciousness.

Yeats is at the centre of this study, for he is at the centre of the modern movement in the theatre. His modernity was obscured for a time partly because he was so far ahead and partly, no doubt, because his experimental drama was associated for many people with fashionable, upper-class patronage and élitist attitudes. The convention of his dance theatre—musicians improvising in an empty space, under the same light as an audience which is invited to collaborate in constructing the illusion—is just what we think of nowadays as most modern and open, but it was not so easy to see it like that when the plays were performed in places like Lady Cunard's drawing room or Yeats's own in Merrion Square. Even then, however, his dance drama became a source of inspiration for someone as unlike him in almost every respect as Sean O'Casey. O'Casey began by distrusting this 'drawing room' drama and ended by adopting it. And he in his turn edged the Yeatsian theatre a little nearer to the popular domain in his exuberant variations on Yeats's methods, his comically grotesque, farcical, sometimes tragic expressions of the mind's fantasies.

Through O'Casey there runs a line from Yeats to the musical

[3] *The Letters of W. B. Yeats*, ed. A. Wade (1954), p. 768.

drama of John Arden and 'improvising' collaborative works like *Oh What a Lovely War*. The other main line, which leads above all to Beckett also takes in Pinter, a master of the unspoken and a self-confessed disciple of Beckett, who is known also to admire Yeats's dance plays: we could deduce this, indeed, by looking at *The Collection* or *The Homecoming* alongside *The King of the Great Clock Tower*, that play of oblique sexual rituals. It is, then, in a context bounded not by his poetry or speculative thinking but by the modern theatre of Beckett, Peter Brook, Pinter, that I am looking at Yeats's plays, seeing them as a 'drama of the interior' in a mode which is entirely accessible to modern audiences and does not depend on special knowledge either of Yeats's theories or of his Irish material. The audience should know the Irish epics, says the Old Man in *The Death of Cuchulain*, but that is a joke, a joke against the author, for he goes on to say 'and Mr Yeats' plays', a remark which can only be taken as humorous self-parody. Later, anticipating present-day playwrights like Peter Handke, he insults the audience—'If there are more than a hundred I won't be able to escape people who are educating themselves out of the Book Societies and the like, sciolists all, pickpockets and opinionated bitches'—provoking them into disagreeing with him, which must mean resisting his pedantry. The play certainly supports us rather than him, for it is a fine demonstration of how a dramatic illusion can be built up, seemingly out of nothing, be undermined and recover itself, become totally self-standing. My case is that the plays really do work subliminally, as Yeats designed them to, suggesting their meaning through words, but also through music and rhythm, light and scene, drawing us into an experience with the mysterious reality of a dream. Whether they have an Irish setting or some other, the dance plays are, in Yeats's phrase, 'remote, spiritual and ideal'; they take us into a kind of no-place inhabited by figures who are more often than not, anonymous—Old Man, Young Man, Queen, King— archetypal beings, essentially free of period and nationality.

I have not aimed to give a comprehensive account of Yeats's drama nor to keep a chronological course except in the opening chapters where I trace the evolution of his total theatre technique, nor have I attempted a general history of the 'drama of the interior' outside the limits set by Yeats himself. Strindberg, for instance, was not a direct influence in the same way as Maeterlinck, though obviously Strind-bergian elements fused with Maeterlinckian in the development of the European theatre and must surely help to form the background to

Beckett's drama.[4] Any general discussion of the European interior drama would have to include, for instance, Artaud's brilliant interpretation of *The Ghost Sonata*: he planned to emphasise the 'interior' effect by making the house transparent and having the characters converse with their own doubles, some of which would be represented by dummies; the play was to end with the doubles disappearing and the characters shaking themselves as if emerging from a deep sleep; perhaps at the very end, he thought, the audience would see the dummy of an old man on crutches hobbling into the dark. There are clear pointers here to the drama of Beckett, Ionesco and others, but that development is not part of my matter: I have dealt with the French theatre, chiefly the theatre of Maeterlinck, only so far as it affected Yeats, Wilde and Synge in forming their techniques; I have not considered later experiments such as those of Copeau or Artaud, though I have touched on Cocteau in discussing the dissolution of frontiers between dance and the drama which has made the performance of Yeats's plays more of a practical possibility today.

The perspective I am taking on the Irish drama enforces its own emphases. One great Irish playright, Shaw, does not come into the picture. Although he had many points of contact with Yeats and the others—he too was fascinated by the music drama and talked a great deal of the musical principles he followed in writing, and in rehearsing his actors—his true mode, as he said himself, was the rational, rhetorical mode of the eighteenth-century tradition. Lady Gregory too, though so important to Yeats and the Irish theatre, is closer to Shaw's mode than to Yeats's, as one can see by comparing *The Unicorn from the Stars* (which she largely wrote) with Yeats's original version, *Where There is Nothing*. On the other hand an Irishman who is not usually thought of when phrases like 'The Irish Dramatic Movement' are used makes his way in here. Oscar Wilde's *Salomé* was a high peak of the symbolist theatrical movement, an experiment in using musical phrasing and dance to express the movement of soul. 'Soul' was one of Wilde's words, but in this context it belongs above all to the playwright he most admired, Maeterlinck. Maeterlinck's saying, 'The soul has senses as the body has', provided inspiration for the many different playwrights who were attempting to construct a great new theatrical language around 1900. No study of the Irish drama in its

---

[4] For a discussion of this subject, see A. Swerling, *Strindberg's Impact in France, 1920–60* (1971).

European aspects could afford to leave out Maeterlinck, for he was the greatest single force operating on it in its formative period. He had a very direct impact on Yeats, Wilde and Synge; there are striking similarities too between certain of his plays—*The Sightless, Interior*— and Beckett's. This is not a direct influence: at any rate, Beckett has told me he does not know Maeterlinck's plays, except for *Pelléas and Mélisande*: the likenesses between his drama and Maeterlinck's are, rather, I believe, a sign that a 'modern' tradition has established itself so that it becomes natural—even for so great an original as Beckett— to write in a style that proclaims without conscious intention flashes of a family resemblance. The family look stems from a fruitful marrying of Irish and French. All the Irish playwrights I am considering, with the single exception of O'Casey (who looks more to the German expressionists and their American heir, O'Neill), fed their imagination from Paris as well as Dublin. There is remarkable consistency in this history, beginning with Yeats's attachment to Paris in the days when Maud Gonne lived there and Arthur Symons, that important catalyst, was introducing him to Mallarmé and other symbolists and to theatrical experiments like *Axel* and *Ubu Roi*. Synge was even more attached to Paris, according to Yeats's vivid account of how he had to prise him away from that city and his 'decadent' subjects of study, to send him to Aran. He certainly spoke better French than Yeats, was indeed bilingual, and never lost his feeling for French themes and style: Maeterlinck remained one of his most admired playwrights. As for Wilde, he was in a way more at home in Paris than in London; *Salomé* was written in French and had, as it turned out, its first production in Paris. And now, most strangely, the web is drawn together by Beckett whom it is hard to place as either Irish or French, so totally bilingual has he made himself.

Yeats's intellectual relationship with Wilde and Maeterlinck was an important one. I spend some time on it, and on the connection between Synge and Maeterlinck, because it is part of the movement from his earlier drama, where the 'interior' is represented as a dreamlike, unselfconscious process, to the mature plays where he found a technique for including self-conscious perspectives, usually ironic. At that stage, we might say, the drama of the interior became fully modern, and indeed 'modernist' might then begin to seem an appropriate term for it. There are already hints of that more complex configuration in the drama of Maeterlinck and in *Salomé*. *Interior* is particularly suggestive, with its intricate arrangement of the stage as a distant but brightly lit interior into which unseen onlookers are gazing; an impression of possibly infinite recession develops; the child sleeping in the room is unaware that he is being watched by the father, who is unaware that he is being watched by the spectators in the garden, who begin to experience an uneasy sensation; 'We too are watched'. The line heralds the Beckettian drama of self-consciousness as clearly as, in its different way, the invocation that opens *At the Hawk's Well*: 'I call to the eye of the mind'. Yeats, however, went far beyond Maeterlinck and Wilde, though he drew from them both, as he did also from Synge, who gave him a very useful demonstration that the Maeterlinckian technique of melancholy stillness and passivity could be infused with Irish energy and humour. Synge was in a way the most complete Maeterlinckian of them all; indeed it was partly for its Maeterlinckian aspects, the 'stilling and slowing which turns the imagination in upon itself', that Yeats so admired *The Well of the Saints,* and that play has Maeterlinck's *The Sightless* obviously in its background. So it was particularly encouraging that Synge could bring into a dream-laden context the irreverent Rabelaisian humour that puts such a sardonic perspective on the dreaming and in doing so asserts more strongly than ever the power of dreams, for they take their way in the teeth of the realism; Widow Quin's scepticism cannot hold back Christy's metamorphosis into the Playboy.

The theatricality is so flamboyant in Synge's drama, the language so strange, so much an artefact, that his characters often seem well on the way to being as conscious as Beckett's of what they are doing in their fantastic improvisations. But the endless story-telling which is their method of projecting images of themselves does not quite cross the borderline of self-consciousness any more than the action crosses the border of the proscenium stage. Synge never broke away from that convention, nor, for all his scenic experiment, did O'Casey: it seems a measure of their special interest in the unselfconscious kind of fantasising that they should always have left their characters fixed in a frame, never allowed them the extra self-awareness that gets into the play when the actors show they know that they are actors. Yeats did take that step, with the aid of great visionaries like Gordon Craig whose screens and masks helped him to achieve some peculiarly modern distancing effects.

That is the process I trace in the second of two chapters on the evolution of Yeats's theatrical syntax. In the first, which deals with the earlier phase of that evolution, Arthur Symons and Maeterlinck are crucial figures; Symons as the most perceptive of guides to the European movement in the arts, Maeterlinck as a pioneer who offered Yeats suggestive models for an interior drama. Maeterlinck also has a chapter to himself in which I attempt to give a rather fuller picture of his drama, since it cannot be assumed that English-speaking audiences or readers will be familiar with it nowadays; a sad state of affairs which I hope will soon be remedied as new translations begin to appear and the lead given by the BBC with their radio production of *The Death of Tintagiles* in 1975 is followed up. Wilde then comes into the discussion with *Salomé*, a play I examine as an important oeuvre in the symbolist theatrical movement and in its curious and interesting relationship to Yeats's *A Full Moon in March*. After looking at Yeats's complex responses to Maeterlinck and Synge, I then focus more closely on a number of his plays (all dance plays except for *Purgatory*), trying to bring out how flexible was the form he evolved to explore the 'deep of the mind', how intricate mental processes are shown in terms of the 'improvising' convention, with movements of feeling and imagination represented as a collaboration among performers each of whom knows only a part of the play though all move through their scenes as if they know from the start what the end must be. In the chapter, 'The Vitality of the Yeatsian Theatre', I have sketched in features of today's theatre which suggest that the time is now most favourable for Yeats's plays to achieve recognition in performance and indicated, in a brief outline, the share taken by playwrights in changing the climate within the English theatre; Eliot and Pinter are here the leading names. I have looked at some of the difficulties involved in producing the plays and at the prospects that seem to be opening up as more companies, semi-professional and amateur, show interest, and the opportunities offered them by television are increasingly explored. I close with a discussion of the two great inheritors of this Irish/French legacy, Sean O'Casey and Beckett. For O'Casey as for Yeats, the time now seems opportune. The growing interest of actors and directors in a drama that uses dance and music, farce and music hall, should be favourable to him; so too, the new styles of staging; the stage in the Olivier Theatre of the National Theatre, with its great revolving disc and immensely sophisticated lighting equipment might have been designed for the purpose of showing O'Casey as he should be shown, while the Cottesloe Theatre, it may be hoped, with its studio intimacy will be the right place for Yeats's dance plays. No such plea has to be made for Beckett, who has amazingly broken through the barrier which has in the past separated Yeats and the late O'Casey from popular audiences. With him, modernism clearly arrives in the theatre; all the elements scattered through the plays of his predecessors seem to coalesce in his drama: it is a natural resting place and conclusion for my study.

In the course of discussing this drama I shall hope to bring out the characteristics that make it not only strikingly original but also accessible, humanly sympathetic and appealing. The words need to be defended, I imagine, when used of Yeats or Maeterlinck and cannot be taken for granted of O'Casey, Beckett and Synge; their plays too have often been thought difficult, O'Casey's late plays so much so that they have hardly had a showing in the English theatre and we seldom see anything of Synge other than *The Playboy of the Western World*.

Among these characteristics two above all stand out for me. First, there is the adventurousness that has opened up the stage for subjects which might have been thought intractable to dramatisation; the simple subjects that are also the most difficult; the experiences of solitude; remembering and dreaming, dying, being born, looking into one's own dark, growing old. Maeterlinck's vision of a static theatre, built round some unremarkable figure, 'an old man, seated in his armchair, waiting patiently, with his lamp beside him', has been realised in an astounding diversity of forms in the period between his own *The Intruder*—where the old man sitting in the lamplight is at the centre of the play—and Beckett's *That Time*, where there is nothing at all but an old man's face in the dark, drawing laborious breath and listening to his own voice telling of times past. The stage of the Irish/European theatre fills up with a set of characters such as the theatre had not starred before; unheroic, unglamorous, often grotesquely so; Maeterlinck's twelve blind people lost in the ancient forest; Synge's ugly, blind, inventive tramps, O'Casey's limping down and outs; a great host of the blind and the maimed, sometimes mysteriously yoked together like Yeats's Blind and Lame Beggars in *The Cat and the Moon* or Hamm and Clov in *Endgame*. The company includes many strange old men; the wise grandfathers, who helplessly try to protect the young souls on Maeterlinck's stage and, the more violent old men of Yeats in their imperious masks, who are so irresistibly drawn to their youthful opposites. Old women too play their part on Beckett's universal stage; he gives us a 'bevy of old ones' to borrow a phrase from the old man in *That Time*; the wry, affectionate, gently self-mocking tone is typical of the human feeling Beckett and, in their different ways, the others, manage to diffuse in the solitary, remote regions they so audaciously penetrate.

And then there is the other audacity, the wholehearted commitment to the methods of total theatre which means that often the plays can hardly be 'read' from the page: it is peculiarly difficult, after all, to imagine the dramatic effect of music that cannot be heard, a dance or a scenic effect that cannot be seen. There are obvious hazards in the technique—as the long undervaluing of Yeats's plays when they were not being seen, reminds us—but great virtues too. These concrete plays lure us towards the concrete experience, turn us into producers or performers; so I found myself producing Beckett's radio plays in order to hear sounds and music, *Eh Joe* to see the silent face, *Salomé* and *A Full Moon in March* to find out about the two related and yet so dissimilar dances and *The Death of Tintagiles* to see the great door that shuts off Tintagiles from the living and hear the music as Ygraine goes down the labyrinthine corridors in the dark castle which is Maeterlinck's house of life. It is in their capacity to excite us in this way, make us realise the inadequacies of the written text and long for the concrete experience that the vitality of the Irish/European theatre proves itself. It seems to me that this excitement is becoming more widespread and that we should before long have more chances of seeing the plays in performance in a theatre which owes so much to the inspiration of this Irish/European drama.

This is a book about the pushing out of frontiers—frontiers of the drama and of the 'interior'—a process which took Ireland into Europe long before the term EEC had been heard. I first glimpsed the theme when I saw the production of Beckett's *Play* at the National Theatre in 1964, in a double bill with Sophocles's *Philoctetes* and was struck by the likeness of *Play* to Yeats's *Purgatory*—remembered too how Maeterlinck had taken *Philoctetes* as his great classical illustration of 'static drama'. Shortly after, I was invited by T. R. Henn to lecture to the Yeats International Summer School at Sligo on the topic, which I had by then begun to explore in print. It was very pleasing to me and seemed most fitting that my first lecture on Yeats as a European playwright should have been given in Sligo, his home which is also Europe's most westerly region, its furthest reach into world space. It is also fitting, I believe, to be writing as I do, out of the context of the English theatre, for it was always a tale of three cities—Dublin, Paris and London. And now it is a tale of Europe.

1 ⌖ Towards Modernism: a New Theatrical Syntax

Yeats's desire for a theatre of all the arts went very deep: it was an expression of his belief in the essential unity of being—'The arts are but one Art'[1]—and of his need to explore, illustrate and know his own depths by acting them out to the full. 'To the full' meant going as far away from the conscious self as it was possible to get. The furthest down, or the furthest out; for Yeats the two things were one, as they were for some of those who were most important as models or stimuli for his drama in its early stages, Maeterlinck and Arthur Symons chief among them.

For them all going down into the deep of the mind meant also reaching out, making contact with the mystery of the universe, galvanising into active life the part of the mind that dreams and is passive and has intuitive knowledge the conscious mind is blind to. Their mystical approach was shared by many of the most original practitioners of theatre arts around the turn of the century, when the Yeatsian drama was taking shape. Isadora Duncan dreamed of rebuilding the temple of Paestum to train young dancers as priestesses of a new religion; when she listened to music in preparing a dance, she felt its vibrations, she said, in some spiritual centre where the vision of the dance was forming. Gordon Craig, who would not have described himself as a mystic, still wrote of his ideal theatre of light and movement in a visionary's terms: of his open air theatre in Florence he said, 'if to experience beauty and not merely to *see* it is Mysticism, then this place can be called the most mystic of places'.[2] His phrase, 'theatre of revelation', has an obvious appropriateness to the drama of Maeterlinck and Yeats.

The nourishing source of the Yeatsian revolution was the symbolist movement which, in the years around 1900, was producing some fascinating practical demonstrations of its exponents' ruling ideas: performers were testing Rimbaud's dream of a language 'of the soul, for the soul, containing everything, smells, sounds, colours'; Pater's

---

[1] 'The Theatre' in *Essays and Introductions* (1961), p. 167.
[2] Letter to Jacques Doucet in Denis Bablet's *Edward Gordon Craig* (1966, English translation by D. Woodward), p. 168.

dictum that all art aspires towards the condition of music; the Nietzschean concept of Dionysiac unity 'wherein actor becomes transformed into dancer, dancer into musician, musician into lyric poet'. Georgette Leblanc, Maeterlinck's 'incomparable' Mélisande, was reciting, or as Arthur Symons saw it, 'acting' poems of Mallarmé and Maeterlinck to the music of Fauré: 'miming and singing the part of a music statue' was how Mallarmé described her unique performance. Sarah Bernhardt was inspiring the symbolist painters, Moreau and Mucha among them, and feeding back to them the stage images— Salomé, La Princesse Lointaine—they had helped her to create. Reverberations were even reaching London, partly through the American, Isadora Duncan, who in 1900 was illustrating lectures on the relation of dancing to painting by dancing Mendelssohn's *Welcome to Spring* in a costume copied from Botticelli's *Primavera*.

And by 1900 two plays had been performed which projected the symbolist drive towards concreteness and a synthesis of the arts into the centre of the European theatre. Wilde's *Salomé* (1893) used dance, Maeterlinck's *Pelléas and Mélisande* (1892) visual and musical effects, to give the frontiers of drama a spectacular extension. Wilde's Salomé, dancing out her complex passion on stage, was the embodiment of an icon dear to the symbolist painters, their glamorous belle dame sans merci, realised in the thicker texture of a human drama built round the interestingly unglamorous, self-aware and self-deprecating Herod.

And *Pelléas and Mélisande* was still more nearly a realisation of the symbolists' dream. Even in its pre-Debussy form 'musical' was the word that came naturally to its admirers. Early critics pointed out that the dialogue was built on musical principles with recurring motifs and intricate patterns of words, pauses and silences. This startlingly original dialogue opened up for responsive critics like Symons and Desmond MacCarthy the sense of a great hinterland of unexpressed thought and feeling behind the little that was expressed with such pain, hesitation and difficulty. Symons could rightly claim it as the fruition of symbolist longings: Maeterlinck's art had 'come nearer than any other art to being the voice of silence'.

Here is the beginning of the theatre's move into symbolist territory, a most unlikely move on the face of it, when one thinks of the emphasis in symbolist literature on everything that is secret and hidden; Yeats's 'half lights', Verlaine's 'rien que la nuance'. 'Secret' is a favourite word with Maeterlinck, with Yeats, with Symons, who is fascinated by that aspect of Maeterlinck's art: 'The secret of things which is just beyond the most subtle words, the secret of the expressive silences, has always been clearer to Maeterlinck than to most people'.[3] Both Maeterlinck and Yeats were deeply involved with the occult and worshipped at the feet of Villiers de l'Isle Adam, that most esoteric and élitist of playwrights.

How was such an exotic bloom to survive transplanting to the rough and ready soil of the theatre? Yeats's determination to find out set him on the road that led in the end to a modernist drama: in its Beckettian forms, which so clearly derive from his, it has proved remarkably open and accessible to all kinds of audiences. Whatever Yeats might say from time to time about his wish for an audience of the élite, in practice he laid his plays before very mixed audiences and learnt from the experience, especially perhaps from the knocks, hazards and irritations. It was his ability to learn in such ways, to acquire an ironic perspective on his characters and build the perspective into his drama that gives his later plays their modern look. The search for concreteness, which began in a symbolist inspiration, took him far into the theatrical process of collaboration and improvisation; and from that came a realisation of how the process itself could figure in a drama of complex self-consciousness. In the end he is playing with the stage illusion, breaking and remaking it, with a masterful ease which relates him to Brecht as well as to Beckett.

Yeats was temperamentally disposed to roam freely among the arts: it came naturally to him to register a mood or feeling in terms of painting, say, or music. He described the impact Maud Gonne made on him when they first met as 'the middle of the tint, the sound of a Burmese gong, an overpowering tumult that had yet many pleasant secondary notes'. With charming unexpectedness, the sight of Oxford colleges inspired thoughts of opera; they were places where you might expect to find people singing instead of speaking. And always, under these impressions and reactions, there was the binding philosophy, 'The arts are but one Art'.

The strength of these natural drives and his talent for translating them into action made him the one person of his time able to move the English-speaking theatre away from its not-so-long established tradition of realism, which he detested so much. He was the great iconoclast, and yet he was also of all poets the one who most craved an ancient tradition to work in; a piquant tension, here, which no doubt helps to account for the astonishing energy of his move to a

[3] *The Symbolist Movement in Literature* (1899), p. 153.

new 'tradition' and his speedy assimilation of elements from so many scattered sources, ancient and modern; Greek tragedy, Japanese Nō, symbolist explorations in the concrete, Maeterlinck. . .

From these heterogeneous materials came a unified technique for the modern theatre. It is the European elements in it I want to examine in this and the following chapter, trying to bring out in the process how central Yeats was in the experimental movement, how he drew in the early stages from the French avant garde and from Maeterlinck, especially through his connection with Arthur Symons, then received from Gordon Craig an inspiration which launched him beyond the French experiment till he arrived in the end at a technique of total theatre which not only begot the dance plays but had a liberating effect on his technique generally and has been a crucial influence on playwrights as diverse as Beckett, Eliot, O'Casey.

His feeling for the concrete arts of the theatre was apparent in his earliest plays: long before he had the artists to carry through his ideas, he could imagine startling and evocative stage uses of sound, visual effects, music and dance. That most Nietzschean of his plays in theme, *Where There is Nothing* (1902), is Nietzschean too in the intermittently violent physicality of its technique. Never was there a stranger dance than the dance of the friars in the fourth act when the Zarathustra-like hero is lying in a trance and in the dim light of the monastery crypt the figures of the silent, dancing friars are just discernible. The lack of preparation for the scene—it opens abruptly after a break of several years in the action—and its total silence create an unsettling effect highly appropriate to the rapt state of the dreamer and the alarming impact he has on other minds. He returns to consciousness possessed by a sense of revelation: '[God] will make of my silence a great wind that will shatter the ships of the world'. It was a difficult thing, Yeats knew, to get the force of that silence into the play, especially as Paul Ruttledge, the visionary, is a man much given to rhetoric; in the earlier version of the play, said Yeats, he was far too opinionated and inclined to 'ram his ideas down people's throats'. The corrective for this volubility lay in the silent dance and the extraordinary ritual which follows when, to the sound of the friars' psalm-singing, Paul blows out the candles one by one, a concrete demonstration of his abstract thought, 'We must put out the Laws as I put out this candle'. It is easy to see why Gordon Craig was attracted to this play, tantalising to think that he so nearly designed for it, as Yeats told John Quinn, apropos Granville Barker's production with the

Stage Society (Royal Court, 26–28 June 1904) in which Edith Craig
played Sabina Silver: 'And now Gordon Craig, her brother, wants to
produce it with elaborate scenery instead of the Maeterlinck which
they had asked him to do.'[4]

In another early play, *The Land of Heart's Desire* (1894), a dance
was again important. Characteristically, Yeats responded to an external
pressure—Florence Farr's request to him to provide a part for her nine
year old niece, Dorothy Paget—by turning what was uncomfortable
in the situation ('for I knew nothing of children', he groaned) to
subtle advantage. The child becomes the Child, a being set apart
precisely by the qualities that might mark a young dancer, childishness
and self-possessed virtuosity; in the stage character they are mixed and
exaggerated to the point where they become uncanny. The Child is so
poignantly 'young and like a bird' that she can charm everyone on the
stage into indulging her; even the priest lets himself be blandished into
taking down the crucifix, so making all vulnerable to her spell. She
has to work this spell by her dance, a severe test for a young dancer;
here again, Yeats can be seen at his most practical, doing his best to
help her make the dance seem, not just a pretty performance, but the
art of a 'mighty spirit' by inviting the audience to hear what the stage
audience think they hear: 'Other small steps beating upon the floor, /
And a faint music blowing in the wind, / Invisible pipes giving her
feet the tune'. Some obvious opportunities here for subtle musical
effects, but even without actual music the lines create an atmosphere
helpful to the dancer, making it easier for us to believe her when she
declares triumphantly that whatever part of the stage she has danced
on has become her sphere of influence, so that priest and family are
helpless to prevent her from luring the young wife away from her safe
domesticity into the mysterious region outside the door 'Where
nobody gets old and crafty and wise'.

The same feeling for the physical potentialities of theatre comes
through in that earliest play of all, *The Shadowy Waters* (Acting
version 1911), the piece Yeats began as a boy and remained obsessed
by for years, constantly revising after seeing it in performance.[5]
Despite all that re-writing, *The Shadowy Waters* has commonly been

---

[4] Extract from letter to John Quinn quoted in the *Variorum edition of the
Plays of W. B. Yeats*, ed. R. K. Alspach (New York 1966), pp. 1166–7.

[5] See the transcription of the Mss and a comprehensive account of the rewriting
in M. J. Sidnell, G. P. Mayhew and D. R. Clark eds., *Druid Craft: The Writing
of The Shadowy Waters* (1972).

thought of as a not very theatrical piece, closer to dramatic poem than full-blown play. Yeats himself worried about the effect its publication might have on his reputation as a practical man of the theatre and actually told Frank Fay in 1904 that he had abandoned that particular dramatic style: it was too remote and impersonal, and might well be the worst possible for the Abbey at that stage of the theatre's existence (*Letters*, pp. 424–6). The play has some dramatic affinities which are unlikely to allay any doubts one might have about its theatrical practicability. As has often been observed, it is so very close to Villiers de l'Isle Adam's *Axel* (1890), that fascinatingly unplayable piece, five hours long and heavy with its occult symbolism, which Yeats saw in Paris in 1894 and read painfully in French as a 'sacred' book.

Actors playing the lovers in these two pieces might well think it a hard task to win belief for their strange characters; Axel and Sara committing suicide in an intensity of unconsummated passion, because ordinary living is beneath them; Forgael and Dectora, expressing the discovery of their love for each other by cutting the cable that binds them to 'real' life and drifting off into the unknown on an unmanned ship piloted only by sea birds. Some of the romantic detail *The Shadowy Waters* has in common with *Axel* would not make their task easier; all that languorous play of the heroines with their abundant pre-Raphaelite hair, for instance; Sara tempting Axel—'Cover yourself with my hair and inhale the ghosts of perished roses'—Dectora voluptuously enfolding Forgael—'Bend lower, that I may cover you with my hair, / For we will gaze upon this world no longer'.

It might seem unfair to look at such aggressively romantic material from a naturalistic angle, but that is just what the plays in a way encourage us to do. There is quite a solid context of 'real life' in *The Shadowy Waters* and Yeats in fact worked hard at increasing the solidity, especially in the characterisation of the sailors: he told Quinn, in 1905, that he had at last got them 'rough as sailors should be . . . I am now correcting the last few lines, and have very joyfully got "creaking shoes" and "liquorice-root" into what had been a very abstract passage'. So we have real sailors carrying off a real woman from a ship passing by in a real ocean to bring her on to Forgael's ship of dreams. An uneasy mixture, even if Yeats was right in thinking that he had managed to increase the realism without losing the lyrical moments. In a letter of 1905 to Florence Farr, however, he implied that the effort was hardly worth while: 'The play as it was came into existence after years of strained emotion, of living upon tip-toe, and is only right in its highest moments—the logic and circumstances are all wrong' (*Letters*, p. 454). This is surely it. A play of high moments, a play calling not for more realism, but less, a play that needs to become more wholeheartedly what Yeats had in his mind when he wrote to Fay: 'It is almost religious, it is more a ritual than a human story. It is deliberately without human characters' (*Letters*, p. 425).

There is evidence in the play itself and in the many comments Yeats made on it over the years that the shadowy form taking shape in his mind was the dramatic form of the future, the musical dance form that he finally evolved in *At the Hawk's Well* (1917). There were good reasons why he could not carry through such a major experiment in 1904. As his comments to Frank Fay on *The Shadowy Waters* imply, the Abbey had not the facilities nor the expertise to give him the unusual effects he was after. The well-known tale of the harp that wouldn't blaze to order is a particularly comic illustration, but all those great plans for marvellous scenic effects, 'burning jewels on the harp and twinkling stars in the sky', did, as Yeats said they would, fade and dwindle as the night of the performance drew near. It was true too that he needed to move away for a time from lyric and practise collo-quial forms, as he attempted to do in the sailors' dialogue.

But even in abandoning it, he defended the method of *The Shadowy Waters* in a way that interestingly brings out its seminal quality. It was, after all, he said to Fay, in the same letter, a 'legitimate' art; and then, referring to the stage scene: 'The whole picture as it were moves together—sky and sea and cloud are as it were actors'. This is promis-ing, though obviously difficult in the context of the Abbey Theatre in 1904. More promising, and more difficult—so much so that it remained abortive—was the precipitating vision of the play, the vision of the birds, as Yeats described it in his autobiography. It had come to him, he said, as a boy at Sligo, rising early and going down to the sea to find what birds stirred before dawn: 'I had wanted the birds' cries for the poem that became fifteen years afterwards *The Shadowy Waters*'.[6]

Those real birds turned into the supernatural creatures that circle round the masthead of Forgael's ship. They should have been, like the sea and the cloud, more completely 'actors' in the piece than Yeats could contrive at the time. How far he would have liked to go is suggested in his casual remark to Lady Gregory, which understandably baffled her, that half the characters in his new play had eagle faces.

[6] *Autobiographies* (1955), pp. 73–4.

The Hawk Woman of *At the Hawk's Well* comes a little nearer with that saying, can be sensed waiting in the wings, not yet able to enter the scene. The birds of *The Shadowy Waters*, as it turned out, had no such dynamic presence; they are only there when spoken of, so there has to be a great deal of talk about them, some of it rather unconvincing, like the sailors' lurid account at the opening—which really calls for musical accompaniment in operatic style—of the spirits they have seen rising from floating corpses and turning into birds with human faces.

More introspectively and persuasively, Forgael broods on the birds. They are his obsession, from his opening line, 'Have the birds passed us?', to the ending when he refuses the chance of ordinary love with Dectora in 'some sure country, some familiar place' in order to pursue the transcendent experience the spirit birds could lead him to, the dream country 'Where no child's born but to outlive the moon'. The poetry is winning, but the amount of clear-cut exposition Forgael is forced into makes it hard for us to get the sense of a man possessed by apprehensions of a world so alien to ordinary, everyday living that it can hardly be put into words. It is harder still to get close to that experience, understand something of its fascination, when the mystical birds have no voice. No masked being here, as in the later plays to express a hidden world by dancing to the hypnotic sound of drum, gong and flute. The supernatural beings of *The Shadowy Waters* remain frustratingly off-stage presences. However passionately Forgael questions them, as in the long monologue—'Why do you linger? / Why do you not run to your desire, / Now that you have happy winged bodies?'—he always has to answer himself, tell himself they cannot hear, 'Being too busy in the air, and the high air'.

The effect is to make him seem helpless and distracted; in the curious scene of Dectora's first appearance it may even begin to look as if the play is a study in delusion or madness, his reaction to her is so wild and odd:

> You are not the world's core. O no, no, no!
> That cannot be the meaning of the birds.
> You are not its core . . .
> I'd set my hopes on one that had no shadow:—
> Where do you come from? Who brought you to this place?
> Why do you cast a shadow? Answer me that.

Yeats was especially pleased with this scene: 'I have done a good bit where he sees her shadow and finds that she is mortal', he wrote to Florence Farr while he was revising the play in 1905. If the visual effect worked as well on the stage as in his imagination, the sense of a mind losing control, perhaps breaking down, must have been accentuated. And Yeats was certainly interested in the shadowy region between poetic vision and madness, as *The Words upon the Window Pane* (1934) and *Purgatory* (1939) demonstrate. He only glances that way in *The Shadowy Waters* however: Forgael at one point insists to Dectora, 'queen, I am not mad', but the emphasis in this play is on the reality of the poet's vision, above all on the extraordinary power it has to move and change the feelings of others. Yeats sets himself the difficult task of persuading us on our pulses that Forgael's vision is real and that in making love to Dectora, he is not abandoning it: still, through the woman of flesh and blood, he is pursuing the shadowless, unearthly beauty the birds have promised. She is not the world's core, but she is his way into it, and through the intensity of their love scene, Yeats aims to make it our way in too.

At this point notes begin to sound that were mute for the birds. The play moves into a musical mode: Forgael's harp becomes the instrument which is to convince us of his power. When he touches the strings, all the characters on the stage are drawn into his dream. Time, place and painful reality are blotted out: the brutal off-stage event, the killing of Dectora's husband at her feet, recedes into legend; the dead husband merges and is lost in the image of a mythical being conjured up by the music, and that image in its turn creates new reality, and it seems to her as if she has had no lover but Forgael. The spell of what Yeats called his 'fine sleep verses' is so strong that it survives his conscience-stricken attempt to allow her a real choice by reminding her of reality. In her turn she makes a faint move to draw him back to the ordinary world but when Forgael is adamant, she goes with him into the dream that has swallowed hers—'We two—this crown— / I half remember—It has been in my dreams'—and as she embraces him at the end and he gathers her hair around him, the harp comes alive and burns 'as with fire'.

Before we can assess the effectiveness of this strange transformation scene, we need to hear how the music would sound. Yeats has got us into the position he deliberately sought as a playwright; words have become only one of the applied arts; the play is a synthesis which can hardly be understood, still less judged, until it is heard and seen in the theatre. There are strong echoes in *The Shadowy Waters*, if we are alert to its musical element, of that most famous love scene in music drama, Act One of *Tristan and Isolde*. In his more attenuated and muted style, Yeats relies as much as Wagner on the power of music to suggest the transcendental nature of the sudden irrational passion that seizes the only half-willing lovers. The harp music is his love philtre. The situations in play and opera are strikingly similar: lovers isolated on a ship drifting to an unknown future, the woman drawn by enchantment away from her husband, accepting the idea of death as ecstasy in a lyrical Liebestod. More peripheral likenesses abound; in the play, Forgael is responsible for the killing of Dectora's husband; in the opera, Tristan is said to have killed Isolde's betrothed and then come to her castle in the disguise of a harper. There is even a sailors' chorus in each piece: Act One of *Tristan* ends with the sailors singing their relief at returning to land; in the play Forgael's wooing of Dectora is accompanied by far-off strains from the sailors on the other ship.

And though it does not touch *The Shadowy Waters* at quite so many places, *The Flying Dutchman* is not far off either: again a ghostly ship and a lover who draws a woman out of the ordinary world to a 'death' in the sea which is an achievement of ecstasy. Senta and the Dutchman are yet more strangely separated from mundane life; their fated passion is expressed in a musical mode defiantly proclaimed in haunting leit motifs which the other characters cannot get access to. Attempts to establish a more familiar language (opera buffa and so on) are swept away by the lovers' swelling strains, as the jovial earthy sailors' chorus at the end is obliterated by the uncanny parody echo from the enchanted ship.

Wagner was very much in Yeats's mind during the re-writing of *The Shadowy Waters*, certainly in 1903, when he was working out the stage scene for a new production. To Sturge Moore, who was designing the décor, he suggested that the costumes should be in 'Wagner's period more or less'. And in a letter of a few months later to Arthur Symons he spoke of the help he had received in the arduous revision of the play from Symons's recently published essay, 'The ideas of Richard Wagner', saying that it had brought to his mind Wagner's advice on concreteness, above all his suggestion that a play must appeal directly to the emotions as a 'piece of self consistent life' (*Letters*, p. 460).

The force of that advice was clearly registered in the revisions of *The Shadowy Waters*, which, as S. B. Bushrui says,[7] in their move

[7] S. B. Bushrui, *Yeats's Verse-Plays: the Revisions 1900–1910* (1965), p. 28.

towards greater simplicity and concreteness bring out sharply Yeats's 'hostility to disembodied emotion'. Intention is one thing, however, dramatic effect another. How well did that concreteness work? Accounts of the play in performance often draw attention to imperfections, and Yeats had his own disappointments, as we have noticed. But he often records his pleasure too, as in his comment on Robert Gregory's colour scheme which made the players like people in a dream.

The sense of being in a dream is what the play should give us, a dream that lifts us above ordinary life and yet grows out of it, for the idea of sexual love lasting for ever in some 'mysterious transformation of the flesh' must surely be a common as well as a strange vision. Forgael and Dectora, Yeats says, are 'an embodiment of every lover's dream'. No doubt about this in *Tristan and Isolde*; we must all want to drink the love philtre when those lovers sing. A few ripples on harp or psaltery can hardly give us that kind of intoxication, nor do Yeats's characters sing, though already in *The Shadowy Waters* there are indications in Dectora's dreamy, chanted cadences of that interest in song-speech which possessed him all his life. It was not a Wagnerian type of music drama he was aiming at, however. He drew from Wagner, like a wonderfully selective magpie, only so much. The model was important for several reasons: he thought poets acquired power and virtue from working in an ancient tradition, and Symons in his essay on Wagner had drawn attention to the antiquity of music drama; behind Wagner, Nietzsche, and his call to the modern theatre to revive the classical tradition of a dancing and singing chorus in a new burst of Dionysiac energy. Also Yeats liked demonstrations that things worked, even though what he took over he always made work differently.

So Wagner was important for that kind of support and stimulus; in other ways he was not persona grata. Like Maeterlinck and Mallarmé (who thought Wagner had only half achieved the symbolist's dream, climbed 'halfway up the holy mountain'), Yeats disliked conventional opera: it was the apotheosis of that noisy exteriority they were all trying to escape from, the 'bondage of rhetoric and the bondage of exteriority', in Symons's phrase. They were haunted by the idea of a new synthesis of music and words which meant remaking opera in a form nearer to their common dream of a delicate, infinitely suggestive art of the interior.

That dream had already found a stage incarnation. The year before Yeats wrote to Symons about his Wagnerian essay Paris had seen the first performance of the Debussy/Maeterlinck *Pelléas and Mélisande*. Debussy/Maeterlinck: the difficulty of knowing how to separate the names is a measure of the marvellous fusion achieved in this first symbolist music drama which impressed its early audiences by seeming 'all recitative'. The pure line of the music follows the dialogue of Maeterlinck's play with scrupulous care, creating a remarkable double effect; conversational naturalness and the strange, intense concentration of a dream. It is a style that can take in the whole play, give equal life and interest to what in romantic opera would usually seem 'flat' scenes—Genevieve's quiet reading aloud of Golaud's letter to the family group at the beginning, for instance—as to more obvious operatic material like the moonlight meetings of Pelléas and Mélisande. The purely orchestral passages, those exquisitely delicate sequences of sound in the intervals of dialogue, seem the necessary continuation of the characters' stammering, unfinished sentences, as if the silence into which the speech is always running, were filling up with a mysterious essence that is more easily expressed by music than words. That fragile essence can be captured in the play itself, but only if we listen as intently to the spaces between the words as to the words themselves. This, supremely, is what Debussy's music helps us to do by registering sharply the significant repetitions, hesitations, pauses, tailings away, which make up the rhythmic structure of Maeterlinck's dialogue. The love scene at Mélisande's tower (Act III, Scene 2) illustrates the process. It opens with an unexpected musical effect, Mélisande singing a haunting little folk song with a calm fluency extraordinary in this timid being who can usually hardly finish a sentence: the music suggests that new confidence and fullness of being which is touchingly accounted for when Pelléas appears with his musical 'Holla, holla, ho' to pour out his delight at the sight of her, with her unbound hair shining in the moonlight. The music points too the contrast between his buoyant entry—the repeated 'I, I, and I' he calls out in answer to her 'Who is there?'—and the loss of equilibrium in the unfinished sentence he ends with. To Golaud's angry question, 'What are you doing here?', he can only reply, 'What am I doing here? I . . .'. The full note given it in the music points up that 'I' left hanging in the air, delicately draws attention to the sad reversal which has taken him nearer to the frightened inarticulacy of Mélisande's usual style.

With or without its music, *Pelléas and Mélisande* shares with *The Shadowy Waters* many echoes of *Tristan and Isolde* and of Villiers de l'Isle Adam's *Axel*; the situation of the fated lovers, the Rapunzel-like scene with streaming hair, the sea scene, when Pelléas and Mélisande stand by the dark castle watching the ship that brought her there glide away. It would be hard to say which of these echoes, from Wagner, from *Axel*, from Maeterlinck, are strongest in Yeats's play. But it is clear that Maeterlinck, with Debussy's aid, had provided a model of the way music and words could fuse in the service of a less rhetorical drama than Wagner's, a dream much closer to Yeats's own idea of a theatre of the interior. If we listen with the ear of the mind to the harp sequence in *The Shadowy Waters,* and have *Pelléas and Mélisande* also in mind, the effect Yeats was aiming at begins to seem more possible.

The musical method may not have altogether worked at the Abbey in those early productions. But Yeats's attempt to make it work is not a sign of theatrical naïveté: he was inexperienced, and groping, but he was groping in the direction of all that was most lively and original in the European scene.

'Groping' must be the word, for of course he knew the odds were rather against him in those early days so far as music drama was concerned. He had no Debussy to write for him, and indeed, even at a later stage, when music had become still more important to his drama, he did not find his Debussy or his Kurt Weil. A comment he made in 1906 shows how accurately he recognised his problem: 'If the harp cannot suggest some power that no actor could represent by sheer acting . . . the enchanting of so many people by it would seem impossible'. He goes on, 'perhaps very wonderful music might do that if the audience were musicians, but lacking the music and that audience it is better to appeal to the eye'.[8]

'Appeal to the eye' also had its practical difficulties, as we have been observing. But Yeats was in a stronger position to know exactly what he wanted on the visual side. He had an exceptionally lively visual imagination, not surprisingly, coming as he did from a family of talented painters; he himself trained at an art school for two years. He was acutely sensitive to the power of stage pictures, knew how they could enhance the spoken word or distract from it, by wrong grouping, perhaps, or by dim lighting which put a strain on the eye. He could produce expressive sketches of his scenic plans, like the ship designs that accompany his re-writings of *The Shadowy Waters*. Always too he had close contact with the art world: from the time when *The Land*

---

[8] *Variorum edition of the Poems of W. B. Yeats,* ed. P. Allt and R. K. Alspach (New York 1957), p. 342.

of Heart's Desire was advertised along with Todhunter's *A Comedy of Sighs* in a poster by Beardsley, he never lacked distinguished artists to produce illustrations, stage designs and costumes for him. Beardsley just before his death, was engaged on a set of illustrations for *The Shadowy Waters*, and his fellow illustrator of *Salomé*, Charles Ricketts, was an important figure in the development of scenic art at the Abbey Theatre. Charles Shannon, Sturge Moore and the versatile Edmund Dulac were among the talented group who expressed his scenic ideas for him.

I want now to look at the part played by the scenic art in Yeats's new theatrical synthesis and at the relation between his experiments and those of European artists, notably Maeterlinck's, because this was Yeats's own starting place. Before he met Arthur Symons and came directly under French influences, he was independently pursuing a line in scenic art that led naturally to Europe. French literature may, as he said, have been a closed book to him in those days, but his visual taste was already European, inasmuch as his deep feeling for the English romantic painters, the pre-Raphaelites and contemporaries of his own like Morris, Watts, Burne-Jones, Crane, was shared by Maeterlinck and continental symbolist painters such as Khnopff and Moreau who both drew from and fed into the avant garde theatre.

Yeats's visual imagination was active in his theatre experiments, as we saw in *The Shadowy Waters*, even before he had had opportunities to see his plays well staged. The stage scene was always an immensely important means of dramatic expression for him. True, he listed scenery last in the theatre manifesto he wrote in 1902: 'I think the theatre must be reformed in its plays, its speaking, its acting, and its scenery. That is to say, I think there is nothing good about it at present.'[9] But all the same it was with scenery that he first saw his way clearly. The changes he made in *The Land of Heart's Desire* after seeing it in performance show how he tried to make the stage scene work more subtly. In the first version minimal stage directions call for a naturalistic set with doors and windows indicated for purely practical purposes. Later directions are more in Maeterlinckian style; the door of the Bruins' kitchen is left open so that through it a moon can be glimpsed, or a late sunset, some light that 'carries the eye far off into a vague, mysterious world'. Even when he had not been able to test his

---

[9] 'The Reform of the Theatre', *Samhain* (1903); in *Explorations* (1962), p. 107.

ideas he could see in his mind's eye with remarkable vividness how the visual elements might be made to function as part of the dramatic rhythm: 'The whole picture as it were moves together—sky and sea and cloud are as it were actors'. The human actors came first: Yeats had no doubt about this priority: 'The actor and the words put into his mouth are always the one thing that matters'.[10] He was delighted with Gordon Craig's screens because they gave the actor 'renewed importance'. But he loved them too for their own sake and for the new stage beauty they made possible, especially under the play of light, when fine colour changes made an 'extraordinary beauty of delicate light and shade': this was a visual language corresponding to the language he used as a poet and opened the way for theatrical communication at an equivalent level.

He approached the stage scene like a painter, seeing very precisely the colour effects he needed—'I want the dark dress and the dark curtain to fix themselves on the minds of the audience before the almost white stage is disclosed'—and painting over if need be, turning a dark green sail bronze, replacing a dim impressionistic view of a wood with stylised trees 'painted in flat colour upon a gold or diapered sky' (in *The Countess Cathleen* (1892)). He worked out systematically the dramatic effect of different colour arrangements: one dominant colour throughout gave a good sense of concerted movement; a two-tone harmony—the convention that became established at the Abbey in his day—needed touches of a third colour to make full impact; hence the Fool's red-brown dress in the purple-olive green design of *The Hour-Glass* (1914). Even when an experienced professional artist like Sturge Moore was designing for him, Yeats would give extraordinarily precise advice: 'the play [*The Shadowy Waters*] is dreamy and dim and the colours should be the same—(say) a blue-green sail against an indigo-blue backcloth, and the mast and bulwark indigo-blue. The persons in blue and green with some copper ornament.'[11] Décor and costume always had to express the deep mood of the play: blues and greens for the fey, withdrawn atmosphere of *The Shadowy Waters*; for the more violent eroticism of *The King of the Great Clock Tower* (1935), stronger colours, orange, red and black; in *The Green Helmet* (1910) a still more aggressive mix of orange-red, dark purple and dark green

[10] 'The Play, the Player and the Scene', *Samhain* (1904), in *Explorations* (1962), p. 179.
[11] Letter of March, 1903 in *W. B. Yeats and T. Sturge Moore: Their Correspondence 1901–1937*, ed. U. Bridge (1953), p. 7.

exploding in a surrealist spectacle, a man in all-red costume and green helmet with branching horns increasing him to giant height, an effect 'intentionally violent and startling'.

Everything the audience saw, from costumes to curtains, had to establish itself as part of the play's meaning. Curtains were very important. The Abbey's olive-green stage curtain was a determining element in the colour scheme of *The Hour-Glass*, and for *The King of the Great Clock Tower* Yeats imagined behind the stage curtain another one, pale purple with a stencilled pattern of dancers, creating a recessive visual effect, corresponding to the inward movement of the action. Even when he was writing plays to be performed in an open space, without scenery, he still kept a kind of curtain, the decorative cloth folded and unfolded by the Musicians at the beginning and end of each play, which was a device of his own invention, not taken over, like other features of the dance plays, from the Nō drama. These curtains, so decorative and stylised, with their emblematic patterns of dancer or hawk, were an important means of establishing the world the audience was to move into; a timeless world, below the level of the daylight consciousness. The more stylised the visual effects, Yeats found, the easier it was to create this sense of timelessness; a forest pattern rather than a forest painting became his ideal. Form and colour were to work subliminally, in the way that Maeterlinck thought the European painters of his day were doing, conveying 'meanings' that could not be put into words.

He seized on the dramatic potentialities in visual art with a confidence and thoroughness rather remarkable in a poet who had evolved such an elaborate literary symbolism. How easily that all went overboard is amusingly shown in his reaction to Sturge Moore's first designs for *The Shadowy Waters*. He did not like the colour scheme— 'The white sail will throw the hounds into such distinction that they will become an irritation'—but realised that Sturge Moore had been misled by his own complicated directions. The pattern on the ship's sail—three rows of hounds, the first dark, the second red, and the third white with red ears—was a piece of colour symbolism which in the days before he had practical experience of the theatre Yeats expected to be 'read' along with other minute visual symbols, like the lily and the rose emblems worn by Forgael and Dectora. But by the time he saw Sturge Moore's designs he knew better; the theatre was not the place for that kind of close reading, and that was the end of the hounds; they kept their place only as a decorative feature of the whole pattern;

'They must be all in some one colour and be almost lost in the main colour of the sail'.

This is the very opposite of the over-literary approach to drama which some of Yeats's critics in the past have attributed to him. His feeling for the visual side of theatre was, in fact, sensitive beyond anything found in other playwrights writing for the English theatre of his time. He was in this respect a European even before he encountered the experimental Continental theatre in action (in *Ubu Roi* (1896), for instance), was, indeed, imaginatively at the centre of the European *fin de siècle* movement to create a more sophisticated and expressive scenic art. An interesting two-way relationship had grown up during the nineties, in Paris especially, between the arts of theatre and painting; the fated production of *Salomé*, which was rehearsed but never performed at the Palace Theatre, London, would have been a fine expression of that fusion, with Sarah Bernhardt as Salomé, and Gustave Moreau as designer. But although that production did not materialise, another did, which offered a similar kind of inspiration in a mood closer to Yeats's own at that time; Maeterlinck's *Pelléas and Mélisande*.

Maeterlinck had close connections with some of the most original European painters of his time and was active in the avant garde movement which tried to involve easel painters in scenic art. The decorative schemes of his own plays were sometimes inspired directly by paintings; in the production of *Pelléas and Mélisande* at the Théâtre d'Art in 1892, for instance, the costumes were based on Memlinc's picture, *Saint Ursula*. Interestingly, after seeing the play in performance, Maeterlinck wrote to Lugné-Poë, the co-producer, offering suggestions for a different style: 'Don't you think that, instead of green for Mélisande, something mauve from Liberty's might be better? Pelléas for his part should be in green—a very simple, very long dress, hanging loosely round the body, with a jewelled belt, and purple ribbons plaited into the hair, or just a little unusual foliage'.[12] The unexpected reference to Liberty's—so many miles away from the dream world of Pelléas, one might think—connects Maeterlinck with that whole world of romantic painting, pre-Raphaelite, symbolist, art nouveau, early surrealist—one leads into another and there is a recognisable homogeneity of interests—on which Yeats and Wilde

---

[12] Letter to Lugné-Poë quoted in P. Jullian, *Dreamers of Decadence* (1971) (translation of *Esthètes et Magiciens*, Paris 1969), p. 63.

also drew heavily. The *fin de siècle* painters were often interested in the stage, took subjects from there, painted actresses (Bernhardt above all, in famous roles like her Melissinde in Rostand's *La Princesse Lointaine*) and sometimes designed décor and costumes. Burne-Jones, who had great influence on continental painting, collaborated on settings for *La Belle au Bois Dormant* by Henri Bataille and Robert d'Humières at the Théâtre de l'Oeuvre in 1892 and designed costumes for the production of *Pelléas and Mélisande* by Forbes Robertson with Mrs Patrick Campbell as Mélisande and Martin Harvey as Pelléas at the Prince of Wales Theatre in 1898. In 1894 he designed scenery and costumes for J. Comyn Carr's play, *King Arthur* (Lyceum, 12 January 1895), in which Henry Irving played Arthur, Ellen Terry Guinevere, and Forbes Robertson Sir Lancelot. He would have been a natural designer for Yeats, to judge from his design for the tableau of weeping queens in their hazy blue-green draperies gathered round the dead Arthur. He certainly had a potent influence on the designer who did work for him, Charles Ricketts, and also on the Flemish and French symbolist painters admired by Maeterlinck.

Burne-Jones defined a picture as a 'beautiful romantic dream'; Wagner talked of his dramas as deeds 'made visible' by music; Satie, one of those who competed for the commission to set *Pelléas and Mélisande* to music, imagined the play in production as a perfect fusion of the arts, with 'musical scenery' and an atmosphere like a painting by Puvis de Chavannes. The move to total theatre can be sensed getting very near in such statements. There is so much talk of this kind in the period that one begins to lose the sense of plays, pictures, poems having separate identities. Images merge; a name may conjure up a picture or a play: Maeterlinck shares *The Seven Princesses* (1891) with Klimt, *Monna Vanna* with Rossetti. Everybody has a share in *Salomé*, so that one begins to wonder who invented her, was it Wilde after all, or Klimt or Gustave Moreau, who painted her so obsessively? And that other girl who haunts the *fin de siècle*, the delicate creature with the flowing hair, which she lets down, Rapunzel-like, to enfold and perhaps entrap her lover. Is it a poet or painter who first imagines her, does she spring to full life in Morris's poem *Rapunzel*, or in Waterhouse's picture, *La Belle Dame sans Merci*; should not his frail, wan nymph, spreading out her fine web of hair round the young knight, really be called Mélisande? But many pre-Raphaelite paintings might have given birth to Mélisande: the romantic painters were fascinated by the ambiguous zone of being she represented and tried continually to evoke it in all those paintings of Undines and Dryads, delicate, spiritual beings, only half separated from their natural element, and in epicene figures like Burne-Jones's Arthurian knights and ladies whose 'tall, unvoluptuous forms' delighted Yeats.

One of the many affinities between Yeats and Maeterlinck was their feeling for the romantic painters and the theatrical use they made of it. Both were inspired by Morris, Burne-Jones, Walter Crane: Yeats knew Crane personally, and Maeterlinck read the Grimm fairy tales in the edition he illustrated, as many details in his plays suggest: Crane's Goose Girl, combing out her abundant, sinewy hair, or his Rapunzel in her miniature tower, hair cascading over her lover, could easily be an illustration for *Pelléas and Mélisande*. Only to look at Maeterlinck's stage directions or read accounts of his stage scenes is to see how important a model he provided. Symons thought him the most pictorial of playwrights, a term of praise, for the dramatist's art, in his view, rested in the first place on an ability to make stage pictures; Maeterlinck's were a superior, modern kind 'in which the crudity of action is subdued into misty outlines'. Many other admirers shared this view. It was as 'a procession of dreamy pictures' that W. L. Courtney enjoyed Martin Harvey's 1911 production of *Pelléas and Mélisande*, a compliment Martin Harvey would have relished, for as he says in his autobiography,[13] the play always presented itself to his mind pictorially. Courtney saw the actors in terms of paintings: Pelléas was one of Carpaccio's knights, Mrs Patrick Campbell one of Botticelli's wistful women; the stage scene evoked now *Morte d'Arthur*, now the pictures of the Italian Primitives. Maeterlinck's visual vocabulary was no doubt, as another admirer, J. W. Mackail, suggested, drawn from an actual Flemish landscape, with its canals, bridges, 'trees in long files and avenues', water everywhere. But this real landscape of castles, towers, canals has an atmospheric film drawn over it which gives it the look of the romantic, painted worlds of Rossetti, Burne-Jones or Walter Crane. Maeterlinck's stage pictures call up many visual echoes: his prince gazing through the glass at the seven princesses, sunk in their strange sleep, his Mélisande weeping by the spring in which her golden crown has been lost or watching with Pelléas the departure of the boat that brought her, so mysteriously, to his country, seem anticipated in the ambiguous encounters between pallid knights and ladies in Burne-Jones's briar rose entanglements and marble terraces or in illustrations

[13] *The Autobiography of Sir John Martin Harvey* (1933).

of Arthurian romance like Rossetti's *Morte d'Arthur*.[14] Likenesses
are sometimes so close as to seem like deliberate visual quotation; the
description of the drowned girl in *Interior*, for instance, whose hair
'had floated up almost into a circle round her head and was swaying
hither and thither with the current' must surely evoke Millais' flowery
Ophelia: the same artist's Blind Girl, gazing unseeingly at the rainbow,
glimmers in the background of *The Sightless*, where another girl with
similarly luxuriant hair looks up towards a starry sky she cannot see.

In his other vein, the homelier style of his 'everyday' drama,
Maeterlinck still draws on the painters, especially the symbolists who
were so active in Belgium during the nineties, investing the quiet
observing style of Flemish realism with strangeness. Maeterlinck gets
a similar strangeness by focusing on some luminous detail in a setting
of perfect ordinariness: the four doors of the living-room of *The
Intruder*, for instance, one of which opens at the end in a silent and
chilling moment of great power; or the memorable tableau in *Interior*
when the two young sisters of the drowned girl take up positions at
two of the three windows looking onto the garden, as if they were
drawn there by the watchers they cannot see, a piece of silent visual
pathos the watchers draw attention to: 'No one comes to the middle
window'. Scenic details of this sort, a significantly closed door, figures
at lighted windows, have the strangeness that comes from the sharp
juxtaposition of the solid with the nebulous, as in symbolist pictures
like Khnopff's *The Abandoned City* with its heavy Flemish buildings in
the empty town square, its solidity invaded by a blur of water, and a
mysterious sense of over-hanging silence. The affinity between their
styles was felt by both painter and playwright: Khnopff was one of
those many continental artists who illustrated, among other works of
Maeterlinck, *Pelléas and Mélisande*.

It was paintings like his that Maeterlinck had in mind when he
wrote in 1896[15] of the advances made by artists and musicians in
subliminal techniques, beyond anything the writers of the time had
achieved. The painter had learnt how to bring out the spiritual gravity
in the 'obscure phases of daily life' by means of seeming simplicity:
'And therefore will he place on his canvas a house lost in the heart of

---

[14] P. Jullian comments on Rossetti's picture: 'The whole of Maeterlinck's
world is already to be seen in this illustration to Tennyson', op. cit., p. 55.

[15] In *Le Trésor des Humbles* (Paris 1896). Quotation from *The Treasure of the
Humble* (1897), p. 102.

the country, an open door at the end of a passage, a face or hands at rest. . .'

In seeking to transfer these techniques of visual subtlety to the stage, Maeterlinck did of course make himself dangerously dependent on scene designers, who varied greatly in their ability to realise his directions. It is not always easy to tell from contemporary accounts how closely they got to his intentions. Arthur Symons, for instance, responded enthusiastically to Burne-Jones's décor in *Pelléas and Mélisande*: the stage pictures were equal to the beauty of the play, making Mrs Patrick Campbell, 'in her wonderful clothes of no period', seem 'a plaintive figure out of tapestry': her art had never been so pictorial. For Graham Robertson too, this Mélisande, in her gold dress, was exactly right, as if she had stepped straight out of a Burne-Jones canvas. For another critic, Virginia Crawford, the effect was less happy: to her mind the play sank under the weight of its scenic splendours; 'its weird, elusive beauty seemed to shrivel up in contact with the material accessories of the stage'.[16] She was more impressed by Lugné-Poë's production of *Pelléas and Mélisande* and *The Intruder* in 1892 which relied less on painted scenes than on dim lights, slow rhythmical movements and lengthy silences heightened by the simple but apparently effective device of a gauze scarf stretched across the stage to separate audience from actors. That same production[17] was likened by Desmond MacCarthy to 'such stuff as dreams are made on'. He also felt that the décor was usually too heavy in London productions of Maeterlinck. He was impressed by Ricketts's designs for the production of *The Death of Tintagiles* (Brussels 1894) at the St James's Theatre in 1913—who could fail to admire the austerely decorative, Japanese/Medieval dress Lillah McCarthy wore as Ygraine?—but thought they did not make up for other too solid effects. His description of Ricketts's costumes and cobweb-silvery curtains', however, suggests that in this artist Maeterlinck had found an ideal designer. Ricketts was also, of course, the painter on whom Yeats relied and whom he singled out, along with Moreau and Dulac, as the great mask and myth makers of his time.

Yeats owed his early familiarity with continental movements

[16] V. M. M. Crawford, *Studies in Foreign Literature* (1899), p. 166.

[17] John Todhunter expressed the same preference in an interesting context, the discussion following Yeats's lecture in London in 1899 on 'The Ideal Theatre'. See J. P. Frayne and C. Johnson, *Uncollected Prose by W. B. Yeats 1897–1939* (1975), ii, 153–8.

entirely to Arthur Symons, whose importance in the evolution of the Yeatsian theatre has been given curiously little attention, despite such suggestive leads as Frank Kermode offered in 1957 in his seminal study of key images in Yeats's poetry, *Romantic Image*. Symons was the John the Baptist of the modernist theatre, a voice crying sixty years ahead of his time for a technique of total theatre which would put the arts of dance, mime, song, scene on an equal footing with words; in all his writings on theatre and his own practice as a play-wright he aimed at 'the concrete expression of a theory or system of aesthetics, of all the Arts'. As early as the nineties he was putting a modern kind of emphasis on the virtues of improvisation, demanding for the ephemeral arts of performance the same sort of serious attention that was given to the written drama, and asking provocative and modern-sounding questions; could not a sculptor's modelling in snow be thought as perfect as a work in marble, a dance be as subtly expressive as music or poetry; was the theatre the invention of the dramatist or was it the other way round; when the right mechanism had been achieved, would theatre be able to dispense with the dramatist altogether 'except perhaps as a kind of prompter?' That most exciting collection of theatre criticisms, *Plays, Acting and Music* (1903), opens with a manifesto that seems to belong to our time rather than his:

> Art has to do only with the creation of beauty, whether it be in words, or sounds, or colour, or outline, or rhythmical movement; and the man who writes music is no more truly an artist than the man who plays that music, the poet who composes rhythms in words no more truly an artist than the dancer who composes rhythms with the body, and the one is no more to be preferred to the other, than the painter is to be preferred to the sculptor, or the musician to the poet, in those forms of art which we have agreed to recognise as of equal value (p. 4).

Yeats acknowledged his literary debt to Symons—he had learnt whatever he knew of continental literature from him, he said—but did not make quite so much of his value as a theatrical guide. And yet Symons was so absolutely, providentially one might say, the guide he needed. When they first met, Yeats was repelled by his way of taking 'life and art as a series of impressions', but that soon changed; they became close friends, sharing rooms in the Middle Temple for some months in 1895 and in the following year visiting Ireland together: Yeats came to trust his taste so well that he even proposed him to

George Moore as a referee in those preposterous quarrels over 'putting style' into *Diarmuid and Grania* (produced 1901). Symons's impressionistic approach to things made him in fact an ideal catalyst. He was the most concrete of critics: in his vivid impressions of stage performances in *Plays, Acting and Music* or *Studies in Seven Arts* (1906) he moves rapidly from one topic to another, always illuminating what he so lightly touches, seldom developing much, but rather leaving his scattered responses and reflections to put out shoots in the mind of his reader.

Another of his great assets, especially from the point of view of an experimental playwright working so far from the main stream as Dublin, was his cosmopolitanism. He was equally at home in Paris as in London; Yeats recalls in his *Memoirs* how he guessed that Symons gave up coming to the Rhymers' Club because the conversation was so inferior to what he was accustomed to in the avant garde circles round Mallarmé in Paris. The news he brought back from trips abroad, seeing Wagner at Bayreuth or Munich, puppets in Rome, Sarah Bernhardt or Loie Fuller in Paris, was exactly what Yeats in his Abbey eyrie most needed. It was one quick magpie feeding a still more marvellous one. Symons could give him exactly the right kind of theatrical nourishment because he shared so many of Yeats's literary and intellectual interests: he was the scribe of the symbolist movement as well as one of its poets and playwrights and was remarkably free of any tendency to compartmentalise his interests. His critical study, *The Symbolist Movement in Literature* (1899), ferments with the same kind of excitement as his reviews of performances; in each type of writing he draws his illustrations with spontaneous ease from literature, theatre, painting, opera. No wonder that Yeats found him such a sympathetic and helpful listener: '. . . Arthur Symons, more than any man I have ever known, could slip as it were into the mind of another, and my thoughts gained in richness and in clearness from his sympathy' (*Autobiographies*, p. 319).

For Symons, as for Wilde, with whom he had some literary connections,[18] symbolism was an essentially modern movement towards greater self-consciousness: 'what distinguishes the Symbolism of our day from the symbolism of the past is that it has now become conscious of itself'. Because it contained so many different arts, theatre offered

[18] They shared a passion for French art, agreeing (in conversation) that no other was worth discussing. Symons published an early article on Villiers de l'Isle Adam in *Woman's World*, the journal Wilde edited (December 1889).

the most rich means of expressing this self-consciousness: Symons was the man to see this, for he brought together supremely the symbolists' love of self-scrutiny, of fine shades and nuances and their feeling for the popular theatre arts, dance, music hall, melodrama. 'All actors should be sent to school in melodrama', he said, 'as all dramatic authors should learn their trade there'. He sought always in the performing arts that special truth which Pater defined as 'the power of distinguishing and fixing delicate and fugitive details'. The theatre must become a 'theatre of revelation' in which wordless arts like music and dancing would combine with words to extend and refine human perceptions. In this synthesis music was crucial, a way of stilling the striving of the individual will, freeing the mind to 'dream awake'. So too were the visual arts; for him, as for Yeats, the power of visualisation was essential equipment for a playwright: 'all drama began with the ordering of dumb show, and should be playable without words'.

One of Symons's most striking virtues as critic and above all as catalyst was his ability to observe, respond to and register theatrical experiences even when he did not find them particularly congenial. In his review of Jarry's *Ubu Roi*, for instance, his extremely vivid and acute account of what he actually saw brings the production sharply before us and also illuminates the essential nature of the play. It was 'a sort of comic antithesis to Maeterlinck'; Jarry was satirising humanity 'by having human beings squeaking with the squeaky voices traditionally assigned to puppets against fairground music—piano, cymbals, and drums'. Those 'painted, massacring puppets' were 'the destroying elements which are as old as the world, and which we can never chase out of the system of natural things'.[19] And yet he disliked the play, thought Jarry 'a young savage of the woods'. Although he describes it so well, it was left to Yeats, whom he took to see the performance in Paris, to pick up the implications and develop from them, as later on he so interestingly did. That was the characteristic pattern of their intellectual relationship. Again and again one can see in Symons's reviews and critical jottings the starting places of Yeatsian experiment, the lines sketched out, waiting for the master hand to fill them in. Just a glance at the list of contents in *Studies in Seven Arts* or *Plays, Acting and Music* is like a glimpse into the theatrical future: 'The World as Ballet', 'Apology for Puppets'; 'Maeterlinck, *Everyman*, The Japanese Players'; what a fine scatter of intuitions, pointing the way Yeats was to go. Well before Ezra Pound, Symons was drawing

[19] *Studies in Seven Arts* (1906), pp. 371–7.

attention to the ritualistic strangeness of the Japanese drama and the remarkable power of the Japanese actors to represent 'moments' of spiritual intensity. In the death scene of *The Geisha and the Knight,* he said, 'the whole woman dies before one's sight, life ebbs visibly out of cheeks and eyes and lips; it is death as not even Sarah Bernhardt has shown us death'.[20]

Through Symons Yeats made his first personal contact with the people and happenings of the European avant garde. He was introduced to Mallarmé, presiding genius of the French movement towards total theatre, whose advocacy of a new synthesis was backed up by powerful demonstrations of his own understanding of the performing arts. Mallarmé wrote brilliantly on the art of dance—'perceptions phenomenally imaginative and phenomenally acute', says a modern practising ballet critic[21]—and supported experiments in linking words and music, including readings from his own poems to the music of Fauré and others. All this was massive encouragement for Yeats, who in the nineties launched the first of many explorations in arrangements of words and music with Florence Farr's readings of his poems to a psaltery accompaniment. He needed Symons as interpreter as well as guide, his own French being, as he said, so poor that he had a struggle to read *Axel* and then only half understood it. Through Symons, translator of Mallarmé, Verhaeren and many other French writers, habitué of theatres like the Théâtre de l'Oeuvre, he was able to extend his imperfect acquaintance with French arts by seeing performances of stage plays in Paris, hearing poems read to music, acquiring the sense of the concreteness of symbolist art. Paris had a compelling attraction for him in the nineties, partly of course because Maud Gonne was living there—'the old lure', as he said—but also because there was such a lively avant garde. Especially there was the Théâtre d'Art (founded by Paul Fort in 1891 in reaction against Antoine's naturalistic Théâtre Libre) and its successor the Théâtre de l'Oeuvre whose director Lugné-Poë produced so many of the seminal plays of the new movement, including, in 1893, *Pelléas and Mélisande.*

Symons supported the idea of a symbolist drama with plays of his own, which may not have had much to offer Yeats—nothing, certainly, in comparison with the wealth of his criticism—but which helped to create a sympathetic context, provided some interesting

[20] *Plays, Acting and Music* (1903), p. 77.
[21] Edwin Denby, *Dancers, Buildings and People in the Streets* (New York 1965), p. 235.

reflections of Yeats's own experiments and may even occasionally have offered him hints. Wagnerian notes are strong, for instance, in Symons's creative writings; he was inspired by a performance of *Tristan and Isolde* in 1902 to write a poem, 'Tristan's Song', which later grew into a play, *Tristan and Iseult* (1917); this at the time when Yeats was revising *The Shadowy Waters* and trying to make it more Wagnerian. Another play, *The Dance of the Seven Deadly Sins*, which also grew out of a poem, is full of interest as a scenario for a dance drama in symbolist style. It was obviously affected (as Yeats's *The Hour-Glass* may have been) by William Poel's revivals of the medieval morality, *Everyman*, and Marlowe's *Dr Faustus*. The real hour-glass which figures in Symons's stage properties seems indeed to make implicit reference to this fertilising process, and the play in its tentative way curiously anticipates the drama of both Yeats and Beckett. A striking feature of the play is its setting—an ordinary room (as it is described in the stage directions), given a sinister charge by its absolute bareness. In an empty space an Old Man and Old Woman, who, we are told, represent Body and Soul, sit on either side of an open fireplace, he with the hour-glass, she stirring the dying log fire 'where the world's last ashes slowly char' (hard not to think of *Embers* as well as *The Hour-Glass* at such a moment). Another device which in 1913 could well have given Yeats ideas is the on-stage presence of a stage manager, who draws attention to the illusoriness of the event, introduces the dancers who perform the dance of the deadly sins and hints at an off-stage presence in the wings, and the approach of the 'end', a kind of last day or Day of Judgement. Symons's feeling for dance drama, so advanced for his time, comes up again in his slight but interesting piece, *The Fool of the World* (1906), where Death is represented as a dancer of a sort, shaking her staff of seven bells in a climax which strikes a curiously modern note of bleak absurdity.

Symons's *Tristan and Iseult* is one of those pieces which even in their imperfections clearly illustrate the impact made on the symbolist playwrights by both Wagner and Maeterlinck. There is an interesting attempt to find an alternative for Wagner's musical climaxes in a Maeterlinckian orchestration of words with silences, pauses and long slow scenes of 'intense quietness'. Eleanora Duse, who was to have played the part of Iseult, was another chief source of inspiration: if the production planned around her had materialised, the play might have revealed dimensions it is hard to envisage from the text alone: sadly it was given up at the time of Symons's tragic collapse. Duse was supremely the artist of silence: her capacity for suggesting inner spiritual activity through stillness, for being 'the artist of her own soul' as Symons put it, was for him the apotheosis of the performing art: in her acting, he said, in memorable phrase: 'there is no transition from the energy of speech to the energy of silence'. For how many present-day playwrights—Beckett, Pinter, Albee—would not this account of a style seem appropriate?

I want now to look at the early stages of Yeats's move to total theatre in the context of the European influences that flowed to him through Symons and through Symons's most admired playwright, Maeterlinck, focusing on areas not so far examined where continental models were most important: acting style; music and movement.

The interior drama required an acting hardly known in the English theatre, a style of stillness and quiet intonations such as Yeats thought his Irish actors had almost miraculously achieved in *The Shadowy Waters*. Their model had to be French, for as Symons was continually pointing out, the London theatre seemed positively afraid of immobility and silence, light emphasis and low key. An actor like Coquelin could stand motionless for five minutes, as Symons said, without change of expression; 'and yet nothing can be more expressive than his face at those moments'. No English actor—with the possible exception of Charles Wyndham—would have dared to try this; if he had, Symons darkly added, the stage manager would have found 'business' for him. 'Business', making 'points', indulging in fussy, unnecessary movements; these were the banes of the English theatre, along with a propensity to exaggerated vocal emphasis and inflated tone. For a radically different style one had to go to the French: the extraordinary force of Sarah Bernhardt's crescendos, so Symons thought, derived from her subtle refusals of emphasis along the way, her 'smooth and level' manner of speaking, her habit of gliding over even significant individual phrases for the sake of the whole effect, the 'ensemble'. For Symons, as for so many of her admirers, her acting was not far removed from a musical performance: 'Her voice is itself an instrument of music, and she plays upon it as a conductor plays upon an orchestra'.[22]

Yeats took his actors as close as he could to the French style. He thought their 'way of quiet movement and careful speech' had given the new Irish plays 'some little fame'. That most perceptive of English critics, C. E. Montague, would have agreed: he was immensely struck by the stillness of the Irish actors, their ability to leave well alone; if

[22] *Plays, Acting and Music*, p. 33.

need be to 'fade into the background like mists at a dawn' or to fix their attention on a central figure so intently that the audience was held more surely than by limelight. 'The Irishmen keep still and white', he said, 'and tragic consequence enfolds them; set on that ground of grave and simple composure, the slightest gesture carries you far in divination of what prompts it'.[23]

Yeats followed Symons in looking to Coquelin and Sarah Bernhardt as models—'We have learnt with devout humility from the players of *Phèdre*'—and deplored, with him, the over-emphatic, restless acting that prevailed outside Paris. He too studied Lugné-Poë's methods; it was these, rather than the play, he told Lady Gregory, that interested him in Maeterlinck's *Monna Vanna* when the French company brought it to London in 1902. In moments of frustration, he indulged in fantasies of rehearsing his actors in barrels to cut out excess movement and no doubt understood the enthusiasm for marionettes which led Symons to ask, Craig style, 'why we require the intervention of any less perfect medium between the meaning of the piece as the author conceived it, and that other meaning which derives from our conception of it?'

Maeterlinck did indeed describe one of his collections as plays for marionettes, perhaps as Symons suggested 'to intimate his sense of the symbolic value, in the interpretation of a profound inner meaning, of that external nullity which the marionette by its very nature emphasises'.[24] The best performers of Maeterlinck managed to suggest something of that 'external nullity', so Symons thought, by a 'fine monotony' of style. 'Monotony' is a word that constantly recurs as a term of praise in criticism of Maeterlinck; Max Beerbohm, for instance, reviewing a revival of *Pelléas and Mélisande* at the Royalty Theatre in 1900, and comparing Frank Mills's Golaud with Forbes Robertson's two years before, found Mills's performance 'quieter, more monotonous—more Maeterlinckian, in fact'.[25] Beerbohm felt some nostalgia for Forbes Robertson's uncouth violence; it was 'out of the picture', but, then, so was the character, it was his fate to be so. That particular effect, however, depended on there being a recognisable 'in the picture style' and for Beerbohm as for Symons and Yeats this was bound up with the notion of monotony, the suppression of external variety and emphasis for the sake of spiritual expressiveness.

[23] *Dramatic Values* (1941), pp. 50–6.
[24] *Plays, Acting and Music*, p. 196.
[25] M. Beerbohm, *Around Theatres* (1953), pp. 93–4.

In this dream-like mode, there was no place for commonplace manifestations of personality or of sex. Symons saw Maeterlinck's characters as child-like spiritual beings, 'at once more simple and more abstract than real people';[26] like marionettes, they were in a way free of the fleshly solidity, the sexual density of the everyday adult world. This idea of 'external nullity' has obviously much in common with Yeats's concept of 'impersonality' in tragic acting, his fascination with the mask as a means of transcending 'commonplace' expressiveness. And indeed there was considerable encouragement for this view of characterisation in the various successful Maeterlinckian performances around the turn of the century. For even in a theatre so dominated by voluptuous, and often vulgar sexual display, it proved possible to find actors capable of suggesting those tenuous, indeterminate creatures, 'at once more simple and more abstract than real people'. Sarah Bernhardt as Pelléas and Mrs Patrick Campbell as Mélisande might not strike us as the most likely casting to achieve that effect; bizarre images rise up of Bernhardt in late years playing Hamlet—how hard not to find this risible (Hamlet, Princess of Denmark, was Beerbohm's reaction)—or of Mrs Pat declaiming Mélisande in the florid mode of the second Mrs Tanqueray. Symons indeed admitted that in the Maeterlinckian role Mrs Patrick Campbell needed to 'prune her luxuriance'. Yet still he admired her; in spite of all, she was able to reach that somnambulistic, other-worldly quality the play required. The testimony of so subtle and experienced a critic, almost enough in itself, found plenty of backing. The authors known as 'Michael Field', for instance, were entranced by the production and especially by Sarah Bernhardt; she seemed to them 'an elfin travesty of man', who played Pelléas so that sex was forgotten 'as an accident' and only the ideal lover remained.[27]

Though it is hard to take the theatrical transvestism of the late nineteenth century as a serious art—except, paradoxically, in the comic music hall forms which are so much more familiar to us—yet we have to recognise that for many of Bernhardt's most perceptive critics these male roles—Pelléas, Hamlet, L'Aiglon—were persuasive and affecting, no more of a freak than Ella Shiels as Burlington Bertie,

[26] Review of *Pelléas and Mélisande*, *Plays, Acting and Music*, p. 72: 'Maeterlinck's theatre of marionettes, who are at the same time children and spirits, at once more simple and more abstract than real people. . .'
[27] 'Michael Field', *Works and Days: From the journal of Michael Field*, ed. T. Sturge Moore (1933).

if more astonishing, calling for more explanation of their curious power. As described by 'Michael Field', the effect was a Platonic freedom from narrow definitions of the 'real' exactly such as Maeterlinck and Yeats were aiming at as playwrights. For them both the ambiguity or asexuality of the transvestite performer offered one way into the world behind the appearance of things, a way of allowing sex itself to be seen in its numinous aspect, as a force in a complex, shifting, essentially spiritual process.

So those casting choices of Yeats which now seem so odd—voluptuously beautiful Florence Farr, for instance, as the poet Aleel, lover of the Countess Cathleen—are not necessarily the sign of amateurishness they have sometimes been taken for. On the contrary, in recognising the potential value to the interior drama of the transvestite, he was using the conventions of the professional theatre to follow up the hints long propounded by the French symbolists: Baudelaire had dreamed of a drama performed by actors on stilts, wearing masks, the women's parts taken by men. That dream had to wait till Genet and Lindsay Kemp for full realisation, but Yeats is firmly there at the start of this modern process, with his complete openness to the idea of playing against the sex of his performers.

First it was women in men's roles. There were no inhibitions about this, even in the English theatre of the Wilde era. William Poel notably cast a woman as Everyman in his influential revival of the play in 1901—neatly reversing thereby the transvestism of four hundred years earlier. Yeats may well have had that in mind when he envisaged a woman playing the Angel in the early versions of his own play on the Everyman theme, *The Hour-Glass*: later he thought a man might do it, if someone with the 'right voice' could be found. References to 'she' in the text were then to be changed throughout to 'he', so a thoroughly androgynous stage effect was not being aimed at, but the concept of a sex that could be taken on at will led easily into the impersonality he wanted for his Angel. This uncommitted being is unknowable in an ordinary human way and will have to be taken as a performer, so Yeats hints in the early prose version (1903) where the Wise Man 'recognises' the visitant by its stage costume:

I think I saw some that were like you in my dreams when I was a child—that bright thing, that dress that is the colour of embers!

By 1914 the depersonalising had gone further; a metal halo was called for, and a golden domino; the human features were vanishing; perhaps even, Yeats suggested, 'the whole face may be a beautiful mask'.

Whoever wore the costume and mask, in fact, would be the Angel. The transvestite idea and the marionette idea seem to be touching here, offering a double inspiration for the technique that was to be perfected in *At the Hawk's Well*, another play where the supernatural role involves an ambiguous sexuality and was thought of by Yeats as open to a performer of either sex; the Guardian's role was created by the male dancer, Ito, and later played, equally, if not more to Yeats's satisfaction, by Ninette de Valois (wearing Ito's costume which fitted her well, he being so small!). Yeats was prepared to go a long way with these explorations; he could envisage the part of the Young Woman in *The Dreaming of the Bones* (1919) being taken by a man—by then masks were regularly in use on his stage—and he gives directions for a specific marionette effect when the Old and Young Man enter the scene of *At the Hawk's Well*.

These were vital means to a vital effect; an impression of the impersonality of the forces governing the personal life and its passions. But he aimed to keep in too the sense of the personal; it was the quality of a passion after all, that made the exploration of it worthwhile: actual marionettes would not have done for him any more than for Maeterlinck. Yeats had some difficulties here such as were not likely to trouble Maeterlinck. He complained to his father that Irish actresses lacked passion, attributing the fact to the inhibiting influence of Irish Catholicism (his father thought it more likely due to 'the false lady-like that is early Victorian'). It is a curious thought—and perhaps a useful reminder of the robustness of the interior drama—that he found his ideal Deirdre in the actress who had her major triumphs as Pinero's Paula Tanqueray and Shaw's Eliza Doolittle—the part of Deirdre was only once played, he said, and that was by Mrs Pat.

She was also Maeterlinck's Mélisande; here, as in the visual sphere, Yeats and Maeterlinck came very close. So too in their musical feeling; the musicality of their dramas is perhaps their most striking common element. Again Maeterlinck provided an important early model. From the start of his playwriting career he attracted the musicians: Satie, Vincent d'Indy and Debussy competed to set music to his first play, *The Princess Maleine* (1889), and there was still more intense competition over *Pelléas and Mélisande*. Debussy triumphed, and his great musical re-creation of the play was first performed in Paris in 1902 and in London in 1909, by which time several other composers had been drawn to the work; Sibelius in 1905 and Schoenberg in 1902. Fauré had written incidental music for Forbes Robertson's production (Prince of Wales Theatre, 21 June 1898) which was considered by Mrs Patrick Campbell a vital source of Maeterlinckian atmosphere. Schoenberg's tone poem is an elaborately orchestrated piece which interestingly points up the musical affinities of the symbolist play-wrights. He was intrigued by what he called the 'inherent brutal strength' underlying Maeterlinck's 'weird and twilit drama' and his music, with its strong suggestions of both Wagner and Richard Strauss, powerfully conveys that strength. The descent of Golaud and Pelléas into the subterranean cavern is a darkly lurching, sinister passage which brilliantly suggests the feelings unspoken by the characters and also, I think, sets up anticipatory vibrations of that other terrible descent, Jokanaan going down into the cistern in the Strauss version of *Salomé*. It says something about the range and variety of Maeterlinck's drama—a doubtful quantity in some eyes—that he was able to strike responses from composers so different from each other and so imaginatively original as Fauré, Schoenberg, Debussy and Sibelius and to draw from them all music which fruitfully reflects the play; the graceful, idyllic lilt of Fauré's spinning song (in the incidental music referred to above) does this no less than Schoenberg's stormy sound.

Composers were drawn to the whole oeuvre, from melodramas like *Sister Beatrice* (1901) and *Monna Vanna* (1902) to such intensely inward pieces as *The Seven Princesses* and *The Death of Tintagiles*, and continued to be long after the plays had ceased to excite the theatre. *The Intruder* (1890) was set to music by Pannain in 1940 when Maeterlinck seemed hardly more than a note in history, to the English theatre at least. An exhaustive list of composers he inspired would be very long; I have said enough, I hope, to suggest how right Schoenberg was in maintaining that Maeterlinck's art was especially attractive to musicians. His view that it was an inherently musical drama was shared by Strindberg who described the plays as 'profoundly musical master-pieces', 'chamber music transferred to another shape': the right production style for them would be close to the manner of Beethoven in his late quartets, a suggestive remark for a whole important develop-ment in modern drama from Maeterlinck to Beckett. Critics of the time also observed the musical aspects; the classical scholar and critic, J. W. Mackail, for instance, saw affinities between the speech patterns of *Pelleas and Mélisande* and the choruses in Greek tragedy. And the supreme accolade was given by Mallarmé, who praised Maeterlinck's drama as 'operas without musical notes', 'a succession of linked chords', and drew attention to his unique method of 'creating silence around his characters'. Maeterlinck, he concluded, 'had linked music and poetic drama in a way that no one else had ever achieved before or since'. Not all the musical settings of the plays of course come within the sphere of drama: many are self-standing pieces like Schoenberg's tone poem. But Maeterlinck did, uniquely, inspire the composers of his time to attempt new collaborations of words and music, sometimes so new indeed that a term like 'music drama' really is needed to describe the fascinating hybrid. Debussy's *Pelléas and Mélisande* is the masterpiece in this genre, but there were other interesting experiments, such as *Ariane and Bluebeard* (1907), which was written as a 'libretto' for Dukas. And in 1913 Vaughan Williams wrote linking sequences for *The Death of Tintagiles* which subtly enhance the expressive pauses and silences of that play, a musical effect I shall be returning to later.

There was great encouragement in all this for Yeats's own endeavours to marry words and music in new ways and make audiences listen with a new intentness. The Maeterlinckian model of music drama was before him constantly in this early stage, both in the theatre and, as ever, in the talk and writing of Symons who was constantly on the look-out for performing styles appropriate to the drama he admired so much. At Bayreuth, for instance, watching Wagner, he would typically be struck by the thought: 'These people move like music . . . Maeterlinck should be acted in this solemn way.' And he was quick to sense wider dramatic possibilities in sideline or highly specialised musical activities, like Arnold Dolmetsch's revival of antique instruments which, as he said, revealed 'an exquisite lost world . . .'. It was some such world, he knew, that Yeats was hoping to create from those recitals of his verse by Florence Farr to the psaltery made for her by Dolmetsch: in that strange half-song with its monotonously insistent accompaniment there might be the germs of a new technique for a music drama, as Symons could see (despite his reservations about Florence Farr's actual achievement) because he carried in his mind such a vivid image of a technique that worked in something like that way with overwhelming success. Georgette Leblanc's verse recitals in Paris solved the problem which always vexed him critically, as it was to vex Yeats in practice, of getting the right balance between words and music. She sang poems of Verlaine and Mallarmé and 'mysterious songs' of Maeterlinck, he said, so delicately that 'it was impossible to think more of the words than of the music or of the music than of the words', so realising Mallarmé's dream of a form that would fuse music and poetry theatrically without falling into the vulgarity of conventional opera, the 'gross recognised proportions of things'. This was a more 'subtly intoxicating elixir'.[28]

From the time when he speculated on the possibility of 'very wonderful music' working stage magic in *The Shadowy Waters*, Yeats was in search of just such an elixir. He did not find a major composer to work as closely with him as Debussy with Maeterlinck,[29] but in a way this was not what he needed. His composer had above all to be theatrically-minded, an improviser, someone capable of working continuously in collaboration with choreographer, dancer and singers as well as poet, and allowing the music to grow out of all those different needs. Edmund Dulac, who acted as designer and mask-maker as well as composer for some of the dance plays, was from this point of view the ideal musician. His music, though admired by Yeats's most distinguished choreographer, Ninette de Valois, has not survived in the way that, say, Fauré's incidental music for *Pelléas and Mélisande* has. Yet there is a certain rightness about this: the dance plays were designed as acts of improvisation and should, perhaps, always be created entirely afresh; for each new production, a new dance, new music.

On the whole this is how it was during the time Yeats was writing the plays; Symons's principle of perishability seems to have ruled, for only exceptionally has the music written for productions been recorded, sometimes rather tantalisingly, as for instance with Elgar's setting for the song 'There are Seven that Pull the Thread', written for that curious work of collaboration, *Diarmuid and Grania*; fine, haunting music, this, which makes one well understand Yeats's wish that Elgar had done more for him. An immense amount of music has been composed for the plays, however, if not always recorded, between then and now; settings to stand on their own, or for specific productions—notably Havelock Nelson's for Mary O'Malley's company at

[28] *Plays, Acting and Music*, pp. 18–22.

[29] Debussy was so in tune with the ideas of the symbolists that in contemplating the collaboration with a poet he hoped for, he vowed he would not, 'follow the errant path of opera, where poetry takes second place, stifled by too heavy a musical clothing'. He hoped instead to graft a dream of his own on to the dream of the poet he worked for.

the Lyric Theatre, Belfast—or adaptations like the operatic *Purgatory*
of Gordon Crosse. The early plays have always drawn attention, from
Hart's setting of *The Land of Heart's Desire* in 1914 to Kalomoires's
The Shadowy Waters and Eck's *The Countess Cathleen* (*Irische Legende*)
in 1954, and the dance plays have inspired some arresting music, such
as George Antheil's for *Fighting the Waves* and the Japanese settings
for *At the Hawk's Well* by Koscak Yamada and *The Cat and the Moon*
by Teiji Ito.

One present-day composer with a special devotion to Yeats, Ray-
mond Warren, has written on the problems of composing for the plays
and the qualities which attract him to the task.[30] The composer
meeting the drama for the first time, he says, will find himself 'in
curiously familiar territory', a remark that recalls Schoenberg on the
inherent musicality of Maeterlinck's drama. Musicians have indeed
often been ahead of theatre people and critics in their appreciation of
Yeats's ideas on song-speech and the dramatic values in pitch, rhythm
and intonation. Some of the music he best liked for his dance plays was
George Antheil's for *Fighting the Waves* (Abbey, 13 August 1929),
which was aggressively modern, drawing as it did on the strident
sounds of urban life in the twenties. He found the dance that was
performed to this revolutionary music a transcendent experience, the
whole piece deeply satisfying. It was also a realisation of ideas long
before expounded in 'Speaking to the Psaltery', for Antheil too sought
'monotony in external things for the sake of an interior variety'. As
Yeats delightedly wrote to Olivia Shakespear, Antheil meant to have
all the singing within the range of the speaking voice, 'for my old
theories are dogmas, it seems, of the new school' (*Letters*, p. 760).

I have looked ahead to that moment in 1929 because the music led
there, and it is pleasant to draw an account of early experimental effort
to an end with a glimpse of fruition. I want to conclude this chapter,
however, with a reminder of what was still missing from the Yeatsian
synthesis in the period of Maeterlinck, Symons and the French
symbolists, before the influence of Gordon Craig had been fully
assimilated or Ezra Pound encountered. Dance was still an undeveloped
element but that is not what I have principally in mind. It is true that
Yeats had to wait for Pound and the idea of the Nō and acquire a
Japanese dancer, before he could make dance an integral part of his
dramatic structure, but his vision of a dance drama goes back to the
earliest phase when he created a dancing role for the Child in *The*

[30] 'An Idea of Music', *Threshold*, 19 (Autumn 1965).

Land of Heart's Desire and the strange, near-surrealist scene of dancing friars in the remarkable fourth act of *Where there is Nothing*. That vision had never lacked encouragement from sources Yeats most valued; Mallarmé and the symbolists, and above all, Symons, who loved dance so much and who kept before Yeats's eyes both the practice—Loie Fuller, Isadora Duncan—and the supporting ideas of Mallarmé and of Nietzsche. What was still needed however, was a technique for opening up more complex regions of self-consciousness. Symons had pointed to the magical fusion of arts attained by Leblanc: 'It is as much with her eyes and her hands, as with her voice, that she evokes the melody of a picture; it is a picture that sings and that sings in all its lines', and it was associated for him with self-consciousness. In that room where she sang Maeterlinck, there was a facing mirror on the wall; once she became absorbed in a song, so he said, she saw no-one else in the room, only the image in the mirror. This was the strongest impression he brought away with him: 'I imagine her always singing in front of a mirror, always recognising her own shadow there, and the more absolutely abandoned to what the song is saying through her because of that uninterrupted communion with herself'. The image brilliantly hints at the special role the idea of performance might be given in a modernist drama of self-consciousness. The performer studying her own reflection seems like an embodiment of all those self-obsessed beings in pre-Raphaelite and symbolist paintings, Hylas looking into the water, the Lady of Shalott living in shadows and reflections and the dancers who acted out the theme, Isadora Duncan dancing Narcissus, Loie Fuller in her mauve and green, colours of Yeats and Maeterlinck, her drapery whirled round by sticks and changing colour under the lights as she danced Salomé on glass, portraying, in Mallarmé's phrase, a marvellous 'frenzy of the self'.[31]

It was that self-communion of the performer sunk in his dream, that Yeats was seeking to realise in *The Shadowy Waters*, the play in which he took his first tentative steps towards a synthesis of words and music, picture and movement. But that was only one half of what was needed. Modernism required a more complex acting out of the self; it was not enough to have 'the dim unconscious nature, the world of instinct, which (if there is any truth in Darwin) is the accumulated wisdom of all living things from the monera to man . . .' (*Letters*, p. 31).

[31] For an illuminating account of this performance see Frank Kermode, 'Poet and Dancer before Diaghilev' in *Modern Essays* (1971).

It also needed the self that watches and receives signals from the unconscious and struggles to deal with and interpret them.

That 'double effect' called for images other than those offered by performers engrossed with their own reflections, another model than the totally enclosed, inward-turning drama of Maeterlinck. Yeats had to find theatrical means of standing outside the dreaming mind as well as of registering the process of dreaming. It is this second phase of his explorations which I now want to consider.

2 ⌁ The Syntax Achieved

The inspiration for a more complex, modernist technique came in the first place from the subtle art of Gordon Craig. It was a marvellous stroke of luck for Yeats that this genius of the European theatre (for Europe was Craig's real home) should turn up on his doorstep to provide just that stimulus his stage art was ready for. From the moment he saw Craig's production of *Dido and Aeneas* in 1901 he knew that this was the beginning of a totally new phase in the art of the theatre: a year later, defending it and *The Masque of Love*[1] in a letter to *The Saturday Review*, he wrote: 'I saw the only admirable stage scenery of our time . . . the staging of *Dido and Aeneas* and of *The Masque of Love* will some day, I am persuaded, be remembered among the important events of our time' (*Letters*, p. 366). There is no more impressive demonstration of Yeats's almost demonic intellectual energy than the speed and thoroughness of his assimilation of Craig's ideas.

The first fruit was the reform of scenic design already referred to. The bold, stylised simplicity of Craig's settings stimulated him to accentuate his own tentative stylisations, as, for instance, in the 'missal' effect which replaced the more realistic décor called for in early versions of *The Countess Cathleen*. One can see already in this stylising process a hint of the extreme formalism to come in the dance plays. In Craig's production of *Acis and Galatea* (10 March 1902) there was much visual symbolism; the tent effect of the opening scene changed from white to grey to express Galatea's grief over the death of Acis, and his metamorphosis into a waterfall was indicated, as Denis Bablet says, in his valuable book on Craig, by 'a decorative, stylised design of curved, dotted lines on the backcloth'.[2] Apropos a contemporary critic's surmise that the inspiration for such effects came from Japanese art, Bablet points out that it was not until three years after the production of *The Masque of Love* (which prompted the remark) that Craig became fascinated with oriental theatre, but agrees that he might unconsciously have come earlier under the Japanese spell.

[1] *Dido and Aeneas* was first produced by the Purcell Operatic Society 17 May 1900 and revived, in the double bill with *The Masque of Love*, 26 March 1901.

[2] *Edward Gordon Craig*, p. 51.

Surely this must have been so. And for Yeats and Maeterlinck also those colours they were addicted to, dull mauves, indefinite greens and blues, must have had Japanese associations. They were colours of the 'Liberty style' which came into being when Arthur Liberty, first at the Oriental Warehouse and later in Regent Street, laid out the coloured silks from the East which delighted so many artists, including William Morris and Burne-Jones. Yeats, we know, was already aware of the possibilities in Japanese art in 1904; writing to Lady Gregory about the different kinds of stage wing required for her comedies and 'remote' plays like *The Shadowy Waters,* he said: 'I have found that the exact thing I want is the sort of tree one finds in Japanese prints' (*Letters,* p. 445). I want to touch for a moment on these early 'Japanese' influences, for, like those from the Continent I have been discussing, they must have helped in the confident assimilation of the Nō inspiration later on.

Gordon Craig's father, Edward Godwin, the architect, was a pillar of Liberty's from its opening ('an enchanting cave', he said of it, 'literally crammed with objects of oriental manufacture') and a lover of Japanese art, two states of mind that were virtually synonymous at the time. He carried both enthusiasms into his theatre criticism and practice: the highly formal beauty of his costumes for an open-air *As You Like It* was much admired by Wilde, and his reviews, which commonly focus on the visual aspects of productions, have a good deal of Japanese allusion. Theatre people, indeed, felt especially strongly the pull of what Arthur Liberty called the 'Japanese impressionistic side of things'. Isadora Duncan and Ellen Terry bought veiling and saffron silk from Liberty's for their stage performances and, with a rather amusing irony, Gilbert used their fabrics for his skit on the style in *Patience.*

Some of Yeats's closest associates in his early days had a strong feeling for Japanese art and theatre. Symons, as we saw, reviewed enthusiastically the performances in London of artists like Sada Yacco. And Ricketts, that most important designer, was fascinated by the theatre arts of Japan. His designs for *Salomé* (for a production taken to Japan) have a suggestion of Japanese line, elegantly combined with the crinkled silk Liberty look and his own bold, decorative stylisations. Often these theatrical impulses towards the 'Japanese impressionistic side of things', especially in Godwin's thinking, anticipate Craig's passion for Japanese austerity in scenic design as well as his feeling for the effects to be got from the play of light on colour and moving surfaces. When Godwin talked of 'the exquisite play of light that one gets from rich and rippling folds', he was expressing a sensibility which his son managed to realise in terms of total theatre. Craig's use of light made a great impact on all his early critics. 'Under the play of this light', says one, of *Dido and Aeneas*, 'the background becomes a deep shimmering blue, apparently almost translucent, upon which the green and purple make a harmony of great richness.'[3] In a later production, *Bethlehem* (December 1902), a remarkable impression of the supernatural was created by light streaming up from the crib into the faces looking down, a long familiar painters' effect which the theatre at last could capture: Craig was deeply influenced by Rembrandt and thought him 'the born dramatist, though he writes no words'. Interesting shadow effects also became possible. The lowering shadow cast by Polyphemus made him, according to Max Beerbohm, 'the one and only real and impressive giant ever seen on any stage.'[4] In Craig's later experiments, with moving cubes, light became even more important, indeed the dominant actor in the scene.

Yeats learnt from Craig how to exploit to the full the potentialities of light; it became one of his most powerful instruments for achieving 'the distance from life which can make credible strange events, elaborate words' (*Essays and Introductions*, p. 221). In each revision of *The Shadowy Waters* the lighting directions became more precise, and after *Deirdre* (1907) had been played in Craig's setting which, as Yeats said, made possible 'natural and expressive light and shadow', he revised his idea of how the sinister 'dark-faced men' in the background should be shown; in 1911 he was thinking of having instead of solid figures 'passing shadows and standing shadows only'. 'Perhaps the light that casts them may grow blood-red as the sun sets', he went on, 'but of that I am not sure' (*Variorum Plays*, p. 396). This eagerness to try variations sometimes took him well away from Japanese austerity: the 'golden spirals' of light in *The Green Helmet* (their elaborateness smacked of the commercial theatre to Arthur Griffiths) were used for jazzier surrealist purposes. But the austere ideal returns in *Purgatory* which is perhaps the supreme instance of Yeats's subtle use of stage lighting.

Craig reinforced in many ways the Maeterlinckian influence. His

[3] M. Cox, 'Dress', in *The Artist* (July 1900).
[4] 'Mr Craig's Experiment', *Around Theatres* (1953), pp. 198–202. Beerbohm expressed a wish that Craig would undertake the production of a Maeterlinck play: 'how hauntingly mystical [it] would grow under his hands'.

too was a theatre of silences, music and marionettes. He began with music—his first productions were all of opera, in collaboration with Martin Shaw—and he announced the dominant theme of his great manifesto, *On the Art of the Theatre* (1911 French edition), in that line from Pater so beloved of the French symbolists, 'All art constantly aspires towards the condition of music'. Music, paradoxically, made silence possible, and for silence Craig had a truly Maeterlinckian reverence. He might almost be quoting from *The Treasure of the Humble* when he says:

All great Drama moves in Silence—
Events of the greatest magnitude and significance pass in silence. . .
There were no words wasted in the creation of the Universe, neither can words create so much as an ant. All Nature is silent when it acts, and speech cannot take the place of action.[5]

His theory of the über-marionette (the actor plus fire, minus egoism) is well known. But there were significant differences in Craig's view of the stage which separate his scene from Maeterlinck's and provided perhaps the most important stimuli Yeats had from him. One of the distinguishing features is his continual emphasis on the dynamism of drama, another his stress on the need to somehow reflect in structure the sense of distance and impersonality he felt there should be in the relation of the creator to the action. In his designing he moved away from pictorial effects to a more austere, structural scene which he himself called 'architectonic'. Interestingly, one painter who had been associated with the pictorial style of the Théâtre d'Art recorded the favourable impression Craig's 'cube' arrangement made on him (when he visited him in Florence in 1910): 'By means of a number of cubes which can shrink or expand, the cube of the stage becomes either square, oblong, or tall in proportion to its width . . . just as a painter selects a square, wide or tall canvas to suit his subject.' And he concluded that this was the direction the experimental theatre must take if it wanted to achieve a full synthesis of the arts, for 'we painters can never give you anything except *pictures*, better or worse; they will never be a real setting for the drama. . .'[6]

Craig cut Yeats free from the picture frame and so encouraged all that experiment with the confrontation of actors and audience, the process of improvisation, the stage illusion itself which was to give his

---

[5] Quoted in E. Craig, *Gordon Craig* (1968), p. 276.
[6] Quoted in Bablet, op. cit., pp. 122–3.

later drama its so modern look. The set of ivory-coloured screens Craig gave him in 1910 along with the miniature model 'to play with', were not often used on the Abbey stage after the production of *The Hour-Glass* in 1911, though it was there that their practicability was first successfully demonstrated. But they had a vital, freeing effect on Yeats's imagination; they banished, as he said, a whole world that wearied him, for now no attempt need be made to suggest a natural scene: the screens were frankly artificial, were folded and unfolded in full view of the audience, a process so full of meaning to Yeats that he later adapted it to the dance plays, having his musicians fold and unfold a painted cloth to open and close the action.

The new feeling he developed, under Craig's influence, for a bare 'architectonic' setting did not in any way diminish his passion for decorative and pictorial effects. Though in 1911 he was announcing sternly 'Easel painting is no natural part of the theatre',[7] he continued to plan elaborate colour harmonies, and curtains and backcloths kept their importance for him as late as *The Herne's Egg* (1938). His ability to love several contradictory things at once was a vital part of his genius: in 1938 when his scene had become very austere, he was charmed by a revival of *On Baile's Strand* at the Abbey with a setting 'ornate, elaborate, like a Crivelli painting'. Part of the screens' attraction, indeed, was their visual charm; they could provide, he thought, 'a decoration of the stage almost infinite in the variety of its expression and suggestion'.

This was a decorative effect, however, which left the stage bare and gave the actor a renewed importance: 'there is less to compete against him, for there is less detail, though there is more beauty'. And if Craig had slightly reduced visual richness, he more than made up for it by offering another source of interest for the eye which was to have an overwhelming impact on Yeats's art—the mask. Already in *On Baile's Strand* (1904) the Fool and Blind Man are described as having 'features made grotesque and extravagant by masks', and in 1910 Yeats wrote to Lady Gregory apropos *The Hour-Glass*: 'I am very much excited by the thought of putting the Fool into a mask'. From the design[8] Craig made for the Fool's mask it is easy to see what excited him. That figure with its faintly oriental head, wide eyes, wide mouth, 'as wide and wild as a hill', with his shears in one hand, and in the other a great bag, so much too big for the pennies he begs for, is an immensely

---

[7] 'The Theatre of Beauty', in *Uncollected Prose*, ii, p. 400.
[8] A design only, for Craig had not time to execute it.

powerful figure, someone who could easily step out of the picture frame and confront the audience directly without losing a shred of his mysterious and rather sinister force.

This was exactly what happened in the later version of *The Hour-Glass* (1914), written after Yeats had seen Craig's screens in action and assimilated the possibilities they opened up for a new kind of dramatic structure. In the prose version of 1903, the action is totally enclosed; Wise Man and Fool are equally cut off from the outside world; no one in the play is able to detach himself enough to refer out to the audience and so change the dramatic perspective. This is in sharp contrast with the method in two plays which seem likely to have been in Yeats's mind at the time, the medieval *Everyman* and Marlowe's *Dr Faustus*. Lady Wilde's didactic tale, *The Priest's Soul* was his immediate source, but there are irresistible echoes in *The Hour-Glass* from those early plays. 'Ah Faustus, now hast thou but one bare hour to live', we might almost expect the Wise Man to say, when he covers the hour-glass in terror at the thought of sinking into damnation as the sand runs out and shrieks, 'Look at me, tell me if my face is changed, / Is there a notch of the Fiend's nail upon it / Already?'. And there are obvious connections with *Everyman* in the appearance of the Angel as messenger of death and the Wise Man's stupefied reaction to the news that he has only an hour to live—'Give me a year—a month—a week —a day'. William Poel's great revival of the play took place in 1901, and though Yeats does not mention seeing the production (which visited Dublin), Symons certainly did, and wrote of it in a way that Yeats must have found suggestive.

Both *Everyman* and *Dr Faustus* speak out directly to the audience through a chorus character who offers his own perspective on the action and invites or threatens us to apply the moral of what we have seen to our own lives. In the 1903 version of *The Hour-Glass* there was nothing of this sort; the action is entirely set in the Wise Man's study and he is a self-contained character who quite coolly and deliberately chooses the text for the opening debate with his Pupils. Under the stimulus of Craig's inventions for the play—the screens, the design for Fool's mask and costume—everything changed. The version published in 1914, after the vital production, has an arrestingly new and modern look. Now the direction calls for a stage to be built out over the orchestra and for the Pupils to appear in front of the stage curtain to make their own choice of theme for the coming debate with the Wise Man. They are nervous, inhibited:

FIRST PUPIL	He said we might choose the subject for the lesson.
SECOND PUPIL	There is none of us wise enough to do that.
THIRD PUPIL	It would need a great deal of wisdom to know what it is we want to know.

Irrational notes begin to sound. One Pupil says he knows the question that must be asked; in a dream he heard a voice telling him to challenge the Wise Man:

> . . . I was to say to him,
> 'You were wrong to say there is no God and no soul—may be, if there is not much of either, there is yet some tatters, some tag on the wind—so to speak—some rag upon a bush, some bob-tail of a god.'

At that point the Fool enters and the forces of unreasoning intuition grow stronger: to the accompaniment of his childish, monotonously repeated, 'Give me a penny', the Pupils abandon rational judgement for chance. In a scene of great visual grotesqueness they balance their books on the Fool's back, making him kneel down and stretch his arms out like 'a golden eagle in a church', a living lectern. Then one of them hears a sound—'the Master has come'—and pulls back the curtain, an inevitably stylised gesture that in drawing attention to the theatrical process raises crucial questions about the different levels of reality on which Wise Man, Pupils and Fool operate.

A new emphasis falls on the stage frame; behind it the Wise Man is apparently quite cut off from the fantasies, intuitions and revelations we the audience have been involved in. And yet he is aware of something going on beyond his view, something threatening to invade his enclosed world, as the Pupils and Fool have literally done by that simple act of drawing the curtain and stepping from the fore stage into the bare interior where he sits, so alone, with the one dominating stage property, the hour-glass. As Karen Dorn points out, in a perceptive analysis, the disposition of the study has also changed in Craig's design; the master's desk has been moved from its original central position to an alcove in shadow, and a corridor of screens curves from it to the light at the centre of the back stage, suggesting 'that his domain of learning is at the dark end of a path moving towards light'.[9]

---

[9] 'Dialogue into Movement: W. B. Yeats's Theatre Collaboration with Gordon Craig', in *Yeats and the Theatre*, ed. R. O'Driscoll and L. Reynolds (Toronto 1975), pp. 109–36.

When the Pupils give him the theme that came up seemingly at random—'There are two living countries, one visible and one invisible . . .'—the violence of his reaction makes it clear that the disturbing thought is no stranger to him; it had already visited him, he admits, in terrible dreams. He tries to throw it away as a theme fit only for beggars, but a beggar takes it up. The Fool, so preoccupied with the need to fill his bag with pennies, confirms, in parenthesis as it were, with terrifying simplicity and matter-of-factness the truth of the text:

> To be sure—everybody knows, everybody in the world knows, when it is spring with us, the trees are withering there, when it is summer with us, the snow is falling there . . . does not everybody with an intellect know that?

His arrogant confidence brings him very close to the man who is saying exactly the opposite thing: it is this essential likeness between them which his more modern technique enables Yeats to bring out so much more sharply in the later versions of the play. That opening scene in front of the curtain plants the idea that some process is under way in a world the Wise Man seems cut off from, though what he says shows that he is somehow in touch with it. It gives a bold hint that the whole action may have to be seen as a dramatic structuring by a mind of its own half-conscious processes. What develops is a movement between two poles, represented by Wise Man and Fool, and a desperate attempt to establish a balance between them.

FOOL   . . . Every day men go out dressed in black and spread great black nets over the hills, great black nets.

WISE MAN   A strange place that to fish in.

FOOL   They spread them out on the hills that they may catch the feet of the angels; but every morning, just before the dawn, I go out and cut the nets with the shears and the angels fly away.

WISE MAN   (*speaking with excitement*). Ah, now I know that you are Teigue the Fool. You say that I am wise, and yet I say there are no angels.

FOOL   I have seen plenty of angels.

The Wise Man goes on denying, but he recognises too. The Fool tells him angels are like the blades of grass, and he instantly remembers, 'They are plenty as the blades of grass—I heard that phrase when I was but a child and was told folly'. He cannot get the thought out of his head now, is compelled to conjure up the being that has appeared in his mind's eye, standing and staring with 'unnatural eyes'.

The Angel who comes through the door, as he imagines it doing, to shock him into 'new sight', is a more equivocal and disturbing apparition than the angel of the first version. There is the ambiguous sexuality I spoke of earlier ('she' could be changed to 'he' throughout —a disorientating stage direction) and the Craig-inspired idea of the 'beautiful mask'. He, she—or should it be 'it'?—no longer introduces itself as 'the Angel of the Most High God', as in the prose version; the subtitle 'A Morality Play' has also been dropped. Now it is simply 'the messenger' or, more strangely, the 'crafty one that you have called'; enigmatic, Beckett-like terms, in tune with the image of the Wise Man's dream, that terrified intuition of what was to come:

> Reason is growing dim;
> A moment more and Frenzy will beat his drum
> And laugh aloud and scream;
> And I must dance in the dream.
> No, no, but it is like a hawk, a hawk of the air,
> It has swooped down—and this swoop makes the third—
> And what can I, but tremble like a bird?

The death sentence the Angel pronounces is the death of personality; if the Wise Man can find no faith, no soul that 'believes' before his hour is up, he will become a shapeless thing drifting in a Lake of Spaces and Wood of Nothing, 'wailing for substance'. The horrific vision crystallises all those earlier hints that the agonised search of the self for completeness is the subject of the play. The Angel too is a part of that self, it seems, outcome of the dreams that have been breaking through into the Wise Man's daylight life since the curtain was so threateningly drawn back at the opening of the play. It is a messenger only, who can get no further than the threshold; an interestingly suggestive inhibition, this, though one wonders whether, if Yeats had had the theatrical means to hand, he would have been tempted to push the Angel nearer to the dancing Hawk figure that seems to want to get into the play.

It is the Fool in fact, not the Angel, who does a dance of sorts; just before the apparition materialises, the Wise Man gives him instructions as if he were a puppet—'Fool, stand there; Fool, go sit in the corner'— and he obeys, like a dazed Lucky responding to the pull of Pozzo's rope. It is a startlingly physical suggestion that the confrontation between these two—so opposite and yet so close—is the climax the play seeks. But first the Wise Man must go through the hopeless routine of questioning family and pupils to find a believing soul, though he knows, really, it is no good: they are only 'mirrors' who will throw back the 'rational' image he taught them. So it happens, with most bitter irony when his children chant in chorus:

There is nothing we cannot see, nothing we cannot touch.

It is one of Yeats's brilliantly uncanny moments when that childish sing-song is taken up into the final passage between Fool and Wise Man and invested with new surrealist intensity. The scene opens with a sinister parody—the Wise Man shrinking in panic from the sight of the hour-glass only to find the Fool measuring out the time by blowing a dandelion clock. This was an effect in the original version, but it is made still more disturbing here when the Fool uses the same childish ritual to taunt the Wise Man with his slowness to realise where he must turn in his extremity: 'Will he ask Teigue the Fool? Yes, he will, he will; no, he will not—yes, he will'. The childish third person, 'Teigue knows everything . . . but Teigue will not speak, he says nothing', uneasily hints at the primitive, unpredictable nature of the consciousness embodied in the Fool. He is by far the most powerful figure on the stage and provides a supreme illustration of the creative interplay between two imaginations, the artist's and the poet's, for it was only after Craig had 'seen' the character in his mask with his shears and great bag that Yeats was able to weave these things into the dramatic texture and give the Fool his suggestive defence of that last mysterious object:

I will not speak. I will not tell you what is in my mind. I will not tell you what is in my bag. You might steal away my thoughts.

The Fool has the upper hand—and yet in a way he has not. As he makes to go, he is turned back by the watcher at the threshold; the 'moment' has come, he may answer all the questions. But he is doomed to remain dumb. Without his aid, it seems, the Wise Man has received his revelation: God is reality; 'the rest's a dream'. Yeats wanted to give his scholar more dignity by removing him from the humiliating position of the earlier version when he went down on his knees to beg the Fool's help: perhaps this heroic stiffening is rather abrupt and not altogether convincing.

Nevertheless the curious three-cornered relationship remains, and is, it seems to me, his great achievement in the play, brilliantly suggesting as it does the indirect path the mind must take in its desperate struggle to 'know' the world beyond the threshold and find its own true form. The Wise Man dies, as he has to: the 'moment' of intense life is only possible within the moment of death; a sombre, ambiguous consummation this, which might even be taken—in spite of the heroic confidence of his conversion speech—as the breakdown of the self under the terrible pressures on it. Yeats strengthens the ambiguity and to my mind makes the play more interesting by giving the Fool's role a decidedly modern extension at this point. He is left alone on the stage to press on the dead man questions and answers which have a part pathetic, part mocking and sinister naïveté: 'Why don't you wake up? . . . You and I, we are the two fools, we know everything, but we will not speak'. It is he, not as in earlier versions, the Angel, who catches the dead man's soul in his hand; then he hands it over to be placed in the Angel's golden casket. How alarming that moment is; what would happen to the soul if it remained in his possession? It is with that sort of question about the Fool and his power that Yeats leaves us. And he forces it on our attention in one of the most exciting additions he made, the scene at the end when the Fool steps right out of the enclosing proscenium frame, to stand in front of the curtain where he began and address the audience directly:

> He is gone, he is gone, he is gone, but come in, everybody in the world, and look at me.

Would we dare to take up that invitation, and what chance would we have if we did of making contact with the slippery, elusive being who exults in the knowledge he has and will not give? His last line taunts us with his dumbness: 'But I will not speak, I will run away'. The Fool was the character Yeats did not inherit from his source, and whose part, as we have seen, steadily grew during the revision. He made his radical break with the naturalistic convention, the enclosed action and the illusion of real life through this figure in Craig costume and mask.

I have dwelt on *The Hour-Glass* at some length because it shows so well how in Yeats's development as a playwright everything flows together; one break out into a new convention or dimension inspires another, there is a steady widening out into freer and ever more radical experiment. The move towards total theatre need not, after all, have led away from the enclosed drama of the proscenium frame or into the deliberate breaking of the illusion of realism represented by the Fool's stepping in front of the curtain. In the supreme example of total theatre Yeats had before him—the Gesamtkunstwerke of Wagner —it did not happen so: the music drama remained totally encased in the picture frame, its characters sublimely unaware of their own theatricality. And this has remained the convention of opera and music drama from Wagner till quite recent times.

Yeats's further step, out of the proscenium, is a measure of his driving originality, an originality which is bound up with his extraordinary capacity for picking up hints and assimilating them and for allowing one part of his mind to fertilise another. The ideas he had received from the French, from Maeterlinck and Symons and then, differently, from Gordon Craig helped to give him the outline of his modernist drama; there it is, in 1914, in the revised version of *The Hour-Glass*. Then came another enormous lift, comparable to the impetus he received from Craig and Maeterlinck, though this one was rather more fully acknowledged as a source of inspiration. The Nō drama, which Ezra Pound made him vividly aware of, was a revelation of the greatest importance, for reasons we can easily understand. It was the first complete proof that total theatre techniques could be used in the service of an interior drama such as he had defined many years before when he spoke of Florence Farr's verse readings to the psaltery as 'a monotony in external things for the sake of an interior variety, a sacrifice of gross effects to subtle effects, an asceticism of the imagination'. There was support now from an ancient tradition for the ideas he had long held. It was because he had held them for so long, travelled so far already by a European route toward a theatrical style close to the Nō, that he was able to recognise instantly what he needed in a drama he saw only on the printed page and learnt of from others, Fenellosa and Ezra Pound and, no doubt, Charles Ricketts, who had been so much impressed by performances of the Nō in Japan. It was not necessary for him to see the masks of the Nō in use on the stage—he never had that experience—in order to take them into his imagination: the idea was enough to help him realise at last, to the full, his total theatre technique.

The impact of Nō on his drama has been very thoroughly charted by Yeats himself and by others.[10] I do not want to recapitulate a history

[10] Yeats in 'Certain Noble Plays of Japan', *Essays and Introductions*; S. Oshima, *W. B. Yeats and Japan* (Tokyo, 1965); R. Taylor, *The Drama of W. B. Yeats: Irish Myth and the Japanese Nō* (1976).

that has become so well known, but to recall briefly features of the new model that must have been specially valuable to him. For one thing, Nō was a totally musical structure such as the symbolists had dreamed of; low toned, oblique, a chamber form, but one that worked with Wagnerian force. Yeats instantly seized on one vital notion; the presentation of the drama by the musicians. This was certainly one of Nō's greatest gifts to him. Another revelation was the dance; for the first time he encountered a drama where dance had a central place and was expressive in just the way he had imagined in *The Land of Heart's Desire*. The Nō dance too was a ghostly communication between man and supernatural being, coming at the point where words fail, offering a transcendental experience. It was fortunate, of course, that the abstract information he received from Japanese texts in translation could be supplemented from the practical experience of the Japanese dancer, Ito, who created Yeats's first complex dancing role, the Hawk Woman. Masks he had already begun to use with great boldness, as we have seen, but here again the Nō offered backing and encouraged a much more thorough-going practice; not just a solitary mask here and there, but all the actors masked in some way, the protagonists in full masks usually, the musicians in a mask-like make-up.

One of the most impressive things about the Nō form is its complete self-sufficiency, and this above all, it seems to me, must have excited Yeats, shown him a way of setting his drama of intense inner 'moments' into a sharp perspective—the further step he had to take to arrive at a modernist technique. In the Nō everything is there on the stage, visible from the start; musicians to initiate and frame the action, actors who are also dancers, able to represent in their fine movements the finest shades of interior being; marvellously beautiful or grotesque masks to create and project the dramatis personae without benefit of scenic complexity, lighting or stage tricks of any kind. The play seems to be absolutely the creation of the performers: it was this self-standing, improvising effect that Yeats so delightedly took to himself and reproduced in his own dance plays—with remarkable success, as anyone who has produced or performed in them will know. Once the performing expertise has been found—musicians, dancers, choreographer—the play begins to grow, a wonderfully independent entity that can be set up anywhere, on any kind of stage, or best of all, as Yeats wanted it, in a room with audience and performers under the same light, no barrier between them. For it is surely true, as he said, that 'these masked players seem stranger when there is no mechanical means of separating them from us'. Certainly the sense of the play as play is strongest then.

When *At the Hawk's Well* was given its first performance in 1916 in Lady Cunard's drawing-room, the audience were seeing 'theatre in the round' fifty years before the term came into general use. The opening of the action was represented by the Musicians' unfolding of the black cloth with its stylised hawk's motif; the actors were played in through the audience with drum beats and the action brought to its end by the folding of the cloth, all done in full view of the audience. *At the Hawk's Well* is so important in Yeats's oeuvre that I shall be returning to it in discussing the remarkable variety he achieved within the narrow limits of the dance form. Here I want only to glance at it as a model of the technique whose evolution I have been tracing from the time of *The Shadowy Waters*. That early play comes naturally to mind at this point, for *At the Hawk's Well* achieved what it could not, the admission of the non-human world to the cast list: at last Yeats has a bird for a character! Paradoxically, this can happen with ease and naturalness exactly because of the highly self-conscious theatricality in the dance form. The hawk's dance is consciously performed, the hawk cries imitated by an actor—sex uncertain—who has in a way always to be seen as just that, the virtuoso mimic, without identity of his own.

From the start the play is presented as a thing 'made' by the three Musicians, who work on the audience with words and music, hypnotic sounds of drum, flute and gong, to make us see what they see. That square blue cloth on the floor is a well where water may appear because the mind makes it so: everything that happens is to happen in the mind, as each in his own mind will settle what is meant by the cryptic saying:

> He who drinks, they say,
> Of that miraculous water lives for ever.

They begin with a magical invocation, whose opening line echoes through all Yeats's plays and is still echoing in Beckett's drama:

> I call to the eye of the mind
> A well long choked up and dry
> And boughs long stripped by the wind,
> And I call to the mind's eye
> Pallor of an ivory face,
> Its lofty dissolute air,
> A man climbing up to a place
> The salt sea wind has swept bare.

'Bare' is a key word. The mind is to be laid bare by means of a theatrical performance which is always showing its bones, so to speak. We are invited into the actors' preparations and routines, the slow unfolding of the cloth, the casual position of the Guardian, who crouches on the floor, almost as if in rehearsal, covered by a black cloth, waiting for his/her part to begin, a Hamm-like posture that indicates one of the many interesting lines of connection between Yeats and Beckett. We see the actors taking up different roles; the Musicians act, stage manage and produce; with words and music they call up the chief figures from some off-stage place. Both the Old and Young Man come on to the scene from among the audience, the Old Man standing motionless for a time, seeming unable to move until the first drum tap is heard, as though he really were the marionette waiting for a pull on his string which the stage direction says he should suggest in his movements. Old and Young Man both think they are free to make their own choices. We see the opposite, that they are moved like marionettes by the Musicians and by the dancer; it is 'in a dream', says the stage direction, that the Young Man follows her later off the stage.

The silence of the dancer is one of the play's most thrilling effects. That dumb, heavy figure under the cloak is there and yet not there, the actor who can't be made to speak, as the Old Man knows; it is with his hopeless attempt to wrest words from her that the action begins:

> It is enough to drive an old man crazy
> To look all day upon these broken rocks,
> And ragged thorns, and that one stupid face,
> And speak and get no answer.

The only way he can get a dialogue going is by mimicking the lines that she did speak, so he says, *yesterday*:

> You said:
> 'The well is full of hazel leaves.' You said:
> 'The wind is from the west.' And after that:
> 'If there is rain it's likely there'll be mud'.

Not a brilliant contribution to a conversation, but the best 'she'—or the Old Man speaking for her—can do. The Guardian of the Well can't really be imagined as a speaking part. Yeats has wonderfully arrived here, in his own distinctive fashion, at the Maeterlinckian position where silence is an active and troubling theatrical force.

What is that dumb presence under the cloak? A girl, the Old Man

says, but we never see that. When the terrible shivering begins and
the cloak is thrown off, it is a totally ambiguous creature who moves
into the dance, masked and costumed to suggest a hawk. Bird, woman
or witch—we can tell no more than the Young Man what name to give.
The power of the persona depends on the strange lack of definition;
having a male dancer in the role, as Yeats originally did, must have
heightened the sense of ambiguity and has much to recommend it as
a way of avoiding the commonplace eroticism that always threatens
the Yeatsian dances and can be so reductive. Strangeness is above all
what has to be sought. The dancer's power extends in so many
directions: she allures the Young Man, oppresses the old one, sending
him into the unwilling doze of age, and revolts the Musicians. They
play for her but will not look at her; instead they look—and focus
attention—on that small square of blue cloth which only they, the
detached ones, have the power to transform into a well, where the
water finally comes. They hear it come, make us hear and see it too.
'Look' they tell us, 'Look where it glitters.'

Great irony here, for the Musicians are not interested in the water
of immortality; they are content to be 'a mouthful of sweet air'. Yet
they give us the moment the two who dream of the well can never have,
being too much in the grip of the dancer. Still moved by her, the Young
Man returns to the daylight world to act out there the 'curse' she has
put on him, while the Old Man goes back to waiting—for the next
time the dancer will deceive him. Yeats had arrived at the perfect form
for his drama of inner action; the 'moment' or 'crisis of the spirit', as
it is called in *The Hour-Glass*, could be represented in something like
its real complexity as an intricate interaction of will and impulse,
conscious and unconscious drives. Such is the suggestion made by the
convention as he handles it. It is a strange collaboration among actors
who only understand their own parts, though they have to work
together in endlessly repeated routines. One set of actors moves and
controls another set, seeing more than those they manipulate and
giving us their sharp perspective but understanding less in some ways
than the actors in the inner play, who, though unaware of the surrounding frame, are nevertheless closer to the play's centre. And at the
centre is the dumb actor, the equivocal one, who cannot be got at, the
seemingly inert creature which is the source of the terrifying energy
that defeats the Old Man and galvanises the Young Man into the
moment of 'intense life' which is also the moment that decides his
tragic fate and death.

The total synthesis of the arts which Yeats had been aiming at for so long proved all he had hoped for. Masks, music, dance were increasingly allowed to suggest and shape the form his ideas took; he would rewrite a play for a dancer as he did *The Only Jealousy of Emer* (1919) or find his inspiration in a mask; *Emer* sprang in the first place from the extraordinary masks created by the Dutch sculptor, Van Kroop. Subtle alienation effects—in plays like *Calvary* (1920) and *The Death of Cuchulain* (1939)—were encouraged by the practical need to improvise and be flexible in the complicated collaborations the dance drama involved.

The achievement of this new theatrical syntax made for a new freedom in all sorts of ways within and without the dance form. Most importantly, he was able to get more of himself into his plays, especially the sardonic humour and scepticism which Chesterton had once mischievously picked on as his distinguishing trait, at a time when most people thought of him as a dreamer in the Celtic twilight. The self-advertising theatricality of the dramatic structure he had worked out allowed him to reveal dissonances and contradictions, often of an unheroic kind; tetchy old men can appear on his stage as well as young heroes and the relationship between them be explored. There is a splendid confidence in the stage directions of the later plays, a sense of mastery which allows him to mix the conventions in suggestive new syntheses, the formal and grand with the coarse and popular, the balletic with the naturalistic, the surrealist with the poignantly human. It becomes easier all the time to see his drama as a model for the modern theatre; these more mixed, flexible forms open up the way for John Arden as well as Pinter, for Sean O'Casey as well as Beckett. One of the last plays, *Purgatory*, is a virtuoso demonstration of flexibility and of continuity, a last fine fruit of experimental thinking going back over many years. The structure is naturalistic but, as many critics have observed, there is a Nō-like quality in the scene; the bare stage with its two focal points, the ruined house and that leafless tree, which surely originated in the Japanese prints that excited Yeats thirty years earlier, though the old inspiration had been reinforced by all he had learnt of the Nō stage, with its bridge and stylised tree. It is also, of course, a development from the Craig scene for *The Hour-Glass*, which had a similar bareness and a similar focusing on one or two symbolic objects —the hour-glass, the Fool's bag and shears. A new element comes into play in *Purgatory*: the light. It is one of the great haunting effects of Yeats's drama, a psychic climax equivalent to the dance in *At the*

Hawk's Well, when the window of the ruined house lights up to show the girl who has been dead for so many years—'A body that was a bundle of old bones / Before I was born', the Boy says—standing in the window, waiting for the arrival of the lover who has not yet given her a child, and yet that child and his child stand before us in the flesh. The fading in and out of the light bringing the ghostly figures before us and taking them away again, the beating of the horse's hooves horribly returning after the murder when the Old Man thinks he has extinguished them, form marvellous images of the hallucinated mind, churning over its painful memories and imaginings.

I want to close this account of the evolution of Yeats's modernist technique with a look at *The Herne's Egg,* for it strikingly illustrates the dance form opening up into a 'mixed' convention, near-Brechtian in its aggressively cool, comic control of tumultuous material. It is a technique for the absurdist theatre, or the surrealist, or for a 'popular' musical didactic theatre like Sean O'Casey's or John Arden's; a modernist technique in fact, which allows Yeats to set a self-conscious perspective on the unconscious without damaging its plausibility or vitality.

There is a great sense of confidence and freedom about this 'madcap Rabelaisian extravaganza' as Austin Clarke calls it. Yeats feels free, for instance, to revert to the scenic method of his earliest drama, turning from the bare 'round' of the dance plays right back to the picture frame and painted scene of his first love. But everything suffers a sea change. The stage decoration here is not harmonious, hypnotic; on the contrary, it is designed to keep us alert and continually adjusting our impressions. The stage is dominated by back cloths painted to suggest symbolic objects; a throne, a misty rock with a great bird standing on it, and on a mountain top a 'moon of comic tradition, a round smiling face'. In reading the play we have to try to keep these pictures in mind, for they supply some ironic contradictions which, when we see the play in a theatre, must change and subtly affect our mood. In the opening scene, for instance, when a roughly humorous, sceptical mood is in the ascendant, the romantic strange bird image is there to counteract it; when the action turns tragic, there is a reverse effect; it is under the round smiling moon that Congal fights to his death.

The technique is very close to that of the dance plays proper, but there are crucial differences: most important, there are no chorus characters, no masks. It is as if Yeats were setting out to show that he can do without these things now and still get the distancing he needs through structural means, by subtle shifts from one style and convention to another which force the audience to change imaginative perspective. The rituals look at first to be quite in the old mode; men fighting without touching, coming together 'as if in a dance', to a clash of cymbals or a drum beat which represent the meeting of swords and shields. The sacrilegious stone-throwing is mimed with invisible stones, and seven drum beats count out the number of men taking part in the rape of Attracta. But from the start the technique is 'degraded' to match the wholesale degradation Yeats so interestingly imposes on his heroic world in this play. A small but telling illustration is the admission of a new strain to the stately consort of drum and flute; that noisy popular instrument, the concertina, comes in appropriately, to suggest the heroes' vandalistic breaking up of Tara Hall in their drunken feast. This is a blackly comic phantasmagoria with a strong pull to bathos and a powerful flavour of nursery rhyme and nonsense tale. The opening battle is fought like a boys' game in Looking Glass land, with unchanging rules, equal losses and wounds of perfect neatness—Congal's in the right shoulder blade, Aedh's in the left: it finishes whenever they like, though not before Aedh has provided a satisfactory ending to his funny story about the two fleas who retired and kept a dog. Almost we might expect those other mirror images, Tweedledum and Tweedledee, to appear over the horizon, complacently arranging to have a bit of a battle, starting at half past four and knocking off at half past six for dinner. The drum/flute ritual, in other plays solemn or lyrical, is here associated with the absurd: the drum beats in the Tara scene represent drunken blows with table legs, the ritualistic counting out of the seven leads into the grotesque scene when they stand in line tossing caps to see who will be first in the sexual encounter with the virgin priestess.

The juvenile theme is repeated in the visual imagery with its fantastic nursery motifs, the round, smiling moon, and, above all, the donkey, a wooden donkey on wheels 'like a child's toy, but life-size', with the creel of eggs painted on its side to represent the eggs stolen from the Great Herne. It is as if the immature heroes wander into the nursery kingdom and are destroyed there—or forced to change and develop. There is immaturity in the female world of Attracta too, but another kind which suggests not the arrested development of the males, but rather its opposite, a huge and terrifying potentiality for change. The onset of change—inevitable after Congal takes the Herne's eggs and has the Herne's curse said over him—is represented by a dance which must be one of the oddest in any of the plays, certainly the hardest to make conventionally seductive (that trap for directors). In a trance-like state, to the sound of an off-stage flute playing the uncanny tune, 'The Great Herne's Feather', Attracta moves into an embryonic dance, all the time clutching the hen's egg given her by one of the watching adolescent girls. To them it seems as if she has been taken over, become a 'puppet'; it is

> As though her god were there
> Thinking how best to move
> A doll upon a wire.

The awkwardness and pathetically childish stiffness observed by her stage audience should not be lost from our view of Attracta. Yeats has provided in this odd dance a perspective on her which is not open to Congal: he cannot see the human pathos of the virgin, only the weirdness which seems to threaten him, the 'loony' who must be brought closer to his stereotype, made 'all woman, all sensible woman'. The dance shows how impossible his idea is. The dancer moves away with astounding leaps, 'long loops like a dancer', say the girls, or 'like a hare', providing a bizarre confirmation of the image she has of herself, a human woman mysteriously related to the world of non-human nature whose power is beginning to rise up in her. The dance hints at the two aspects of the play which can never be separated, so Yeats has contrived; the absurdity of it all—men fighting to death over an egg, a virgin 'waiting to be trodden by a bird'—and the awesomeness; the Herne's egg *does* represent another order of reality, the virgin does in some mysterious way 'know' the bird and derive power from her knowledge.

The dance and Attracta's substitution of the hen's egg for the herne's are the deliberately bathetic prelude to the central act of the play, the rape. This is real in the way the ritual fights of the opening were not, so Yeats suggests by a daring variation he now introduces into the quality of the stage sounds. When Attracta calls to her supernatural lover to justify his 'darling'—'Great Herne, declare her pure . . . Let the round heaven declare it'—the response comes, not in the stylised form of flute and drum but as a real sound of 'real' thunder, beginning as a low grumble and gradually swelling, in thoroughly naturalistic style, till it has terrified the men into submission, made all

except Congal retract their sexual boasts. In the stage world of simu-
lated sights and sounds the woman who can call up this life-like
thunder has proved the superior power of her 'reality', forced her view
that it was not a rape she experienced but a mystical bride bed where
she lay with the Great Herne and held his thunderbolts in her hand.

The thunder says it is so, and with that sound still in our ears we
go into the final scene where Yeats with stunning virtuosity moves us
deeper both into absurdity and into the sense of awesome revelation
that grows around the figure of Attracta. He has established his
stylised convention so well by this point that he can bring on a new
character, the Fool, with eerie matter-of-factness. Like the comically
round smiling moon he is just there, a necessary feature of the scene,
with his ludicrous, horrific equipment, cauldron lid, cooking pot and
spit, his whistling and his calm knowledge; he had to come because
'Somebody said, "King Congal's on the mountain / Cursed to die at
the hands of a fool".' Yet there is a kind of wild, free, near-Shake-
spearean naturalism in it too:

> CONGAL   What is your name, boy?
> FOOL   Poor Tom Fool
>   Everybody knows Tom Fool.

This is touching and painful in a new way: Congal has changed,
become more inward, as the change of style between his first contest
and this last one finely suggests. The confident balletic performance
he gave with Aedh was the public self, enclosed in defensive masculine
rules, fixed and 'perfect' in the unchanging symmetry emphasised by
the rhythmical drum beats. This one is silent, private, deadly; it is
the acting out of the dark message that came to him from the hidden
region where the Great Herne sits wreathed in mist:

> And to end his fool breath
> At a fool's hand meet his death.

It is a conflict with a crazily distorted mirror image, as he realises in a
flash of wild intuition—'Fool! Am I myself a Fool?'—though he
pushes aside the terrifying thought that would rob him of free will,
asserts his public identity—'I am King Congal of Connacht and of
Tara'—and runs on to the spit to defeat the curse by making his death
his own act. But the silent language of the play says otherwise; the
ritualistic process of the mime, like a slow motion, silent film, puts an

ironic focus on that most incongruous of instruments for a hero's death, the Fool's kitchen spit. And Congal knows the irony, though he refuses it:

> Your chosen kitchen spit has killed me,
> But killed me at my own will, not yours.

There is a child-like bravado in that cry, and a poignancy too, such as everything in the action is acquiring: the play is growing more human as it grows more strange. And now we are called on to 'believe' (in the usual way, of suspending disbelief) in the strangest possibility of all, that the great change we have seen worked out in Congal may not end with his death. The whole of Attracta's prophecy may be true; in his next incarnation he may be forced down a step or two in the ladder of creation, be re-born as an animal or a bird.

How can this grotesque idea provide us with a satisfying climax? Yeats's technique meets its acid test here and splendidly survives it. Partly he works through sympathy, the human sympathy that has so remarkably been built up in the surrealist context: it would be hard for the audience to avoid some contagion from Congal's panic especially, perhaps, as it is the panic of a man, a tough, male chauvinist sceptic, who has nevertheless been brought under the dominion of the unearthly, nursery moon. It is like a child in the nursery that he calls out to Attracta:

> Protect me, I have won my bout,
> But I am afraid of what the Herne
> May do with me when I am dead.

And it is like a mother that she responds or like one of those Strindbergian women, who can release their kind feelings for their lovers only when they feel safely established in maternal power.

So far, so natural, but Yeats now takes a step beyond naturalness and psychology into the metaphysical region which is also the region of the absurd, for we can hardly avoid feeling the absurdity when Attracta calls to Corney to come and lie with her quickly to beget a human form for the dying man's spirit to occupy. Yet can we afford, any more than Congal can, to laugh away this weirdly literal assumption of the maternal role? Surely not: by now the absurd has acquired a sinister and equivocal status: the grotesque dance with the hen's egg had in it the herne's curse, the man's death took place under the absurd moon: from hen's egg to herne's egg proved to be, as the literal nearness suggests, only a step.

Yeats tests us further, however, going to the limits of absurdity and audacity by introducing into this event so dangerously poised over the abyss of the unreal, a shockingly real sound, a donkey's bray. Too late, Attracta cries, the donkey has broken loose and coupled and the female has conceived: 'King Congal must be born a donkey!' And the play ends with Corney's joke about donkeys' long pregnancies:

> All that trouble and nothing to show for it,
> Nothing but just another donkey.

A prospect that is brutally bleak or promising, according perhaps to how much we like the prospect of living for ever—and donkeys!

What beast is this which has suddenly assumed so much character? Nothing but the wooden donkey on wheels that Corney pushed about, though he also addressed it as if it were human, with its 'rapscallion Clareman's eye'. Two levels of reality there, and now another; the donkey existing in its own right, out there braying its real sound in the 'real' off-stage fields and rocks where a real fate awaits the dead hero. Or may await—but once we start to speculate on these ideas we are already caught, are investing with the life of our own mind the hard-to-forget world that was created, we know, out of play materials-birds painted on backcloths and life-size toys.

'One of the characters is a donkey', Yeats wrote to Dorothy Wellesley in 1935 (*Letters*, p. 846). Yes, and what a triumphant conclusion to the search for style which began with the abortive attempt to get eagles as characters into *The Shadowy Waters*. The unlikely reality of the donkey in *The Herne's Egg* is the best of signs that Yeats had evolved a theatrical syntax to suit all his needs. In persuading us to make the fantastic mental adjustments required to establish the donkey as a character, he brings home the fantastic nature of imagination, its power to construct endless versions of reality and invest them with value, for in the theatre after all, the dumb wooden donkey is no less real than the off-stage one braying 'naturalistically'; the hen's egg in the dancer's hand no more real than the herne's egg painted on the donkey's side. We dissolve one reality into another with the greatest ease, at the touch of a drumbeat, a song, a disconcertingly natural sound; the play makes us self-conscious about this strange capacity without in any way undermining it; the illusion re-asserts itself at will.

Here was a technique of virtuoso flexibility for the drama of the interior, a technique we should have no difficulty now in seeing as modern. And it was a modernist drama that he shaped with it as I shall hope to show more fully in my later discussion of the dance plays.

3 ∾ Maeterlinck

'Drama of the interior', 'static drama', 'school of silence' are all phrases that were used by or about Maeterlinck in his own time and yet how modern they seem, as if they had been newly coined for the theatre of Beckett and Pinter. To conjure up a few characteristic scenes and images from his early plays is to experience a quite disconcerting, even ghostly sense of *déja vu* and dissolving identity.

To whose stage, for instance, does this dark place belong, where the twelve blind figures sit in awesome immobility as if they have no further need for the commonplace gestures of ordinary life, waiting for someone to come and save them, straining to hear the footsteps that mysteriously approach and stop among them? Not Beckett's, and yet, in a way, how well it might be: with the forest of *The Sightless* Maeterlinck set the scene for a later generation of lost ones than his own; Vladimir and Estragon would not be out of place there, nor blind Pozzo led by Lucky, though their response to their situation is so much more robust than the cries of terror we hear as the curtain comes down on Maeterlinck's distraught characters:

> They are here!
> They are here in our midst!
> Who are you?
> Have pity on us!

More images from the Maeterlinckian theatre stream into mind, setting up great ripples of echoes. The well there, called 'blind man's well' because its water is said to have cured the blind: Pelléas and Mélisande are the figures who sit by it gazing at the water, but might we not have expected some rather more dilapidated characters in that vicinity, Synge's blind tramps, or Yeats's blind and lame beggars, struggling to a holy well to be cured of their afflictions? Then there are doors: doors laboriously pushed open to let light into a dark interior or slowly opening of themselves to admit someone or something unknown that is yet somehow known and dreaded—how easily they could seem to be opening on Pinter's threatened rooms. And two more recurring images: the watcher at the lighted window, fascinated and horrified by the calm unawareness of the figures silhouetted behind the glass, their ignorance of the suffering he knows is in store for them: an old blind man sitting motionless in his chair under a light he cannot see, listening to presences in the silence, registering his sensations, thoughts, intuitions. There are some long echoes here. Other eavesdroppers come into view; Yeats's Old Man gazing up at the lighted window in the ruined house of *Purgatory*, Eliot's Harry, appalled by the family at Wishwood exposed in the drawing-room window to the watching eyes they have no sense of. And on Beckett's stage, another old man, almost blind, sitting under a strong light, listening to the sounds from a life that is no longer there.

The shadowy forms which evoke thoughts of playwrights as distinct as Synge, Yeats and Eliot, Beckett and Pinter, are the forms of the Maeterlinckian drama at its most haunting and compelling. *The Intruder, The Sightless, Pelléas and Mélisande, Interior, The Death of Tintagiles*[1] were seminal plays which launched into the modern European theatre the powerful images of the well, the blind man, immobile in his armchair, the menacing door, the lighted interior with the eye upon it: they have gone on echoing ever since, from *The Well of the Saints* to *No Man's Land*.

Yet Maeterlinck's own name produces few echoes nowadays. For most people he is probably best known as the author of *The Blue Bird* (1909), the one title of his that is as easily recognisable in its English form as its French.[2] Not seen anything like as often as *Peter Pan*, still it is likely to touch off similar associations; a children's play of magic and 'pantomime toggery', in Granville Barker's phrase, about the search for a blue bird of happiness; a play for Christmas, or, in its latest metamorphosis, a film for Elizabeth Taylor to star in. *Sister Beatrice* is another play that might stir memories, if only of Reinhardt's spectacular version, *The Miracle*, and of course there is *Pelléas and Mélisande*, which everyone knows, though there is a sting here too, for how many would think first of Maeterlinck rather than Debussy or want to argue against Peter Conrad when he suggests that the opera has taken over as the superior form? The English theatre has had no interest in Maeterlinck since his

---

[1] *The Intruder*, 1892 (*L'Intruse*, Brussels 1890)
  The Sightless, 1895 (*Les Aveugles*, Brussels 1890)
  Pelléas and Mélisande, 1895 (*Pélleas et Mélisande*, Brussels 1892)
  Interior, 1899 (*Intérieur*, Brussels 1894)
  The Death of Tintagiles, 1899 (*La Mort de Tintagiles*, Brussels 1894)
[2] *The Blue Bird*, 1909 (*L'Oiseau Bleu*, Paris 1909).

heyday at the beginning of the century when he was included in the Vedrenne-Barker repertory at the Court Theatre and there were all those prestigious productions I spoke of earlier, with Sarah Bernhardt, Mrs Patrick Campbell, Forbes Robertson. He is never produced with that kind of flourish nowadays; the plays are hardly seen at all, nor even easily read; there are no new editions and the old Edwardian translations set up considerable barriers to a modern reader's enjoyment and understanding. Yet I have been suggesting that he has been a pervasive influence on the modernist drama of Yeats and Beckett. How is this discrepancy to be accounted for? Part of the answer, I think, is that the qualities which made him exciting to Yeats and Synge—and could still excite us now—have been obscured by the lush, old-fashioned romanticism which co-exists with his startling modernity. He has some uncongenial nineteenth-century traits, a weakness for florid rhetoric—irony of ironies, in the apostle of silence —and much sentimentality, roused especially by ailing children and frail girls brutally betrayed; his interest in them sometimes has a lip-smacking quality which calls to mind those fleshly, genteelly pornographic Victorian pictures of erring wives, redeemed prostitutes and voluptuous beauties, like Edwin Long's half-naked girls in *The Marriage Market* safely exposed to public view under a caption with a respectable historical association. Maeterlinck was a prolific and extremely uneven writer: exalted melodramas like *Monna Vanna*, *Sister Beatrice* and *The Burgomaster of Stilemonde* are curiously mixed up in his oeuvre with fantastic Shakespearian pastiches like *The Princess Maleine* and *Joyzelle*[3] and with the plays that seem to belong to quite another dimension, where, if the romanticism remains—as I suppose one would have to say it does in *Pelléas and Mélisande*—it is transformed and transcended; a new modern quality has entered. These plays, which are mainly his earliest, have an austerity, a purity of line, a genuine strangeness and subtlety that cut them off from the nineteenth century and led the way into a totally new kind of theatre. It is with these early works, written between 1889 and 1894 that I shall be chiefly concerned.

[3] *Monna Vanna*, 1904 (Paris 1902)
   Sister Beatrice, 1901 (*Soeur Beatrice*, Brussels 1901)
   The Burgomaster of Stilemonde, 1918 (*Le Bourgmestre de Stilemonde*, Paris 1919)
   Joyzelle, 1907 (Paris 1903)
   The Princess Maleine, 1892 (*La Princesse Maleine*, Ghent 1889)

It is true that even they are seldom performed today in the English-speaking theatre. The absence of good modern English editions is the symptom of a neglect which has to do, perhaps, with the strange nature of the plays themselves, for certainly they are a production risk, operating as they do on a knife edge, on the brink of an abyss of the absurd. Intensely concentrated and inward-looking, ironical, but without real humour, at any rate in the Edwardian translations, they depend rather dangerously on the creation of poetic atmosphere and on a finely turned acting style. And here the question of translation becomes crucial. Admirably enterprising though they were in their time, the versions of William Archer, Alfred Sutro and Laurence Alma Tadema seem heavy in the hand today, vague where they should be exact and literal—sometimes ludicrously so—when they should be delicately oblique. Even when it seems from their introductions that the translators have grasped Maeterlinck's methods in principle, they seldom bring out clearly his highly distinctive patterns of words and silences, his 'inarticulacies', the child-like broken speech, the helpless repetitions, the unfinished sentences—all those features of his style which were so extraordinary around the year 1900 and could still, I believe, impress us today, even though—or perhaps because—we have become accustomed to similar techniques in the theatre of Beckett and Pinter. A good demonstration that his drama does keep its power was given in the production by the BBC of *The Death of Tintagiles* in August 1975. Then we did hear the delicately broken, hypnotic, intensely musical speech Maeterlinck calls for. The translation was Basil Ashmore's, and to see it on the page[4]—tiny paragraphs of speech separated by spaces to indicate pauses—was to realise to the full the barrier to understanding set up by the old translations. Visually, the Ashmore text instantly suggested modernity, the style of *Krapp's Last Tape* or *Landscape,* by formalising, as the older translations do not, the typographical lay-out so as to emphasise the important syntax of pauses and silences. Maeterlinck gives some very exact notation for these transitions, with patterns of dots to represent pauses, and careful distinctions as between 'silence' and 'new silence'.

The BBC production used the music Vaughan Williams wrote for the play in 1913, and this again was a revelation: it provided a context of haunting beauty, a string of pure sound on which the episodes of the drama were twined. The words seemed to grow out of the elegiac and wistful cadences of sound and to fade into them; when the music died

[4] In typescript: the translation was not published.

out, one became sharply aware of the vast silence brooding around the characters, the silence that becomes such a powerful dramatic force at the end when Ygraine hammers on the door and shouts into the void that has taken Tintagiles. Dorothy Tutin as Ygraine perfectly caught the child-like notes in the sisters' pathetic determination to hold the little boy back from death, while at the same time suggesting the mature knowledge lying underneath, the premonition of the inevitable event. Though the important visual dimension was missing, this sensitive production proved beyond any doubt that Maeterlinck was playable and must surely have made those who heard it wish also to see *The Death of Tintagiles* either on stage, or, possibly, on television, which seems in some ways an ideal medium for this small-scale, intense drama with its sinister alternations of distancing and close-up.[5]

Here, as elsewhere in Maeterlinck's drama, delicate feeling and the 'inherent brutal strength' that Schoenberg noticed are curiously bound up together; another modern effect which was obscured in the past by the timidity of the first English audiences and critics who often found his more grotesque scenes too strong meat. The invisible queen in *The Death of Tintagiles*, for instance, was too much even for the ardent Maeterlinckian, James Huneker; he could not face the thought of the 'fat panting devil', the 'obscene shape of terror!' conjured up by Ygraine's line in the French text, 'on dit qu'elle n'est pas belle et qu'elle devient enorme. . .' The hint of monstrous growth in 'devient enorme' suggested to him 'a black, dropsical spider shut in the dark weaving the murderous webs for passing flies'. Could there not be ways of softening the horror, he wondered, perhaps by using music to give 'the pathos of distance'.[6] Much cruder means than that were commonly taken to spare the audience's feelings. Sutro as translator and Granville Barker as producer were scolded by Desmond Mac-Carthy for watering down this same effect with the tepid translation, 'They say her form is strange'. And it was not till 1911 that Martin Harvey restored to *Pelléas and Mélisande* the 'terrible scene' in the subterranean cavern which had always up to then been cut in English productions.

Maeterlinck himself, looking back at plays like *The Sightless* from

---

[5] The play lent itself well to adaptation for television, we thought, when we recorded it for the Consortium for Drama and Media in Higher Education in 1977. (The video recording of this production may be obtained from the BUFC, 81 Dean Street, WC1.)

[6] 'Maurice Maeterlinck' in *Iconoclasts* (New York 1905), pp. 367–429.

his more optimistic position of later years, seems to have been as appalled as some of his critics by the blackness of his early drama. In a tone of perplexed detachment he says:

> The keynote of these little plays is dread of the unknown that surrounds us. I . . . seemed to believe in a monstrous, invisible, fatal power. . . Its intentions could not be divined but the spirit of the drama assumed them to be malevolent always . . . The problem of existence was answered only by the enigma of annihilation.[7]

It is strange to find him putting this rather snubbing stress on the negative aspect, for the great achievement of the 'little plays' is precisely that so positive a sense of mysterious potentialities and unexplored faculties is created out of negative conditions—absence, deprivation, immobility, silence. In this drama 'not knowing', 'not remembering', 'not saying' become vital modes of expression. There is a connection with Maeterlinck's mysticism, especially his wish to bring silence on to the stage and give it dramatic force. His ideas on this subject were peculiarly uncompromising, might make us wonder indeed, as we read prose meditations like *The Treasure of the Humble* and *The Buried Temple*, whether as Una Ellis-Fermor suggested, there may not be 'inherent incompatibility between drama and the matter of religious experience':

> No sooner do we speak than something warns us that the divine gates are closing.
> Words can tell us scarcely anything of that which should be told.
> We wander in God like helpless sleep-walkers, or like the blind who despairingly seek the very temple in which they are actually situated.

That last metaphor however already has a little drama curled up in it, as we might well think even if we did not know *The Sightless*, and in fact throughout the prose works the inherently theatrical cast of his imagination constantly shows itself. Maeterlinck had an extremely strong urge to draw ordinary people into the mystical experience; his will to do so was a driving force of his drama. He may sometimes talk about 'mysteries' and the 'elect' as Yeats does, but again like Yeats, he insists also on just the opposite, that the doors of perception are open to all, even, or perhaps especially, in the conditions of everyday life.

[7] *The Buried Temple*, 1902, translated A. Sutro, pp. 109–11 (*Le Temple enseveli*, Paris 1902).

There were signs, he thought, of a general increase in sensitivity; a new, more spiritual epoch was approaching when the ordinary man might begin to realise that he had all the time been an 'inarticulate mystic'. It was entirely appropriate that he should give to his most important essay on the theatre the title 'The Tragical in Daily Life'; it is a kind of assurance to himself that the ordinary men he has in mind could provide an audience for a theatre of a totally new kind, a theatre of revelation.

This celebrated essay, which first appeared in the collection, *The Treasure of the Humble*.[8] is one of the great documents of the modern theatre, its Preface to *Lyrical Ballads,* one might say. In it he seems to wave a wand that conjures up a whole new drama which has *Krapp's Last Tape* and *That Time* at its further reach.

> I have grown to believe that an old man, seated in his armchair, waiting patiently, with his lamp beside him; giving unconscious ear to all the eternal laws that reign about his house, interpreting, without comprehending, the silence of doors and windows and the quivering voice of the light, submitting with bent head to the presence of his soul and his destiny—an old man, who conceives not that all the powers of this world, like so many heedful servants, are mingling and keeping vigil in his room, who suspects not that the very sun itself is supporting in space the little table against which he leans, or that every star in heaven and every fibre of the soul are directly concerned in the movement of an eyelid that closes, or a thought that springs to birth—I have grown to believe that he, motionless as he is, does yet live in reality a deeper, more human and more universal life than the lover who strangles his mistress, the captain who conquers in battle, or 'the husband who avenges his honour'. (pp. 105–6)

The somewhat comical anti-climax of the ending is more easily understood in the full context where Maeterlinck discusses the changes he wanted to see in the theatre of his time. *The Treasure of the Humble* was published in French in 1896, still, that is, in the era of Sardou and 'strong' dramas like *La Tosca, Cléopâtre, La Sorcière*; they made him feel, he said: 'as though I were spending a few hours with my ancestors, who conceived life as something that was primitive, arid and brutal'. He sums up their subject-matter—a deceived husband killing his wife, a woman poisoning her lover, a son avenging his father, a father

[8] 1897 (*Le Trésor des humbles*, Paris 1896).

slaughtering his children—in a contemptuous 'Blood, surface-tears and death!'. Some irony here, one might think, since Maeterlinck's own drama indubitably depends rather heavily on just such events and feelings, especially sexual jealousy and violence. But the similarities only highlight the remarkable differences. We could easily enough summarise *Pelléas and Mélisande* in terms of the boulevard drama— a play of adultery, ending with the husband killing wife and lover— but how misleading that would be as an account of what the play is really about. Golaud's attack on Mélisande, brutally shocking though it is, is not the cause of her death: the wound is a scratch so small 'a bird would not die of it'. The cause is more mysterious, it is to do with the tremors of communing, of loving and not loving, knowing and not knowing, which have formed the real stuff of the action. 'She could not have lived. . . She was born for no reason . . . to die; and now she is dying for no reason', the Doctor says, with a magisterial conviction that is endorsed by the whole action, for from the moment of her arrival by the forest well, able to tell nothing of where she came from, Mélisande has been a figure of mystery in a play where almost everything seems to happen without the characters' intention or understanding. As for the term 'deceived husband', it comes nowhere near describing that terrible need which torments Golaud to 'know' the unknown being he calls his wife.

Physical events, violent or otherwise, become on Maeterlinck's stage an expression of the unknown self with its mysterious faculties for knowing what it must do regardless of a possibly catastrophic outcome; Pelléas and Mélisande must stand and look at each other in the moonlight, Ygraine must oppose the Queen, though she knows, really, that she will not be able to keep Tintagiles from her. Physical sensation for Maeterlinck was bound up with intuition and intuition led into a whole world of the mind which was inaccessible to reason, but subject to blinding revelations. Maeterlinck was an enormously ambitious explorer in that obscure region. He believed his attempt to register the subtle nuances and sifting processes of the human mind faced with the terror of 'ordinary' reality was something totally new to the theatre, though, like Yeats, he looked back to earlier traditions for support and stimulus and found it in the same places. Shakespeare gave him one classical example of 'inaction' in Hamlet, but closer still to his own way of thinking was Greek tragedy. He quotes with approval from the preface to *Bérénice* Racine's defence of that other 'simple' tragedy, Sophocles' *Philoctetes* whose entire subject, says

Racine, 'is but the coming of Ulysses with intent to seize the arrows of Hercules'. Maeterlinck agrees: 'What have we here', he asks, 'but life that is almost motionless?' In such a play, he goes on, even psychological interest—in itself more interesting than mere material action—was suppressed or diminished 'with the result that the interest centres solely and entirely in the individual, face to face with the universe . . . [man] is at rest, and we have time to observe him'.[9]

In that last phrase he anticipates not only his own as yet unwritten plays, but a whole movement in modern theatre. Then he addresses himself to the question of method: 'I do not know whether it be true that a static theatre is impossible.' Rather surprisingly, he finds no help here from Racine, that master of statuesque immobility and subtle discriminations. For Maeterlinck, he is ruined by rhetoric; his characters cannot reveal their innermost being because they are so busy talking. 'What can you tell me', he asks, 'of the soul of Andromache, of Britannicus?', and answers with a damning negative, 'If they were to be silent, they would cease to be'.[10]

But how can dramatic characters be silent? If they were so, would they not all cease to be? In prompting such questions, Maeterlinck is certainly edging us towards that Beckettian territory where Mrs Rooney feels herself becoming a pale blur in risk of disappearing altogether when her words fail her. At the time he asked the question, Maeterlinck could point to one playwright who was already showing a way to an answer. Ibsen in *The Master Builder* had invented, he thought, a 'language of silence': Hilde and Solness were the first characters in modern drama to show they knew they were living in the 'atmosphere of the soul'. How did Ibsen do it? Maeterlinck was inclined to resort to favourite and rather irritatingly evasive words like 'sorcery' when he examined the process, but all the same he does distinguish a method of dialogue: Solness and Hilde speak in a way that is both credible and like nothing we ever heard: their words have a somnambulistic quality, both hiding and revealing the sources of their inner life and suggesting profound movement under a trivial surface. Ibsen has 'endeavoured to blend in one expression both the inner and the outer dialogue'.[11] For Maeterlinck, of course, that inner dialogue was the one to be highlighted. He was confident that it could

---

[9] 'The Tragical in Daily Life', *The Treasure of the Humble*, p. 108.
[10] 'The Awakening of the Soul', op. cit., p. 29.
[11] 'The Tragical in Daily Life', op. cit., p. 119.

be done without losing the sense of common life, for he suggests we all communicate far more than we realise through the unspoken; what we take away from a conversation is not so much the ideas we have heard, but the aura that surrounded them; we are always listening to vibrations from the words that are not spoken. This above all was the speech he wanted to realise in the theatre; it would have affinities with the dialogue in *The Master Builder*, but would go much further into 'silence'; he would explore character under a different light and in a stillness such as no one had yet tried to bring on to the stage. Speaking of the visual charm of *Pelléas and Mélisande* and the impossibility of conveying it by the methods of the Lyceum, William Archer suggested that a whole new stage art was needed for this drama: 'One would have practically to invent new methods of scene-painting and stage-lighting.'[12] We have already seen that this was indeed what happened; Maeterlinck did devise a new stage art, a language of sight and sound, pictures and music, which I have been discussing in the course of tracing the evolution of Yeats's total theatre technique. I want now to look more closely at the drama itself, taking it in the two aspects that Maeterlinck himself distinguished: first, 'man face to face with the universe', looking out into the mysteries of time and death; secondly, people face to face with each other, seeking to look into the depths of personality.

I begin with a play which epitomises the first, more metaphysical genre. *The Sightless* was the earliest and perhaps the most uncompromising expression of Maeterlinck's idea of static theatre. It is a play of the 'moment', brief and unremitting, confining us, the audience, as well as the actors, within almost unbearably narrow limits: we are forced to concentrate with new precision, made aware of the possibility of finer perception by being deprived of sensory richness. It is one of the most awesome and tyrannical examples of Maeterlinck's 'negative' technique: he takes away almost everything we normally look for in the theatre—movement, colour, light, variety of mood—to exercise us in the art of deprivation and bring us to a climax of mystical intensity. The opening tableau makes an assertion that this is indeed 'static theatre'. We are confronted with a dim stage, representing a wintry northern forest where we have to strain to see the twelve blind people who face each other in two statuesque rows, hardly to be distinguished from the tree stumps and rocks they sit on. At the apex of the sculptured

[12] *The Theatrical World of 1895*, p. 116.

configuration is the figure of the dead priest whom the blind are so pathetically unaware of; he is only a degree more static and rigid than they are, for they move rarely, with deliberation and difficulty; it may be quite a long time before we realise that one of these dimly seen figures is not able to move at all.

When we have adjusted to this dark world with its terrifying stillness and scaled down our expectations to accord with the assumptions of the blind, we begin to notice more; like them, perhaps, we discover what we have through what we have not. We learn to discriminate among the blind, recognise the great variations of perception among them. Some are doubly afflicted—there is a deaf man, a woman out of her mind—and some wilfully seem to refuse opportunities of perceiving with their other senses. Slowly an impression builds up of a complex network of receiving modes, through which certain characters, especially the women, experience a fuller dimension: they hear the sea, remember crossing it, can imagine each other's faces, hear the voice of the priest as if he were alive among them. In all this, Maeterlinck does not soften or romanticise: nothing is spared of the pain, humiliation and awkwardness, at times grotesque, of their affliction. When they do move, they often make clumsy mistakes like the man who walks on the daffodils and crushes them in trying to pick them for the girl; all are more helpless than the dog which bounds in at one point and is at first mistaken by them for the old priest returning, a horribly absurd error which emphasises their disorientation and distance from reality. As our time draws on in this claustrophobic world, sight gradually comes to seem a rare and precious condition rather than the norm we take for granted. We may find ourselves, like the stage blind, beginning to exercise our other faculties harder than usual, listening intently as they do for almost imperceptible sounds;

SIXTH BLIND MAN	I am beginning to make out where we are. . .
THIRD BLIND MAN	We ought to go towards where midnight struck.

(All the night birds exult suddenly in the gloom)

FIRST BLIND MAN	Do you hear?—Do you hear?
SECOND BLIND MAN	We are not alone!
THIRD BLIND MAN	I have had my suspicions for a long time; we are being over-heard.—Has he come back?

FIRST BLIND MAN	I don't know what it is; it is above us.
SECOND BLIND MAN	Did the others hear nothing?— You are always silent!
THE OLDEST BLIND MAN	We are still listening.
THE YOUNG BLIND WOMAN	I hear wings about me!
THE OLDEST BLIND WOMAN	O God! O God! Tell us where we are!

We may have begun by feeling a distant pity for the deprived beings who find it hard to tell the simplest thing; who is sitting next to them, whether it is midday or midnight. But the play draws us alarmingly into the centre of their situation, forcing us to exchange our quick, impatient rhythm for theirs, so slow and heavy, with its hypnotic repetitions—'I only hear the dead leaves', 'O God! O God! Tell us where we are'—and its long pauses that fill up with tension as the blind hear the sounds they cannot interpret, of birds, sea, snow-flakes. But can we hear snowflakes or, as one of them does, the sound of someone's hair? We begin to lose the confidence in our own percep-tions we started with; our position of superiority is insidiously under-mined. They seem so pathetically helpless when they ask each other anxiously about the whereabouts of the priest as if he were still alive, when we know he is sitting stone cold among them. And yet how do we know that among the marmoreal figures this one is dead? Only because he does not speak; for us, as for them, the one who is silent has ceased to be. And sometimes we change places with them entirely, as when they try to identify the exact nature of a scent which does not exist for us at all; that experience is as closed off from our senses as the pictorial from theirs; we have to take it on trust:

THE YOUNG BLIND WOMAN	I smell a scent of flowers round about us. . .
FIRST BLIND MAN	I only smell the smell of the earth!
THE YOUNG BLIND WOMAN	There are flowers, there are flowers near us!
SECOND BLIND MAN	I only smell the smell of the earth!
THE OLDEST BLIND WOMAN	I have just smelt flowers on the wind. . .

THIRD BLIND MAN   I only smell the smell of the
                                   earth!

The technique of repetition and incantation works on our senses,
charms us into feeling the girl's hypersensitivity, persuades us, perhaps,
that she—and to a lesser extent the other women—have finer perceptions than the men, may even make us wonder uneasily about the other
powers she claims. Before she lost her sight she was beginning to 'see'
the future—she could tell 'who was going to be unhappy'—and she
has been told that some day she will see again. What would that
'seeing' mean? Sight is an awesome word by the end of the play,
standing for a faculty we are probably no longer sure we have or
aspire to, for that would involve us in facing whatever it is that comes
into the forest at the end and that only the child can see, though what
it sees it cannot tell. The final tableau when the young girl holds the
child high up to 'see' for them all is one of Maeterlinck's most thrilling
inventions, a powerful theatrical image for the terror and mystery of
insight. What do we see in our mind's eye at the horrific moment when
the footsteps stop—if indeed we hear them at all, for on this point the
stage directions are not explicit and the blind may hear more than we
do, as they have been doing throughout the action? We are left just
short of revelation, suspended like them in a void of anxious uncer-
tainty, imagining for ourselves the being who comes to save or perhaps
destroy them. Another God is coming into the world, a new priest, a
new revelation—or in more personal terms, their senses are being
refined to the point where they can receive intimations of another
mode of life that lies all round them, though they know it only through
interpreters like the dead priest and the prophetic girl.

From this first exploration in the unknown, Maeterlinck went on to
open up regions which the theatre has seldom dared to contemplate.
Death and birth are among his audacious subjects, and life at these
extremities merging into some 'other' existence, a mighty continuum
behind recurring cycles of being. *The Blue Bird* is a child's eye view
of this awesome region: the two children, Mytyl and Tyltyl, are given
a magic diamond which allows them to see through the veil into the
deep interior, the soul of things. It is a fairy-tale device but the concept
behind it was something that Maeterlinck took very seriously, and in
certain scenes makes us do too. There are remarkable moments in the
country of the unborn, where the children see many souls clamouring
for life and some trying to refuse it: one who stands apart saying 'I

would rather not be born' is told the moment has come, he cannot choose; another grieves at losing her twin soul. She is comforted, as the boat pushes away, carrying the separated being—'He is not going to die, but to live'—and yet birth in that scene is a kind of death. In the fine episode in the graveyard, it is the other way round. The scene opens full of the terror of death. Mytyl and Tyltyl are waiting nervously for midnight to strike and the tombs to give up their dead; he tells her he once saw a corpse; it was 'quite white, very still and very cold and it didn't talk'. 'I don't want to see the dead!', she cries pitiably, 'I don't want to see them!' Then the magic diamond does its work and they 'see'. Mounds open, crosses totter, slabs heave up and from the tombs rises a subtle efflorescence, white and virginal, 'transforming the graveyard into a sort of fairy-like and nuptial garden, over which rise the first rays of the dawn'. The scene ends with one of Maeterlinck's most moving negatives:

> Where are the dead?
> There are no dead.

This is the optimism of a fairy tale for children, but even in the sombre, tragic drama of *Pelléas and Mélisande* or *The Death of Tintagiles* Maeterlinck wonderfully brings out the sense of life and death touching and of the indestructibility of this thing he calls 'the soul'. In *The Death of Tintagiles*, it is true, the whole action leads up to the moment when Tintagiles is taken behind the door in the vault where the spider-like queen is waiting. That formidable door, which critics from the start of his career thought of as a characteristic symbol of his drama, certainly suggests a fearful dead end. It looms there, vast, iron, a Craig-like fantasy of a door (how easily we can imagine how Craig would have done it; as Symons says, designing for Maeterlinck would have been almost too easy for him). From behind it come the feeble responses of Tintagiles to Ygraine's impassioned calls. Pauses here are a formidable technique for working up the suspense and terror; like Ygraine we strain to hear, guess with a pang the awful meaning of the long pause after his last cry, and feel with her too the implacable nature of the silence that is returned to her entreaties:

> You will open the door, will you not? . . . I am asking so little . . . I want him for an instant, just for an instant . . . I cannot remember . . . You will understand . . . I did not have time . . . He can get through the tiniest opening . . . It is not difficult . . . (*A long inexor-*

able silence) . . . Monster! . . . Monster! . . . Curse you! Curse you!
. . . I spit on you!

And yet in these grim negatives there is the germ of something
positive: the silence is 'inexorable', but there is something there, the
door leads somewhere: and though the emphasis falls strongly on loss
and helplessness, it is equally on the will not to succumb, not to give up.

In *Pelléas and Mélisande* death is still pervasive and painful, but it
is part of a mysterious cycle now, in which its opposite, birth seems
almost the more arduous and doom-laden process. It's easy going,
to borrow a phrase from *Endgame*. Mélisande dies in childbirth with
the simplicity of a child, slipping away 'without a word', the old
grandfather standing over her, protecting her from the ravaging adult
grief of her husband. The approach of death is heralded by strange
silences; first, the servants, who have not been sent for, file silently
into the room and stand around the walls—a most disturbing episode
—and then, as if they hear some order no one else can, drop to their
knees, always in the same somnambulistic silence; that is the moment
of her death. It is inexplicable, bizarre, and yet deeply fitting; the girl
who communicated best in silence has escaped from words at last.
Her death is sombre, but there is a sense of release and relief too: the
delicate spirit had to make so much effort—simply to live, perhaps.
From the start, when she was discovered by the spring, like an Undine
out of her natural element, she was frightened of life. Even in the
brief idyll with Pelléas she was never at home but seemed 'ill' for want
of light in the dark castle which saw so little of the sun. Through her
stammering half remembrances and sense of lostness Maeterlinck
conveys piercing intuitions of another world which is there waiting
to be remembered but cannot ever be quite grasped. Mélisande, we
must feel, will never be acclimatised to the severities of Golaud's
castle: 'I am lost! . . . lost! . . . Oh! lost here . . . I don't belong here
. . . I was not born here. . .' This impression of life itself as somehow
an alien condition is special to her as a character; but Maeterlinck takes
it further into the play as a whole by brilliant stage imagery, and
especially—here again he is strikingly modern—by his use of stage
lighting. As the stage light waxes and wanes, moonlight gives
place to subterranean dark, shadows fall, we look into lighted windows, gradually we begin to recognise patterns of spiritual need;
characters long for light, or like Golaud seek out shadow; the boat
that brought Mélisande to the castle is watched disappearing into the

mist she came from; the lovers bathe in the light of Mélisande's hair, shrink from Golaud's long shadow, go down trembling into underground caves and vaults and return with relief and exultation to the light. Light is fragile, precious, evasive, a condition they aspire to but cannot possess for long; darkness continually draws them down till the castle seems to be an image of the world of matter in which they are trapped.

There is reinforcement for the idea of life as a kind of sad and difficult straying from the path of light in one or two odd little episodes which have a curious shock effect, because they seem so random, inexplicable, having nothing really to do with the main action. Yet at the same time there is a feeling that if we only knew, they would be the key. One such is the scene when Yniold sees the sheep going by and is shaken to see them being driven from the path they want to take back to the fold and hear them suddenly go silent as the voice of the off-stage shepherd calls. He questions him; 'Shepherd! Shepherd! why don't they talk any more?' The answer comes, cryptic, ominous. 'Because it is no longer the way to the fold'. The boy repeats the line, musing 'Where will they sleep tonight, I wonder?' And as if the plight of the sheep had brought it home to him, he suddenly becomes aware of the darkness and silence around him too: an image of lostness the more haunting for being so oblique and delicate.

But perhaps the strangest scene in the play is the first, when the servants are heard inside shouting, 'Open the door! Open the door!' and the door-keeper resists them: 'Out by the little doors, out by the little doors; there are enough of them!' This is an uncanny stage effect which must surely turn our thoughts, as so often in Maeterlinck's drama, to Ionesco and the modern absurdists, and indeed to Strindberg, for the clover-leaf door of *A Dream Play* is very close here. An enormous effort has to be made to open the door; the door-keeper is not sure he will be able to do it; he calls on the servants for help; they all begin to pull as the light comes up on the stage and then suddenly the light is full and the door thrown open. The servants appear on the threshold carrying water to wash the step. 'Yes', says the door-keeper, 'Pour water, pour water, pour out all the waters of the flood; you will never be able to do it. . .' He means they will never be able to clean the step of the stains—an eerie anticipation of the ending when Mélisande lies bleeding on the same threshold. That is an image of death, but it is surely birth that is suggested by the arduous effort to open the door, let in the light and begin the day. Birth is a kind of death, then, or death a birth; we may look at it as we like, but it is certain they cannot be separated, so the enigmatic scene says: they make up a cyclical movement in and out of the light, and this, if we had to summarise, is what the play is about.

I want to turn from *Pelléas* to a group of plays in what one might call Maeterlinck's Wordsworthian vein, for whereas in *Pelléas* he brings out familiar elements in a remote and dream-like world, in *Interior* and *The Intruder* he takes the opposite approach, starting with commonplace materials and investing them with strangeness. *The Intruder*, like *The Death of Tintagiles*, is about the coming of death and as in *Pelléas* it is a death following childbirth. But here everything outwardly is unremarkable. Doors are a focal point, but they are ordinary ones in an ordinary living-room; a glass door opening on to a terrace, a small concealed door leading to a staircase, two doors to bedrooms, one to the new-born child's, the other, which remains closed till the final moment, into the bedroom of the sick woman. No violent event looms up. The family are waiting with increasing anxiety for the arrival of the sister who is a nun: the old blind grand-father and to a lesser degree the three young girls are acutely sensitive to threatening sounds which the other members of the family are at first unaware of. Still a realistic, even prosaic situation, we might say, in that the blind and the very young commonly do have especially sensitive hearing, but in Maeterlinck's hands this hyper-sensitivity acquires a patina of mystery so that by the end we surely feel that some palpable presence has surged into the house, some great force that knows its time, comes when it must, cannot be deterred. We feel it because we are slowed down to the quiet rhythm of the old man, blind and almost motionless, under the light he cannot see with the physical eye; we are made to listen with him and feel his nervousness, become nervous too as the silences fall and small sounds accumulate that are nothing in themselves—a wind, the sharpening of a scythe, the cessation of the nightingale's song, a sigh, footsteps—but gather suggestive force as they pass through his exceptional faculties. He reads the signs: an intruder is approaching; something is taking its course. The intuition grows stronger, spreads even to the less percep-tive members of the on-stage family. In one of those odd, absurd and disturbing scenes which are so quintessentially Maeterlinckian, the Father has an altercation with a servant standing outside the door: he must be leaning against it; the servant protests, he is yards away, has not touched it. 'But you *are* pushing it.' In the moment of that angry, bewildered shout the intruder enters the room to make the savage separation; the prosaic door has become as formidable as those spectacularly nightmarish doors in other plays. The actual moment of death, as in so many of the other plays, is represented by deepening silence; the family turn very still and slowly, in the stillness, the door of the sick woman's room opens. Do we not half expect something to emerge—a pillar of cloud, a dark shadow, bearing away a soul? Maeterlinck hypnotises us, I believe, into having such expectations, but he does it without upsetting normality: there is a quite ordinary explanation, the door is only seemingly opening of its own accord. The nurse is coming to tell the family her patient has died; but so effectively has Maeterlinck attuned us to the nuances of every smallest action and movement, that the opening door becomes a moment of great intensity, which has in it a suggestion of release as well as ending. Death came in as an intruder, but for the woman shut up in the inner room it is the opening of a door—on to what we can't know, but the play has certainly suggested very powerfully that there is another world out there, not always quite out of reach of the senses.

Doors—ominous, threatening, immensely hard to open (and to close) releasing, promising—there seems no end to Maeterlinck's inventiveness in his handling of this stage image. Even in plays of a lesser order than those I am discussing we can see how his imagination was fired by it: *Alladine and Palomides*,[13] for instance, is an uneven piece, but it has one memorable scene when the lovers' death is represented by a view of a long corridor with closed doors on either side and the voices are heard faintly calling from behind them, an uncomfortable physical statement of separation.

His other great visual image, which expresses so much of his feeling about life and drama, and has been so influential in the modern theatre, is the image of *Interior*—figures in a lighted room exposed to watching eyes they are unaware of. In this piece too, doors are important; the family are forced to unbolt the door of their cosy living-room to let in the messengers of death; that scene, to which I shall be returning, is one of the fine visual moments of Maeterlinck's drama.

But here the door is distant, spoken of rather than visually prominent: the focus is on the side of the house that is not bolted, but open to the view, protected only by a sheet of glass. We see the family in their living-room sitting in the lamplight, an undistinguished

---

[13] *Alladine and Palomides*, 1899 (*Alladine et Palomides*, Brussels 1894).

domestic group, father and mother, the two daughters doing embroidery, a younger child asleep. But everything is changed, made strange and dreamlike by being seen through the windows from the viewpoint of the Old Man in the garden. The stage direction indicates the effect Maeterlinck wanted—and that productions often achieved in his time, according to critics like Desmond MacCarthy:

> *When one of them rises, walks, or makes a gesture, the movements appear grave, slow, apart, and as though spiritualised by the distance, the light, and the transparent film of the window-panes.*

It is, again, a 'moment' we are seeing, the long moment before the eavesdropper can bring himself to do what he has come for and break the news of the daughter's death to the family inside. Nothing happens but his hesitation; when at last he goes into the room the play ends. A play made out of nothing, one might say, certainly made in large part out of the evanescent materials Maeterlinck was so great a master of—light and silence.

The dreamlike remoteness of those silent figures behind the glass has one extraordinary effect which takes us into the distinctive Maeterlinckian territory, the hinterland of the mind, with its possibly undeveloped faculties including the sense of the future, which Maeterlinck thought an unused part of our equipment for reading life. The structure of the play curiously disorders our time sense. The present we are in is the Old Man's 'moment': the family are living in another, oblivious present while he stands watching them with the future, which already exists, bottled up in him; to bring it about he has only to tap on the window, as the Stranger, his fellow voyeur, presses him to do. But no, he delays. Compassion is part of the motive, but part of it too, we must feel, is fascination with this uncanny power he has of settling the exact shape the future will take:

> It is better that I should not be alone . . . I thought of that as I came along. . . If we enter together, I shall go roundabout to work; I shall tell them, for example: 'They found her thus, or thus. . . She was floating on the stream, and her hands were clasped. . .'

'Her hands were not clasped', says the Stranger, 'her arms were floating at her sides'; a Beckettian contradiction which heightens the eerie sense of fluidity; everything has happened and yet still has to happen, is still in a way being invented.

The process that is taking its course outside is sensed in the interior.

Maeterlinck achieves a particularly haunting and moving effect when the silent figures within who cannot hear what is being said in the garden nevertheless make signs of tentative response: when the talk is of their drowned sister's Ophelia-like hair, the hair of the girls within seems to 'tremble'; they turn their eyes to the window, one of them looks afraid; in one remarkable moment they move to the window and look out into the garden, one at each side, leaving the centre empty. The Old Man's line, 'No one comes to the middle window', points up the pathos of the grouping and the suggestion it makes that 'the soul has senses as the body has'. The reader who could envisage that scene and its significance was a satisfactory reader of plays, so Granville Barker said.

The simple physical situation—watching and being watched—becomes laden with awesome implications. Only the sleeping child is not looking at anything; it is being looked at however, by the family, and they are being looked at, and soon a possibly endless recession of watching opens up:

THE OLD MAN   They are looking at the child. . .
THE STRANGER   They do not know that others are looking at them. . .
THE OLD MAN   We, too, are watched. . .

In that last remark, which may exceptionally for Maeterlinck look out to the audience, and which certainly points in a direct line to *Endgame,* vast new possibilities can be glimpsed for a drama of modern self-consciousness. It is one of the most impressive illustrations of the lengthening out to the universal that Maeterlinck is able to achieve in these 'little' plays. The watchers in the garden seem immune, but the Old Man reminds his granddaughter, 'Do not weep, my child; our turn will come', and there are reverberations for those other 'immune' watchers, the audience:

MARY   Have pity on them, grandfather. . .
THE OLD MAN   We have pity on them, my child, but no one has pity on us.

In the extraordinary final scene the garden fills up with people trying to peer in, children being lifted up to get a better view, all speculating, pressing closer, while the family are still unconscious of being watched. It is one of the many moments in Maeterlinck's drama when Ionesco and the modern absurdists rush to mind; a bizarre image of violent anxiety and curiosity. There is tragedy too, we know, but character-istically Maeterlinck takes us on from there, silently contradicting in a scene of great visual power the dark message that forces its way into the interior. The Old Man goes into the room at last; the doors at the back are thrown open and the family go out. But what we see is not a blank wall, not darkness, but a marvellous sight; a starry sky, a luminous night, with lawn and fountain bathed in moonlight. So we end in the light, and there is a connection between this and the experi-ence of pain and darkness: as the Stranger reminds us, 'the child has not wakened': it misses both the moment of tragic shock and the silent revelation of starry immensity.

Interior is a wonderfully expressive image for the life of man 'face to face with the universe'. 'Look, my child, look: you will see what life is . . .', says the Old Man to his grand-daughter. Yes, by then the lamplit interior barred and bolted on one side but totally exposed on the other to the pitying and threatening watchers, has become, for us as for him, the little world where man makes pathetic attempts to hide himself from the death-bringing future, haunted by the thought that he is not alone, that a watchful eye is on him.

It is also a fine image of the inscrutability of human character, and this brings me to the second part of this discussion, Maeterlinck's application of his distinctive technique to character; man trying to know himself and the people in his life. Here we might expect to run into difficulty, for his idea of character, as he expounds it in his prose essays, seems rather inimical to drama. Character in the ordinary sense is an illusion, he says; reality is the soul and the forces that move it, far behind the appearance of things; the spiritual world is impersonal; in the shadows of the interior life, where accident and circumstances no longer play a part, all souls begin to resemble one another: the soul of the prostitute could have 'the transparent smile of the child in her eyes'.[14]

But what if we are more interested in the differences between the child and the prostitute? Is it not usually difference and variety of character that holds our interest in theatre as in life? Maeterlinck knows this, but he has another kind of interest to offer; as always it is bound up with seeming negatives; ignorance, deprivation, impotence. Speak-ing in *The Treasure of the Humble* of Shakespeare's characters, he suggests that what really fascinates us is not so much the actions of a

---

[14] 'Mystic Morality', *The Treasure of the Humble*, p. 64.

Lear or a Hamlet as the forces of destiny which can be sensed underlying them. Would it not be possible, he asks, in a modern drama, to
bring these forces into the foreground and 'send the actors farther
off'?[15]

This is one of his great seminal questions, to which he provides
some wonderfully varied answers, full of hints for the psychological
as well as the metaphysical drama of later playwrights, for Pinter as
well as for Beckett. He is inventive in devising techniques for sending
the 'actors' farther off. The lighted window of *Interior*, for instance,
creates a dream-like distance that gives the actors a shadowy, marionette quality. As Arthur Symons said of *The Princess Maleine*, it is
almost like 'a masque of shadows, a dance of silhouettes behind the
white sheet of the "Chat Noir"'. The anonymity of his characters is
another impersonalising device: most commonly they are identified by
the phase of life they have reached—Old Man, Grandfather, Young
Girl. In *The Sightless* the twelve blind people have not a name among
them, but refer to each other in a curiously impersonal way as 'the
deaf one' or 'the woman who is always crying' and so on. Only the
characters in the fairy-tale plays are allowed names, but those sweet,
strange sounds—Ygraine, Pelléas, Ariane—bring in their own
remoteness.

Maeterlinck draws dramatic interest of a very special kind from the
difficulty his people experience in knowing each other and the strange
forms of communication they do achieve. He is fertile in finding ways
of keeping characters remote and inscrutable and exciting us with
thoughts such as the Old Man has about the family behind the window:
'They look like lifeless puppets, and all the time so many things are
passing in their souls'. His invisible figures are potent. The dead girl
in *Interior*, for instance, is very much a presence in the play; her death
is a mystery which can neither be resolved nor left alone. The Old
Man and the Stranger discuss it obsessively, slowly building up an
impression not so much of the girl's personality, but of the troubling
difference between the façade she presented to the world and her
inner life:

> She might have lived as the others live. She might have said to the
> day of her death: 'Sir, or Madam, it will rain this morning', or 'We
> are going to lunch; we shall be thirteen at table', or 'The fruit is not
> yet ripe'. . . And yet, what a strange little soul she must have had—

---

[15] 'The Tragical in Daily Life', op. cit., p. 99.

what a poor little, artless, unfathomable soul she must have had—
to have said what she must have said, and done what she must
have done.

Here again is the characteristic process of making something from
nothing. The dead girl, the silent family are interesting exactly because
we cannot get near them, but are made to contemplate them in a new
way, wonder about them, feel the tantalising reserve and mystery of
people. 'You cannot see into the soul as you see into that room', the
Old Man says, in his usual way generalising the concept for us. The
stage image itself, however, has already embodied it: we know that we
will never know anything about them except what can be known from
looking through the glass, and heard at second or third hand, as the
reports filter through the eavesdroppers.

Invisibility is a great force in *The Death of Tintagiles*. From start to
finish the off-stage queen in the sinister tower looms over the action,
filling our minds as eventually she swallows up Tintagiles. Everything
in the play is simple except the motivation of this destructive character.
Why does she behave so, summoning Tintagiles to the castle only to
kill him? This is a question we must be exercised by as well as Ygraine
and her sister. In a way, of course, the Queen and her servants are
simply a metaphor for death, but there is also a faint suggestion of
some obscure personal connection, for she is, after all, Tintagiles'
grandmother, responsible at one remove for bringing him into the
world; and now she is taking him back, as though some hereditary
illness were rising up, beyond her or his control, or as if—so Ygraine
thinks of it—a monstrous effort was being made to stamp out the
line she has engendered.

Of the plays I have been discussing, *Pelléas and Mélisande* has the
greatest character interest; this is where Maeterlinck looks an important
progenitor in a line of modern drama that stretches beyond Yeats to
Pinter. In this play above all he brilliantly conveys both the fearful
difficulty of knowing people and on the other hand the communication
that takes place without being willed or understood or even wanted.
In Golaud's tormented efforts to 'know' Mélisande the technique of
negative response is seen at its most effective. From the time of their
first encounter in the forest he is always pressing on her questions she
cannot answer:

GOLAUD   Who was it that hurt you?
MÉLISANDE   All of them! all of them!

GOLAUD   How did they hurt you?
MÉLISANDE   I will not tell! I cannot tell!

We see her becoming more and more evasive, beginning to lie for no
obvious reason, as when she tells him that the precious ring he gave
her was lost, not where we know it was, in the palace well, but in an
underground cavern by the sea. It becomes a vicious circle; the
evasions and blanks she meets him with only exacerbate the obsessive
curiosity which is also a masochistic urge to self-torment. So it seems
in the harrowing scene when he uses his small boy, Yniold, child of
his first marriage, to spy on Pelléas and Mélisande, holding him up to
peer into the window of Mélisande's tower where the two are sitting,
terrifying him with questions in which the hysteria is barely under
control:

GOLAUD   But what are they doing?—They must be doing some-
          thing. . .
YNIOLD   They are looking at the light.
GOLAUD   Both of them?
YNIOLD   Yes, father dear.
GOLAUD   And not speaking?
YNIOLD   No, father dear; they have not closed their eyes.
          . . .
GOLAUD   They are making no gestures?—They are not looking
          at one another?—They are not making signs? . . .
YNIOLD   No, father dear.—Oh! oh! father, they never close their
          eyes. . . I am dreadfully frightened. . .

The terrible ambiguity of the silence and stillness is invested with a
special force by this painfully second-hand viewing, in which the
ignorance and fear of the boy unwittingly feed the corroding suspicion
of the man.

The ambiguity is never resolved, either for us or for Golaud. We
see, as he does, the two meetings between Pelléas and Mélisande when
they come closest to seeming lovers in the ordinary sense—though
how strange even that ordinariness seems on Maeterlinck's stage—but
their one kiss which for him is a sign of their guilt, for us seems
curiously innocent. We know it is their first and they say it will be
their last, for now Pelléas is really leaving her, has come to take his
farewell. True, we will never know whether he would have gone of his
own will, for Golaud intervenes to settle the question and—in killing

Pelléas and bringing Mélisande to her death bed—leaves it open for ever. The technique of the final scene between Golaud and Mélisande shows Maeterlinck at his most modern. In a style it is rather hard not to think of as Pinteresque, the focus moves from one character or group to another as they scrutinise and speculate on the tragic event, all giving us angles of vision that seem superior to Golaud's. The servants with their sensitive antennae, the old blind king who has, despite his disclaimer, the insight so often associated by Maeterlinck with physical blindness; all see images of innocence, two children clinging together in death. Golaud is forced to take that vision into his; he scourges himself with the thought of his blindness; they loved like children, he has killed for no reason. Yet still he is burnt up with his question and to the end Mélisande evades him:

GOLAUD	Mélisande! . . . Tell me the truth, for the love of God!
MÉLISANDE	Why have I not told you the truth?
GOLAUD	Do not lie thus in the hour of death!
MÉLISANDE	Who is going to die?—Is it I?
GOLAUD	You, you! and I, I too, after you! . . . And we must have the truth. . . We must at last have the truth, do you hear? Tell me all! Tell me all! I forgive you all!
MÉLISANDE	Why am I going to die? I did not know. . .
GOLAUD	You know it now! . . . It is time! It is time! Quick! quick! . . . The truth! the truth! . . .
MÉLISANDE	The truth . . . the truth. . .

Are those last words said as an ironic echo of Golaud's or a sad one, recalling the time when she and Pelléas first drew together and she asked him what she should tell Golaud about the loss of her ring. 'The truth', he said then, 'The truth'. In knowing of that episode, we know more than Golaud, but we know no more than he does what the cryptic echo means.

Finally, I think, Maeterlinck persuades us that what has been acted out in this fairy-tale context is no more—or less—than what we experience in the common interchanges of life where always, however well we may think we know someone, a part remains reserved, inaccessible. The technique of hesitations, silences, evasions, which make the reserve so interesting is one of his great contributions to the modern theatre.

Throughout this discussion I have been emphasising Maeterlinck's power to use negatives in ways that excite and involve us. But perhaps the most impressive feature of his drama at its best is the emergence from all the negatives of a Wordsworthian assertion and demonstration of the value of common life and common affections. He has a special feeling for the love within a family, parents for children, brother for sister, the old for the very young; some of his most touching scenes show old men pitying and trying to spare the young, as Arkel protects Mélisande, and Aglovale the small boy and his sisters, and as the Old Man in *Interior* tries to shield the young girls from seeing the family reaction to the coming of death. Speaking of that favourite play, *Philoctetes*, Maeterlinck drew attention to the 'primitive psychology' which seemed to him to be 'merely the sides of the vessel containing the clear water; and this itself is our ordinary life'.[16] In his own characterisation the 'clear water' is what he aims at. Too deep an immersion in complicated, exceptional characters would set up obscuring ripples; so Tintagiles, for instance, has no more distinct a personality than is needed to make him seem a real boy and the affection between brother and sisters a real thing; the focus is on the feeling, and how it stands up even to the final ordeal when the loved person has become no more than a thin voice behind the iron door which has no handles or hinges. Still he calls, 'Sister Ygraine', and still she can master her own grief and fear to comfort him in his extremity: 'Do not be afraid. I am here'. This is indeed a distillation of that clear water, an exceptionally pure revelation of a feeling as common as life—and made to seem here as precious.

When Maeterlinck describes his plays as 'plays for marionettes' he is speaking figuratively, indicating the degree of remoteness he wants, and the sense of helplessness and blindness which is so important in his view of life. No doubt about his being a formidable universe, full of threatening, unknown powers which the characters have no hope of understanding; no wonder if they often make, as Symons said, 'the blind gestures of marionettes'. The affinities with the sinister world of modern absurdists like Ionesco are unmistakable, as I have been indicating. But even in what Maeterlinck himself came to see as his most pessimistic plays, he separates himself from the absurdists by the force of his emphasis on the human values that survive the horrors, the darkness, the massive impenetrable doors, the intruders and assassins. In his world, so full of meaningless and accidental events, human love asserts itself and seems all the more marvellous because the conditions of its existence are so tenuous. It is not the end of Ygraine's love for

[16] 'The Tragical in Daily Life', *The Treasure of the Humble*, pp. 110–11.

Tintagiles when he is taken by the messengers of the Queen and, though she has no hope of reaching him, there is no absurdity in her continuing to batter at the terrible door with her feeble lamp that breaks so easily.

The circularity of his dramas sometimes has a nightmarish, *déja vu* quality, but there goes along with it usually a sense of renewal, of life moving in cycles which gather experience in affection as well as in unhappiness and fear. It is characteristic too that his sad actions should so often end with the focus on a child, a new life beginning. It may be fearful and faint—the crying baby in *The Sightless*, Mélisande's frail infant—or more confident like the child who sleeps through the tragic revelation in *Interior*. But there is always tenderness and promise in these quiet reminders of life's power to renew itself.

In his invention of the 'static' technique which allowed him to look through the façade of things deep into the interior and to draw these fine, tremulous positives from such dark negatives, Maeterlinck opened up a broad avenue for the modern drama, not the narrow one he is sometimes thought of as treading. He is both the Coleridge and the Wordsworth of the modern stage, able to persuade us of a strange reality in his enchanted scenes of blind kings, princesses behind glass and magic wells, and, at the other extreme, of the infinite strangeness in the most commonplace-seeming domestic interiors. I see him, as I have said, opening up a way that leads to Beckett and Pinter, and this I shall return to later. He was certainly a great fount of inspiration for Wilde, Yeats and Synge, and it is what they made of it that I now want to consider.

4 ⌖ Salomé *and* A Full Moon in March

I have spoken of Wilde's *Salomé*, along with Maeterlinck's *Pelléas and Mélisande*, as a great starting-point of the modern theatrical movement which crystallised in Yeats's dance dramas. Wilde wrote only one piece in this kind—it still remains *sui generis*—and Yeats did not acknowledge it as an influence. Yet it cannot be left out of a study which seeks to place the Yeatsian drama in a European context. For Wilde was the first of that extraordinary line of Irish-European playwrights who helped to fashion a modernist European drama. It is wonderfully appropriate—prophetic even—that *Salomé*, the play which first took up the influences from Maeterlinck and the French symbolists and projected them into a dramatic form that instantly seized the European imagination, should have been written by an Irishman living out of Ireland and writing in French—as if he were holding out his hand across fifty years to Beckett.[1] French airs play all round *Salomé*. Flaubert's *Hérodias* was an inspiration (and no doubt Massenet's operatic version, *Hérodiade*); so too Moreau's paintings: a French actress, Bernhardt, was to have lent to it the music of her 'flute-like voice', 'the most beautiful voice in the world', as Wilde called it.[2] Also in the background was Maeterlinck, a favourite author, whom Wilde included along with Flaubert and Gautier in the poignant reading list he gave Robert Ross from Reading Gaol.[3] In such a context his writing of *Salomé* in French was natural: French was the language for the drama of 'soul', and this, I want to suggest, is what the play essentially is.

Apart from the striking circumstance of its being written in French, *Salomé* stands out from Wilde's other drama and leans to *Pelléas and Mélisande* most obviously in its musicality. Wilde thought of it in musical terms: it was a 'strange venture' he said 'in a tongue that is

[1] Wilde did not translate himself however, but left the task to Lord Alfred Douglas.

[2] In the event she did not, but the French connection was maintained, for the Lord Chamberlain's ban on her production at the Palace Theatre ensured that the play was first produced in Paris, by Lugné-Poë at the Théâtre de l'Oeuvre (11 February 1896).

[3] In a letter of 6 April 1897 he specifies: 'Maeterlinck: Complete'. *The Letters of Oscar Wilde*, ed. R. Hart-Davis (1963), p. 522.

not my own, but that I love as one loves an instrument of music on which one has not played before' (*Letters*, pp. 330–1). Both his play and Maeterlinck's were almost instantly turned into music dramas—*Pelléas* in 1902, *Salomé* in 1905—by composers who were struck by the musical phrasing of the literary texts: Strauss said that Wilde's text 'cried out for music'; he found that very few changes were needed to turn it into a libretto. The play already had its own leit motifs, as Wilde himself pointed out: writing to Alfred Douglas from Reading Gaol about his discovery of the necessity for pain and suffering in life, he said: '. . . it is one of the refrains whose recurring motifs make *Salomé* so like a piece of music and bind it together as a ballad'.[4] True, the ear begins to listen for the return of the fateful cadences—'I will kiss thy mouth, Jokanaan'; 'Dance for me, Salomé'—as one listens for the great crescendos in the Strauss opera: it must surely be with a shudder of fearful satisfaction such as Salomé herself experiences that we hear the final variation, 'I have kissed thy mouth, Jokanaan': six quiet words with the force of a symphonic climax. We do, I think, need to hear the words, even when we are listening to Strauss's marvellous swell of sound. There may be times when one is glad to lose the English text in the libretto—its floridity can be embarrassing—but even in such an alluring performance of *Salomé* as Josephine Barstow gave with the English National Opera (Coliseum, 11 December 1975), the glorious singing voice did not quite make one stop wishing for a chance to hear that other music of the desperately, monotonously repeated words.

Salomé has qualities of mood, atmosphere, characterisation which connect it with the dramatic world of both Maeterlinck and Yeats. Max Beerbohm, when he saw it in 1905, described it as 'a form compounded, seemingly, of Sophocles and Maeterlinck in even proportions'.[5] Less flatteringly, Graham Robertson, when Wilde read it to him, took it for a burlesque of Maeterlinck: 'very clever, very delicate, but nevertheless a burlesque'.[6] The great terrace of the palace where the action is played out is decidedly a Maeterlinckian set, with its moon so like the supernaturally bright moon that floods Mélisande's tower with light. Here it is a visual image of doom, from the moment when Herodias's page calls attention to it at the start—'Look at the moon! How strange the moon seems! She is like a woman rising from a tomb. . . ' to the

---

[4] Letter of January–March, 1897 ('De Profundis'), *Letters*, p. 475.
[5] *Around Theatres* (1953), p. 377.
[6] *Time Was* (1931), p. 136.

climax when Herod cries, 'Put out the torches! Hide the moon! Hide the stars!' This dominating moon makes the characters who are so obsessed by it seem like puppets moved by forces outside themselves: an effect accentuated by the 'Biblically monotonous style'—Arthur Symons's phrase for Maeterlinck which is even more appropriate to *Salomé*. In other ways too the characterisation recalls Maeterlinck. Salomé herself is a destroyed Mélisande. She has a similar child-like naïveté, which comes out at the beginning in funny and rather touching ways, when she reacts to the sound of Jokanaan's voice, for instance, with childish bewilderment—'Of whom is he speaking?'—and registers with childish satisfaction the vehement denunciations of her mother—'Yes, it is of my mother that he speaks'—a line inviting sympathetic laughter from audiences. When this unformed, virginal creature is frustrated in her first sexual passion, the naïveté becomes a terrifying force, cutting her off from kind human feeling, making her 'monstrous', even to Herod. She has certainly parted company with Mélisande in that last scene when she croons over the bloody head, rocking it in her arms, kissing the unresponding lips. But what gives the scene its tragic quality is the presence in her still, even in this manic mood, of the little lost girl of the opening, who rushed on to the terrace gasping for respite from the world of the lecherous stepfather, sighing for the moon:

How good to see the moon. . . The moon is cold and chaste, . . . I am sure she is a virgin, she has a virgin's beauty. . . She has never defiled herself. She has never abandoned herself to men, like the other goddesses.

'Lost, lost', she might almost be crying, with Mélisande, 'I am lost! . . . lost! . . . Oh! lost here . . . I don't belong here.' Both are bewildered, out of tune with the worldly world: for Salomé too everything went wrong because she was not looked at by the right man.

In their musical handling of dialogue Maeterlinck and Wilde are often strikingly close. Maeterlinck's 'inarticulacies', those gasping unfinished phrases, are certainly a far cry from the sonorous, rounded periods of a Herod or a Salomé, but within each different idiom there is a similarly hypnotic repetition of words, phrases and images, which as Wilde said, bind the action into unity. In the same way that Mélisande's first frightened words to Golaud, 'I am beginning to feel cold', echo powerfully in her death scene—'I am frightened of the cold—I am so frightened of the great cold'—so Salomé's 'I will kiss thy mouth,

Jokanaan' *must* lead in to that dreadful variation, 'I have kissed thy mouth, Jokanaan'. The significant recurrences are part of an oblique, symbolist technique which it was the triumphant achievement of these playwrights to project into the theatre with full stage panache.

Wilde's play has sometimes been disparaged as an essentially literary piece, but in fact, for its time, it made unusually subtle use of theatrical resources. The stage scene has the expressiveness of a painting by one of his favourite artists, Burne-Jones or Moreau; stately marble terrace and escalier form a background to the ominous object, the cistern, and are lit by a moon that changes colour to reflect the changing mood of the play. It hangs there like fate made visible, as Herod, the most imaginative of the characters, reflects:

> Ah! the prophet prophesied truly. He prophesied that the moon would become red as blood. Did he not prophesy it? All of you heard him. And now the moon has become red as blood. Do ye not see it?

Yes, we see it, must feel too that there is some mysterious and fatal connection between what happens to the characters and the moon's sinister changes from brilliant white to blood red and then to black when it is blotted out by a cloud as Salomé broods over the severed head. Finally a single moonbeam breaks through the cloud, 'covering her with light'. It is a sight Herod cannot stand: he is in the act of leaving the stage but when he sees the terrible kiss in the moonlight he breaks into a frenzied shout, 'Kill that woman!', and the soldiers rush forward to crush her with their shields.

So her death is literally brought about by the moon. There is a symbolic rightness in that—for our reading of Herod as well as of Salomé. We might say that it is only when he sees her picked out in the moon's ray that he registers the full horror of her deed; in that hard, clear light Salomé is 'monstrous' and must be destroyed. But the moonlight also reveals a beauty he could not stop looking at and no doubt still desires though it is lost to him forever: she must die, to spare him that pain. We don't, of course, have to choose between these two views; it is just the complex knitting of motives in Herod that gives his character its special density and interest.

Wilde seeks with pictures as well as words to evoke a whole world of visual suggestion—all those paintings of Salomé and John the Baptist from Cranach and Caravaggio to the potent mask and myth makers of his own day, Moreau and Beardsley. Beardsley's black and white vision of Salomé is in fact embodied in the play's symbolic colour arrangement. Salomé sees Jokanaan as a marvellous human picture: 'Thy body is white like the lilies of the field that the mower hath never mowed'; 'There is nothing in the world so black as thy hair'; 'Thy mouth is like a band of scarlet on a tower of ivory'. The colours reflect the changes the moon passes through: she is crying for the moon and **she** achieves it in the only way such perfection can be possessed—as a still-life. The head is presented to her as a beautiful, blood-stained object on a silver platter, held up by a huge black arm, one of the most thrilling visual moments in the play. Black, silver and red: she has her desire and in achieving it tastes to the full her tragedy: 'But wherefore dost thou not look at me, Jokanaan?'

Producers of the play have a problem in striking the right balance between the stylisation it calls for and the fleshly realism which is also a part of it: refine that away and something vital is lost, the tragic incongruity of the characters' desires, the hopeless divisions of spirit and flesh. Certain hard actualities such as the severed head must be there, to give the full contrast with the frustration of the early scenes when Salomé was so totally fended off by Jokanaan's 'Touch me not. Profane not the temple of the Lord God'. The frustration was absolute —it should be unthinkable for the actress playing Salomé to lay so much as a finger-tip on the living Jokanaan. And so in the end we must see her holding the head of the dead Jokanaan—fondling it, threatening, 'I will bite it with my teeth as one bites a ripe fruit'—in order to experience the peculiar tragic irony of this Pyrrhic victory: the more violently she enfolds and devours the beautiful dead thing, the more desolate her realisation of her loss: 'I love thee yet, Jokanaan, I love thee only. . . What shall I do now, Jokanaan? Neither the floods nor the great waters can quench my passion'.

The moon too has to be a real stage object before it can attain its symbolic function as the focus of a universal longing for the unattainable. Through their reactions to its different phases the characters reveal their nature. For the amorous Syrian captain, the moon is a little princess with a yellow veil and feet of silver; for Salomé herself, an undefiled virgin, cool and chaste, the qualities that attract her in Jokanaan: '. . . He is like an image of silver. I am sure he is chaste as the moon is. He is like a moonbeam, like a shaft of silver. His flesh must be cool like ivory'. Herod sees the opposite of that austere image; the moon for him is sex-crazed, 'a mad woman who is seeking everywhere for lovers'. Only for Herodias are there no associations—

'No, the moon is like the moon, that is all'. This materialist is troubled by the actual physical sound of Jokanaan's voice denouncing her, but once he is beheaded she hears him no more and can sit in the place where she was once so uneasy with absolute aplomb. She provides the audience with an outlet for their natural resistance to the extravagantly fantastic, moony world and at the same time undermines it, for her obvious limitations, the coarseness and narrowness of her mind, surely make the moon-struck dreamers more sympathetic.

They command sympathy too as prisoners of the surface, the cold, glittering surface of things; it is their tragedy that they cannot break through the hard façades they present to one another. Only Herodias settles for things as they are, however unlovely. The others are more aspiring spirits, desperately looking at the moon and at unattainable faces. The word 'look' rings through the play, an agonised sound: all are looking or shunning looks or trying to divert them:

THE PAGE   You must not look at her. You look too much at her.
JOKANAAN   Who is this woman who is looking at me? I will not
            have her look at me. Wherefore doth she look at me
            with her golden eyes, under her gilded eyelids?
HERODIAS   You are looking again at my daughter. You must not
            look at her.

Refusals to look bring death: Narraboth dies because Salomé will not look at him, Jokanaan because he will not look at Salomé. Perhaps the most macabre moment in her apostrophe to the severed head is the fearfully naïve question: 'But wherefore dost thou not look at me, Jokanaan? Thine eyes that were so terrible, so full of rage and scorn, are shut now. Wherefore are they shut?' The refusal to look is a wound she is savagely trying to cauterise with mockery, though there is a suggestion too of distracted childish bafflement; even now she can't really believe she can be denied what she desired so intensely. She taunts him, but when her resentment has spent itself, the word 'look' recurs very differently, not as a taunt but a thing of infinite sadness:

Ah! Ah! wherefore didst thou not look at me, Jokanaan? If thou hadst looked at me thou hadst loved me. Well I know that thou wouldst have loved me, and the mystery of love is greater than the mystery of death. Love only should one consider.

For Herod she is 'altogether monstrous' at this moment, but the pathos of that 'Wherefore didst thou not look at me, Jokanaan' is surely too real to allow us to agree with him. It may seem perverse to speak of love in the grim context, but yet it is genuine soul longing that sounds tremulously here, a note of tenderness creeping into the violent intensity of feeling which has made her up to now so akin to the man who would not see her. They were in a way too like to be able to exchange looks with love: in the imagery of the play, they were mirrors, showing each the likeness of a God- or moon-haunted face. In her final recognition of this harsh truth, her move from bitter refusal to sad acceptance, she takes on a tragic quality, becomes what Wilde called her, a 'tragic daughter of passion'. The final kiss is a horrific ecstasy, but there is poignancy in it too, and a sense of an immature but exceptional spirit, spoilt and lost; the authentic sense of tragic waste.

Of course it is a precarious kind of tragedy, balancing on a knife edge, with an all too easy drop beneath to a world of grotesque and absurd melodrama. Wilde's own recognition of that knife edge and the way he deliberately builds his recognition into the play itself, helps to give *Salomé* a modern look. No one is more conscious than Wilde himself—how could we expect otherwise of the master of *The Importance of Being Earnest?*—how close to absurdity emotional intensity such as Salomé's and Jokanaan's must be. Of course it is absurd to long for the moon, desire what does not desire you, be tormented with thirst when there are drinks of a kind within reach. All can be seen as absurd: the young man who kills himself because a girl looks in the wrong direction, the celibate thundering against women, the virgin finding her satisfaction in a blood-stained head. Most absurd of all is Herod. But in him the absurdity is deliberately accentuated and made to serve as a focus on the unselfconscious intensity of the others: it is a distancing technique which has a near Brechtian coolness and aplomb. The moment he enters the scene, flamboyantly striking attitudes and rhapsodising on the moon, he is brutally undermined by Herodias—'. . . the moon is like the moon, that is all'—and later, when he demands in a panic whether they have not all seen the moon turn red, she mockingly brings him down to earth: 'Oh, yes, I see it well, and the stars are falling like ripe figs, are they not? And the sun is becoming black like sackcloth of hair, and the kings of the earth are afraid. That at least one can see.' She has no difficulty in making him seem 'ridiculous'—the word she uses with icy contempt to demolish one of his opulent visions: 'As for you, you are ridiculous with your peacocks'. We are on the edge of comedy here, the classic comic situation of the henpecked husband which Wilde exploited so wittily in his plays of fashionable London life. We see Herod writhing in the toils, enduring his wife's powerful sarcasm and getting his own back whenever she gives him an opening. He remains resentfully henpecked to the end, taking every chance to punish her: even at the height of his rapture over Salomé's dance, his first thought is to score off Herodias: 'You see that she has danced for me, your daughter'. He is undignified in this and in other ways too which are sometimes close to farce; he nearly falls over on his first entrance, slipping in the young Syrian's blood; he makes a fool of himself by ingratiatingly offering food and wine to Salomé while she gives him frosty answers; he reacts to tales of a saviour who raises the dead in the style of the grotesquely vain Herod of medieval theatrical tradition:

> . . . But let them find Him, and tell Him from me, I will not allow Him to raise the dead! To change water into wine, to heal the lepers and the blind. . . He may do these things if He will. . . But I allow no man to raise the dead. It would be terrible if the dead came back.

And yet in that last line 'It would be terrible if the dead came back', there is something that is not absurd. Herod's awe at the thought of the dead and the supernatural life may have a superstitious, childish aspect, but it is a sign too of a larger life in him, a life which relates him unexpectedly to Jokanaan, makes him lean towards that dour opposite. At this point interesting connections between Wilde and Yeats begin to force themselves on our attention; the idea of masks enters the play, the notion of character as an inner drama with a perpetual pull between archetypal opposites. Herod is very much an actor, always conscious of eyes on him, always looking for an audience reaction. He is not content to develop a poetic image for its own sake, like Salomé or Narraboth, but has to provoke a response in the others: 'Does she not reel like a drunken woman? She is like a mad woman, is she not?' He swings from mood to mood with disconcerting speed and with such exaggeration that it is hard to know how much is play-acting, how much the hysteria of a manic-depressive, how much the expression of genuine feeling and intuition. A virtuoso scene of this kind occurs as a prelude to Salomé's dance. At the high pitch of excitement and joy he feels most strongly the presence of the great unseen bird of death which has haunted him since he first came on to the moonlit terrace.

His vacillations of mood issue now in a series of tumultuous contradictions:

> Why can I not see it, this bird? The beat of its wings is terrible.
> The breath of the wind of its wings is terrible. It is a chill wind.
> Nay, but it is not cold, it is hot. I am choking. Pour water on my
> hands. Give me snow to eat. Loosen my mantle. Quick, quick!
> Loosen my mantle. Nay, but leave it. It is my garland that hurts me,
> my garland of roses. The flowers are like fire. They have burned my
> forehead. (*He tears the wreath from his head and throws it on the
> table.*) Ah! I can breathe now. How red those petals are! They are
> like stains of blood on the cloth. That does not matter. You must
> not find symbols in everything you see. It makes life impossible.

He has become a ground for warring opposites, and there is certainly
an element of absurdity in the lightning speed of the changes: it is a
testing passage for an actor. How much one would have liked to see it
done by Robert Farquharson, whose Herod, said Robert Ross, was
'one of the finest pieces of acting ever seen in this country.'[7] But his
acute self-consciousness makes Herod in the end a formidable character,
more master of his own reactions than Jokanaan and Salomé, who are
totally obsessed: they can never get outside themselves, talk to themselves as he does in that wonderfully self-mocking line: 'You must
not find symbols in everything you see'.

In this character who contains so many contradictions and vacillations, Wilde creates a Yeatsian opposition between the self-conscious
self and its opposite, the mask he yearns towards, the mask of the
heroic, unselfconscious, spiritual being. More than anyone else in the
play Herod is sensitive to the supernatural aura round Jokanaan, feels
that the finger of God has touched him, that 'in the palace as in the
desert God is always with him', though characteristically he is unwilling to commit himself and must add a cautious postscript, 'At
least it is possible'. The pull towards the austere, god-centred prophet
is immensely strong: they are never seen together, but Herod is the
one who really listens to what the terrible voice from the cistern is
saying and the death he calls down on Salomé in the end is the death
prophesied by the voice: 'Let them crush her beneath their shields'.

[7] Preface to the French text of *Salomé*, 1909 (limited edition 1908), p. xi.
Even those who disliked the play and its author were 'hypnotised' by the power
of this Herod, according to Ross. There is plenty of contemporary support for
this view. 'Michael Field' found his performance 'Flaubertian'.

Herod himself brings the idea of masks into the play when he picks up the theme of 'looking' which has run through the dialogue and develops it in a typically self-conscious metaphor: 'Your beauty has grievously troubled me, and I have looked at you too much. But I will look at you no more. Neither at things, nor at people should one look. Only in mirrors should one look, for mirrors do but show us masks'. This is a last defensive clutching at the hard surfaces of things before the irresistible onrush of the moon-crazed fantasies which are so triumphantly and disturbingly established by the end of the play as the shaping force of the action. Herodias despises dreams and dreamers, but the thing she most desires, the silencing of Jokanaan, cannot be accomplished till the dreaming faculty has been roused in Salomé and in Herod. They must long for the impossible, she for a lover as chaste as the moon, he for a virgin goddess moving among peacocks 'like the moon in the midst of a great white cloud', before energy can be generated equal to the terrible event. The impossible world of the spirit forces its way in through every crack. The dead will not stay dead; it is surely in the direction of the cistern that Herod looks when he reacts with such deep unease to stories of the dead being raised by the Nazarene and surely we feel the murdered brother stir. And though Jokanaan's mortal voice sounds no more, his spirit acts on Salomé to the end: against all the odds, the Grand Guignol horror is turned to tragedy when she speaks of love with that final sad tenderness: 'The mystery of love is greater than the mystery of death. Love only should one consider'.

Great delicacy of handling is required to get the right balance among these subtly dissonant elements and realise Wilde's symbolist landscape; the mind's fantastic interior under the light of a supernatural moon. It is all too easy, to judge from stage history, to reduce the play to melodrama, and the dance is a testing point. Herod's desire to see Salomé dance should seem an expression of the difficult longing I have been trying to define, but it obviously cannot seem so if the dance is to be no more than a refined strip-tease. This was the reputation it soon acquired, largely through association with the popular versions that flourished at one time on the music-hall stage.

The most serious of these in the years around 1900 was Maud Allan's dance of Salomé. It is hard to know now just how impressive it was as dance, but her account of it in her autobiography[8] is certainly interesting. It was in two distinct parts; first the shedding of the seven

[8] *My Life and Dancing* (1908).

veils before Herod—the pleasurably shocking part—then what she
calls 'The Vision of Salomé', which was quite another thing, a vision
of the severed head and an ecstatic recall of the tragic story. The title,
and Maud Allan's description, suggest that she may have based this
sequence on one of the most celebrated paintings of the subject,
Moreau's 'The Apparition'. His exotic Salomé stands plunged in
dream while the severed head, bathed in faint radiance, hovers in the
air above her. Maud Allan was in touch with continental art movements: like Isadora Duncan, she was an exponent of free dancing who
sought to create poetic effects by drawing on high art forms (classical
sculpture and classical music especially) as inspiration for her dances.
She interpreted Bach and Beethoven in dance and improvised to music
composed for her by the Belgian, Marcel Remy. Contemporary
audiences may have reacted chiefly to the 'shocking' aspects of her
Salomé dance, especially the near nudity, but she herself saw *The
Vision of Salomé* as a kind of spiritual transfiguration. Unlike the
European artists who painted Salomé as a sophisticated, tigerish being
—ideally represented on the stage by Sarah Bernhardt[9]—Maud Allan
stressed the child-like, virginal quality of the character and the poignancy of her too late realisation of what she had done:

> In the mad world of childish joy she is drawn again to dance—
> dance around this strange silent presence . . . craving the spiritual
> guidance of the man whose wraith is before her; but it remains
> silent! No word of comfort, not even a sign! Crazed by the rigid
> stillness, Salomé, seeking an understanding, and knowing not how
> to obtain it, presses her warm vibrating lips to the cold, lifeless ones
> of the Baptist! In that instant the curtain of darkness that had
> enveloped her soul, falls, the strange grandeur of a power higher
> than Salomé has ever dreamed of beholding becomes visible to her,
> and her anguish becomes vibrant. (pp. 126–7)

A flowery effusion, certainly, and yet if we can distinguish the thought
from the style, there is considerable interest in Maud Allan's concept
of the role and her emphasis on the immaturity of Salomé which is so
curiously related both to her cruelty and her final vision. That is one
approach. At the other extreme, the dance in the Coliseum production
already referred to was a sophisticated manoeuvre for handling Herod,
teasing him with a broken sequence of episodic dances, always stopping

___

[9] Even in other plays she called to mind for one of her admirers Jean Lorrain,
the triumphant, coruscating costume of the Salomé in Moreau's *The Apparition*.

before each climax, to make a mockingly flamboyant return in a new costume and style: it was 'a show in a noble night club', as the director, Joachim Herz, put it. There was obviously a good practical reason for this interpretation—limiting the effort required of a dancer who was also the singer—but it expressed a directorial attitude too, fitting in perfectly with the cool perspective kept throughout the production, especially on the absurdity of Herod: a profoundly emotional dance, such as Maud Allan described would have been quite out of place. Yet another interpretation of the dance as a Dionysiac state of total possession was offered by Lindsay Kemp in 1976 (I shall be returning to this later).

The point I want to make is that the dance is an integral part of the action; in deciding what style it shall be in, a director expresses his view of the whole play. He gets no help from Wilde; nothing but the bald stage direction: 'Salomé dances the dance of the seven veils'. There may be a hint of some esoteric ritual, in this cryptic comment, so Wilde himself darkly indicated,[10] but what form it might take it is left to the critic or director to discover for himself. This is, one might say, a real commitment on Wilde's part to total theatre. It is for the artists of the dance, he seems to imply, to carry through in their own language what the play has suggested to them. Wilde is looking very like Yeats again at this point: it becomes natural, even inevitable, to ask questions about the relationship of *Salomé* to those dance plays which are so obviously its near kin, *The King of the Great Clock Tower* and *A Full Moon in March*.

I want to take up those questions and go on to a separate discussion of *A Full Moon in March* by looking once more at the dance in *Salomé* from the viewpoint I arrived at in course of producing the play, in a double bill with *A Full Moon in March*, with a student company. That sense of spiritual anguish in *Salomé* which I have been trying to define was felt independently by our choreographer, Niema Ash, who designed the dances for both plays: for her too, Salomé was a poignant figure, and the dance must somehow express that poignancy. The first step to that was to find the right music: it had to be un-Strauss-like, a music of the moon rather than the sun. Ravel's *Daphnis and Chloe* might have done, we thought, or something by Maeterlinck's own composer, Debussy: it was easy to imagine Salomé in her

---

[10] He inscribed a copy of the 1893 edition for Aubrey Beardsley: 'March '93. For Aubrey: for the only artist who, besides myself, knows what the dance of the Seven veils is, and can see that invisible dance. Oscar.'

Mélisande aspect as a young girl in white dancing to the sound of *Clair de Lune* played on a solitary flute. In the event the girl in white danced to the fuller sound of Ravel's *Alborada del Gracioso*, a piece which proved to have the right division of mood; wild, exotic strains modulating into a deep lyrical melody, full of tenderness and sad longing. To the first strain the dancer performed for Herod, using her yellow veils as scarves in a flamboyant display of erotic energy: to the other, she danced for Jokanaan imprisoned in his cistern, a dance of desire and grief: the scarves became his body, stretched between her hands, to be caressed and mourned over. This dance, it seemed to me, created a reservoir of feeling which Salomé was able to draw on in the final bizarre love scene with the severed head when she revealed the capacity for spiritual anguish which is never quite lost even when the barbaric flood overwhelms her.

Though we did not choose it with that thought in mind, Ravel's music was appropriately named: the Alborada occurs in the sequence called *Miroirs*, making it seem designed for this play of reflections and the pursuit of images. With that appropriateness in one's mind, that sense of the power in the music and dance to extend and project fine shades of character, it became harder than ever to understand Yeats's view of the dance in *Salomé*, which I now want to turn to.

Even before the lessons learned in production, I had always found Yeats's dismissive attitude to the dance in *Salomé* very puzzling. In a letter to Olivia Shakespear after he had completed his own plays on the theme of the moon and the severed head he made an invidious comparison between Wilde's dance and his; Salomé's was 'a mere uncovering of nakedness' whereas his Queen's was 'a long expression of horror and fascination' (*Letters*, p. 827). It is hard to know how he could be so specific on the basis of Wilde's non-committal stage direction. He had seen the play in 1906, and may even have seen Maud Allan's music-hall performance, which did have a striptease element, though its second part, as we have seen, strikingly anticipated his own pattern of 'horror and fascination'. Possibly, then, it was from experience of the play in the theatre that he acquired the notion of Salomé's dance as a commonplace 'uncovering of nakedness'. But it is difficult to avoid the suspicion that he was very ready to take that view—so unsupported by the text—because of a defensive, partially hostile attitude to Wilde, not dissimilar to his love/hate relationship with Maeterlinck.

Wilde's drama too was a model, exerting powerful pressure, and perhaps seeming embarrassingly close at times. It certainly touched on many of his own passionate interests. In the background was the same French inspiration, as he remarked himself in 1911, on rereading Flaubert's *Temptation of St Anthony* in a new translation and feeling the revival of an old excitement: 'How much of what is most typical in our generation, Wilde's *Salome* for instance and much elsewhere in his work has come out of it.' (*Letters*, p. 562). Earlier, as he recalled in 'The Tragic Generation' (*Autobiographies*, p. 321), he had been excited by a different French version of the story, when Arthur Symons read passages to him from his translation of Mallarmé's *Hérodiade*:

> The horror of my virginity
> Delights me, and I would envelop me
> In the terror of my tresses, that, by night,
> Inviolate reptile, I might feel the white
> And glimmering radiance of thy frozen fire,
> Thou that art chaste and diest of desire,
> White night of ice and of the cruel snow!

The appropriateness of those last two lines to Wilde's play is apparent; they might equally be applied to *A Full Moon in March* (1935), a play that explores to the full the cruel 'winter of virginity'. In fact the French and Wildean versions of the Salomé story had a much stronger grip on Yeats's imagination than the Irish legends which he tried to use in early drafts of *The King of the Great Clock Tower* and *A Full Moon in March*. In the later versions, as Curtis Bradford points out, 'this Irishing almost disappeared'.[11] Sometimes it seems indeed as if even the Irish countryside took on in his mind the tints of *Salomé*. It may be, as he says, that it was an Irish tradition to describe the wind as 'the dance of the daughters of Herodias', but it is hard to hear real Irish voices saying the words: they sound more like the imagining of this one Irishman.

Their affinity with French art and literature is only one of many close connections between Yeats and Wilde in the dramatic sphere. Wilde anticipated Yeats as a theorist and to some extent as a practitioner of a modern symbolist drama. 'Modern' is a great word with Wilde; for him too it meant looking back behind the prevailing

---

[11] *Yeats at Work* (1965), p. 291. So too F. A. C. Wilson: 'I imagine that Yeats had intended a specifically Irish play and abandoned the project with reluctance in favour of a more general treatment.' *W. B. Yeats and Tradition* (1958), p. 54.

tradition to ancient sources; only minds steeped in the past, he said, will be able to realise not just their own lives, but the collective spirit of the race, and so make themselves 'absolutely modern, in the true meaning of the word modernity'. He is often startlingly close to Yeats in his philosophy of masks and his fascination with marionettes and mirrors. His haunting poem 'The Harlot's House' sketches a near-scenario for a symbolist shadow play. The watchers outside the harlot's house see shadows racing across the blind like 'strange mechanical grotesques', ghostly dancers spinning, skeleton silhouettes; a clockwork puppet presses a phantom lover to her breast and 'Sometimes a horrible marionette / Came out, and smoked its cigarette / Upon the steps like a live thing'. There is a touch of marionette quality in Salomé, as I suggested earlier, and though Wilde does not use actual masks, he conveys through his characterisation of Herod his sense of personality as a continual exchange of masks, a necessary flow between distant poles: 'The desire of any very intensified emotion to be relieved by some emotion that is its opposite'. He sounds even more modern than Yeats, closer to Beckett, really, when he emphasises, as he so often does, the total fluidity of the self. We are always looking backward or forward, he says, living in a succession of moments, with no possibility of stability or permanence:

> there is no such thing as a romantic experience; there are romantic memories, and there is the desire of romance—that is all. Our most fiery moments of ecstasy are merely shadows of what somewhere else we have felt, or of what we long some day to feel . . . I myself would sacrifice everything for a new experience, and I know there is no such thing as a new experience at all. (*Letters*, p. 185)

Wilde saw the need for a new dramatic method to explore this unstable self; scenic design, colour and music would play an important part in it. In his essay 'The Truth of Masks' he turned an account of Shakespeare's use of costume into an appeal for something like a total theatre technique. The stage, he declares, is 'the meeting-place of all the arts',[12] and it is also the return of art to life: we must bring to it and have gratified our sense of colour and form, our ear for music, as well as our feeling for words and action. He subscribed to the symbolist placing of music as the chief of arts: it was so because it 'can never reveal its ultimate secret' (*Works*, p. 970). And he called for just what Yeats was attempting at the time, a unified approach to scenic effects:

[12] 'The Truth of Masks' in *The Works of Oscar Wilde* (1948), p. 1006.

a colour scheme should always be carefully related to the dominant feeling of a scene, made to express that 'mystery of mood' which it was the business of art to explore and illuminate: without actually recommending those aesthetic favourites, green and blue, he implies a preference for them, or at any rate for muted and subtle shades, rather than 'glaring' colours like 'the hot, violent red' which was apparently popular when he wrote. It would be hard not to think of Yeats when Wilde is in this vein, pondering the value of particular colour arrangements and making specific suggestions, as for instance, that black can be a key colour, a useful means of separating and harmonising other shades: just such a purpose was served, he interestingly points out, by the black frock coat of male actors in contemporary productions of naturalistic plays. He had too a feeling for the potency of light: 'Under certain conditions of light and shade, what is ugly may become beautiful . . . and this, indeed, is the real modernité of art'. Yet despite all this closeness in their thought—or perhaps because of it—it is clear that Yeats was often alienated by Wilde and disliked the turn his ideas took. Perhaps, as Richard Ellmann suggests, he 'could not bear so much impermanence'. Wilde's emphasis on the discontinuity of the self is certainly ruthless, for he does not seem even to feel the need— so vital to Yeats—for a vision of continuity and stability. Nor was Yeats likely to sympathise with Wilde's yearning for a state of detachment and contemplation where the artist would turn into a kind of saint and 'become perfect by the rejection of energy'. For Yeats, as we know, energy was king. It was at this crossroads that he parted company with both Wilde and Maeterlinck.

Perhaps it was for the last reason that he reacted so violently against *Salomé* when Sturge Moore told him that he was planning to produce it in 1906 along with *The Florentine Tragedy*. '*Salomé* is thoroughly bad', he announced: 'The general construction is all right, is even powerful, but the dialogue is empty, sluggish and pretentious. It has nothing of drama of any kind, never working to any climax but always ending as it began'. He then offered a rough sketch of the line the action would take in a 'good' play, a sharp upward movement from climax to climax; by contrast *Salomé* was 'as level as a table'—and it was not 'organic'.[13] Behind this outburst there seems to be the same revulsion he had felt at one time from Symons's commitment to a life and art made up of impressions—also, perhaps, an uneasy sense that

[13] Letter of 6 May 1906 in *W. B. Yeats and T. Sturge Moore: Their Correspondence 1901–1937*, pp. 8–9.

Wilde's ideas and his drama, like Maeterlinck's, cast a parodic shadow on his own; the one by frivolity and mocking exaggerations, the other by sentimentality, undermining his concept of a symbolist drama which might also be a drama of energy and passion.

The fact that he is so totally wrong about *Salomé* being 'as level as a table' and 'not organic' is interesting, for he is wrong with such passion. This is not a dismissal but a protest against something he has to be violent about because it troubles him at a deep imaginative level. He could never push *Salomé* out of his way, or at least not until he wrote it out in *A Full Moon in March*, a play he described to Dorothy Wellesley as 'a fragment of the past I had to get rid of' (*Letters*, p. 843). Like his own Cuchulain, irrevocably bound to his opposites, the Blind Man and the Old Man, Yeats could not get free of Wilde, and often seems indeed to be drawn even against his will towards him, for instance in his use of actors. He employed the services of both the actors who starred in the 1906 production of *Salomé*,[14] Robert Farquharson and Miss Darragh, though his attitude to Farquharson was equivocal, even contradictory, almost a reflection of his ambivalent attitude to Wilde himself. He knew from Charles Ricketts, who designed for the 1906 production, that Farquharson was admired, certainly by Ricketts himself, for the power and subtlety of his performance as Herod, and he cast him for the part of Forgael in *The Shadowy Waters*; yet he described him to Sturge Moore as a 'vulgar charlatan'. Miss Darragh, on the other hand, he admired unequivocally when he saw her as Salomé. His account of her intelligent acting—she had, he thought, more intellectual stature than Mrs Patrick Campbell—makes one wonder still more about those wrong readings of *Salomé* he was so prone to give, almost as if he were denying a value he was really aware of.

This curious background of attraction and repulsion explains the sense of relief Yeats felt, so he told Olivia Shakespear, when he looked again at *Salomé* after completing his own plays of the severed head. *The King of the Great Clock Tower* was more original than he thought, 'for when I looked up *Salomé* I found that Wilde's dancer never danced with the head in her hands—her dance came before the decapitation of the saint and is a mere uncovering of nakedness' (*Letters*, pp. 826–7). And it makes more understandable his slighting and inaccurate reference to Wilde's dance: it was a part of his cutting himself free, feeling that he had arrived at his own distinctive expression of the Salomé theme.

[14] 10 and 18 June 1906, King's Hall, Covent Garden.

And indeed he had done so. He has no need to insist on the differences to persuade us of the distinctiveness of his own play; it is in
observing the striking likenesses that one becomes most aware of
Yeats's originality. He has simply taken the symbolist technique
outlined by Wilde to its furthest reach: almost all that is of the nineteenth century in *Salomé* is cut away, and what is left remarkably takes
us into the twentieth century, indeed, right into our own time.

I want to illustrate this idea from *A Full Moon in March* rather
than from *The King of the Great Clock Tower*, because it was this play
I was able to compare with *Salomé* in production and I chose it then
because it seemed to me the most complete distillation of the theme.
So indeed Yeats himself thought: 'In *The King of the Great Clock
Tower* there are three characters, King, Queen and Stroller, and that
is a character too many; reduced to the essentials, to Queen and
Stroller, the fable should have greater intensity. I started afresh and
called the new version *A Full Moon in March*' (Preface; *Variorum
Plays*, p. 1311). The elements in *Salomé* and *A Full Moon in March*
are strikingly similar: a royal virgin 'cruel as the winter of virginity',
a prophetic figure who speaks to her with a kind of rough scorn that
enrages and fascinates her, a dance of sexual adoration, a severed head.
Art nouveau, still, in a way, and yet how audaciously modern Yeats's
play is, in the self-conscious theatricality that separates it so decisively
from Wilde's enclosed, somnambulistic world. For here the elements
are presented to us as indeed just that, pieces to be put together somehow by the two Attendants who start the play off wondering how
they will ever do it:

FIRST ATTENDANT   What do we do?
                   What part do we take?
                   What did he say?
SECOND ATTENDANT   Join when we like,
                   Singing or speaking.

One is an elderly woman, the other a young man; at the start she is the
more unsure, he confident and masterful: 'Sing anything, sing any old
thing, said he'. At the end these positions are reversed, it is he who is
tremulously asking: 'Why must those holy, haughty feet descend /
From emblematic niches . . . What do they seek for? Why must they
descend?' and she who gives the answer with complete assurance:
'Their desecration and the lover's night'. An ironic reversal which
reflects the paradox in the inner play—the triumph of the female

principle, even in its passivity and ignorance, over the male—and in so doing points up the important though obscure relationship between the Attendants and the protagonists.

We are never allowed to forget the Attendants: they are continually at work, opening and closing the inner curtains to reveal and conceal the Queen, supplying all voices, music and sounds except when Queen and Swineherd confront one another directly. It is they who settle the line the action must take: the First Attendant's 'Come then and sing about the dung of swine' looks forward to the 'desecration' of the Queen when she steps from her throne, unveiled, and dances for the Swineherd with blood on arms and dress. So the action belongs in a way to them—and yet it is mysterious to them, distant, bewildering, an encounter between a veiled woman and a masked man which takes its own course entirely, once the curtain has been drawn back. The Queen knows before the Attendants do that 'some man' is at the door; neither she nor the Swineherd need telling that this is the fatal time, the full moon in March when the virgin must be won by a song from out the 'ignorant forest'. In the story he tells her, he evokes their fate:

THE SWINEHERD   There is a story in my country of a woman
                 That stood all bathed in blood—a drop of blood
                 Entered her womb and there begat a child.
THE QUEEN   A severed head! She took it in her hands;
                 She stood all bathed in blood; the blood begat.
                 O foul, foul, foul!
THE SWINEHERD   She sank in bridal sleep.
THE QUEEN   Her body in that sleep conceived a child. . .

We are deep in the interior now, beyond the perplexed tentative intuitions which opened the play, beyond conscious will, beyond personality. The Swineherd has no urge to strip off the veil, says indeed, 'What do those features matter?' The Queen's face is never seen: when she drops her veil, committing herself at last, she stands with her back to us, and the Swineherd has been taken away; he will not see her and she will see no more of him than his mask when she performs for him the dance of the severed head, the dance of sex in which personality is obliterated or suspended.

Still we have further to go. When the Queen turns round, holding the severed head—in our production, the discarded mask—in hands menacingly covered in red gloves, the dropped veil at her side, words cease; she is dumb, no more dialogue is possible between the lovers. What she is experiencing now can only be expressed in a dance, but she is not yet ready to dance; first she must draw out, with her song, a song from the severed head.

Up to now the Attendants have improvised, managed and framed the inner action: from this point on they take it over almost completely, stepping into the roles of Queen and Swineherd; singing for them, and laughing, for in the tense, waiting silence comes first the sound of Dionysiac laughter and then at last the song; a ghostly ventriloquial sound, a surrealist nursery rhyme from the depths of the unconscious:

> I sing a song of Jack and Jill.
> Jill had murdered Jack;
> *The moon shone brightly*;
> Ran up the hill, and round the hill
> Round the hill and back.
> *A full moon in March.*

Who is speaking, who is performing now? We can no longer tell, no longer distinguish among the elements which have fused to produce the mysterious climax of the Queen's response; her 'crazy' laughter, her dance of longing, triumph and adoration before the severed head —an Artaud-like moment of pure theatre. It ends in a long drawn-out shivering to the orgiastic rhythm of accelerating drumbeats; a sexual climax that is also, as in Wilde's *Salomé*, a summit of some other sort, a reconciliation between the virgin impulse towards the cold perfection of the moon and the voice out of the 'ignorant forest' that spoke of dung and swine. It comes over as something unwilled, never really understood. To the end the Second Attendant asks his distraught questions. And yet nothing can happen until the two who themselves know so little, call up the actors and speak for them. It is not with the Maenad moment that the play ends, but with question and answer between the Attendants and the final assertion of enigmatic purpose and order which the First Attendant can make now, as she could not at the start:

SECOND ATTENDANT   What can she lack whose emblem is the moon?
FIRST ATTENDANT   But desecration and the lover's night.

There is a kind of religious clarity and purity in this ending, so the composer for our production, Dyl Bonner, thought; he set the closing lyric in the style of medieval plainsong, and it was that serene sound we heard as the stage slowly darkened till nothing was visible but the brilliant white round of the moon. Yeats did not suggest an actual moon, but I felt the need for one, perhaps influenced by thoughts of the moon in *Salomé*; Yeats's Queen laughing her crazy laughter in the full moon of March seems almost an embodiment of the moon-mad woman Herod imagines reeling through the sky, looking for lovers. Our moon was, I hope, in the spirit of a play that sets such emphasis on improvisation: it was no more than a prop, a self-standing disc on a stick, in no way meaningful until the light fell on it and it became a glowing source of power. When the First Attendant moved closer, it was as if her inner ear was enabled to register the sounds from the dumb mouth:

> I cannot hear what she is singing.
> Ah, now I can hear.

Only then could she speak for the Queen, express that complex feeling of the virgin for her lover, part maternally tender, part sexually fierce:

> Child and darling, hear my song,
> Never cry I did you wrong;
> Cry that wrong came not from me
> But my virgin cruelty.

In this play Yeats has certainly brought into the foreground Maeterlinck's 'destiny or fatality that we are conscious of within us, though by what tokens none can tell'. The actors have been 'sent farther off' and the lights fall with hallucinatory brilliance on a drama that is really being performed in the shadows of the 'obscure theatre of the soul'. From Wilde's moon to the full moon in March, a long step— but a step on the same path surely.

5 ⌀ Synge

At first sight Synge might well look the odd man out among the innovatory Irish playwrights I am discussing; there is nothing strikingly modernist in his technique, no radical experiments with music, dance and masks, no move out of the proscenium frame, no self-conscious play with the theatrical illusion. It is rather easy to see him as an essentially nineteenth-century figure, looking back to the romantic and rhetorical style of a Rostand rather than forward to the anti-rhetorical drama of the Beckettian era. Yeats once said that he himself, Lady Gregory and Synge were all instinctively of the school of Talma, a style characterised by Gordon Craig as throwing up an arm to call down thunderbolts rather than seeming to pick up pins from the floor. No doubt about there being a touch of the thunderbolt-invoker in Synge; the heroical, romantic strain comes out most strongly in *Riders to the Sea* (1905) and *Deirdre of the Sorrows* (1910), but is never really absent from his drama, even in so darkly ironical and unheroic a play as *The Well of the Saints* (1905). Talma was also the actor who startled his contemporaries by abandoning the conventional stage dress of his time, the brocaded coat and periwig, and playing roles like Racine's Britannicus more 'realistically' in a toga. In this sense too Synge's is a Talma style. His care to get things accurate and lifelike—typified in his presentation of real pampooties from Aran to his actors—is as much a part of him as his flamboyant romanticism. These elements in combination can give him a rather un-modern look, especially when the realism is over-stressed in production, as it so commonly is. His realism is a marvellous thing, but it can be a trap too, as Yeats shrewdly observed when he connected scenes in *The Well of the Saints* he found 'over-rich in words' with the realistic convention Synge was using: 'the realistic action does not permit that stilling and slowing which turns the imagination in upon itself'.[1]

This is surely a very acute comment. Both the realistic detail and the lush rhetoric of Synge can distract at times from the qualities that should make him most interesting to a modern audience, the austere vision of life seen so disconcertingly through the humorous grotesque,

[1] 'An Introduction for my Plays' in *Essays and Introductions*, p. 529.

his 'violent laughter', in Yeats's good phrase. Since Beckett, Synge's modernity has become much more apparent. Who could fail to recognise the family resemblances between Estragon, Vladimir, Hamm and the rest and all those solitary wanderers of Synge, who take their frighteningly free way by ditch and mist-wreathed roadside, cracking their Rabelaisian jokes, telling their endless tales, creating and re-creating an inner landscape that draws even the most unimaginative characters into it, and can come to seem more real than the circumstantial outer world? The Irish line running from Synge through Yeats and O'Casey to Beckett has become the main line of modern drama. One non-Irish figure, Maeterlinck, plays a crucial part in this evolution, as we have seen, and it is at the point where he and Synge touch that I want to begin.

Much has always been made of Synge's stay in Paris and his dramatic recall to Aran, but the emphasis is usually on the Aran side of things, the return to Irish influences rather than the assimilation of French ones, with the implication that in living and working abroad (in Germany as well as in France) he had taken a wrong turn and his creative life only began when he returned to Ireland. But for Synge, as for Yeats himself, an immersion in European thought and art was really a necessity; it saved him from parochialism and encouraged him in his modern attitudes; his scepticism, his remarkable capacity for detachment, his sense of the solitariness of the human self and its strange, virtuoso ability to dramatise and people its solitude.

He was steeped in European literature, and kept all his life a strong feeling for French authors, Molière and above all Rabelais, whose name he invoked when he was driven to defend the mixed mood of *The Playboy of the Western World*:

> . . . the romantic note and a Rabelaisian note are working to a climax through a great part of the play, and . . . the Rabelaisian note, the "gross" note, if you will, must have its climax no matter who may be shocked.[2]

A chief source for *The Well of the Saints* was a medieval French morality play[3] and Robin Skelton has stressed[4] how typical this is, how often Synge's subjects come from or can be related to European

[2] Letter of 5 September 1907 to John Quinn, quoted by A. Saddlemyer in introduction to *Collected Works*, iv, p. xxv.

[3] Andrieu de la Vigne, *Moralité de l'aveugle et du boiteux* (1456).

[4] R. Skelton, *The Writings of J. M. Synge* (1971).

folk art or ancient literary tradition. Synge did indeed resist attempts to introduce more European plays into the Abbey repertoire, but only because he felt the desperate need of Irish playwrights for a stage to experiment on; they had no other. Through Irish experiments, however, Abbey audiences might be expected to become more open to Europe: the ambiguous title, *The Playboy of the Western World,* subtly makes this point, directing the Dublin audience to look west-ward, to their own Mayo, certainly, but beyond that to the wider world of Europe and the West; standing on the West coast of Ireland, looking out to America, it is indeed particularly easy to think of oneself as a European.

Synge had no difficulty in seeing himself in that way. For long after he was recalled to Aran by Yeats, he continued to divide his year between Ireland and Paris, and to write book reviews and articles for French journals like *L'Européen*. He spoke and wrote in French with enough ease to be thought of as bilingual, translated Villon, was always slipping into French in his notebooks; his notes on *The Well of the Saints* are half in French, half in English. No wonder if Beckett in his turn feels at ease with Synge. Yeats, with his bad French, sometimes seems to look half askance at this continuing allegiance, as when he says: 'I have never heard him praise any writer, living or dead, but some old French farce-writer'. If he had in mind, however, the medieval farce about the lame beggar and the blind beggar, on which Synge drew for *The Well of the Saints,* the remark is a reminder that Yeats and Synge both went on sharing and drawing on the French experience, for that play also provided strong hints for *The Cat and the Moon* (1926).

It was not just the older French drama that inspired Synge however. He responded to the modern movement with great intensity. Whatever reservations he later had about the symbolists (they have been some-what exaggerated by critics who wish to stress his Irish commitment), the symbolist playwrights who were important to Wilde and to Yeats exercised a pervasive influence on the mood and style of his drama too. There are echoes of *Axel* in his earliest play, *When the Moon has Set* (not published nor produced in his lifetime), in which a girl gives up a nun's vocation for her lover and 'marries' him in a mystic love rite, and again in the unfinished last play, *Deirdre of the Sorrows,* where the heroine compulsively chooses an act that she knows will almost certainly lead to the death of her lover and herself. Maeterlinck, as we will see, was an important influence, and Wagner, that inescapable genius, hovers in the background too, coming just a little more sharply into view in *Deirdre of the Sorrows*.

In one way Synge was better equipped than Yeats to draw from the avant garde theatre of Europe; his musical ear and training equipped him to appreciate the Mallarméan concept of music drama, and in his own distinctive way to follow it. Music first took him to Europe (he went to Germany to train as a violinist) and when his thoughts turned to the theatre, it was an opera (on the story of Eileen Aruin) that he planned to write. He thought of life and the artist's compulsion to express it as a kind of musical process: 'Every life is a symphony, and the translation of this life into music, and from music back to literature or sculpture or painting is the real effort of the artist.'[5] This was how he approached the dramatic art. He constructed a dialogue so intricately musical that his actors had to learn to read their texts like scores, orchestrating cadences that by no means came naturally to them. Yeats commented, 'I can't imagine anyone getting his peculiar rhythm without being instructed in it', and William Fay endorsed the remark from hard experience: 'They took a cruel lot of practice before we could get them spoken at a reasonably good pace and without at the same time losing the lovely lilt of his idiom'.[6] The special atmosphere created by this elaborately rhythmical, lilting dialogue is obviously a crucial means of bringing us to accept the reality of the inner world the characters project out of the bare, plain or prosaic scenes they factually inhabit: to a great extent Synge depends on making words function like music. That knowledgeable observer of the Wagnerian movement, George Moore, felt this was so: in an enthusiastic account of *The Well of the Saints* he drew attention to the beauty of the dialogue and to 'the fact that one listens as one listens to music, charmed by the inevitableness of the words'.

Synge, like Yeats, brooded on the possibility of working out a speech notation, to preserve that fragile music. It grieved him that a poet's 'subtle and individual intonations' should be lost when someone other than himself read his lines, that the magic of a poem read as he once heard a Gaelic poet movingly read by an old man, should vanish in translation. He toyed with the idea of applying musical notation to speech—ff, ral and so on. Nothing came of this, nor were Synge's actors called on to accompany themselves in the style of Florence Farr,

---

[5] *Collected Works*, ed. Alan Price (1966), ii, 3.
[6] W. G. Fay and C. Carswell, *The Fays of the Abbey Theatre* (1935), pp. 167–8.

with psaltery or harp. But the work they had to do on their dialogue was in itself a musical exercise; Fay's jottings include stray directions like 'pianissimo'. And Synge worked out the structure of his plays in a strikingly musical way, feeling for the right 'tune' to a scene, indicating the weight and rhythm he needed, often by reference to other plays: a Molièrian climax; a Rabelaisian—very strong; a *Riders* note here; a diminuendo ironical. Like Yeats again, he attracted his fair share of composers, including one, Vaughan Williams, who wrote for them both (*Riders to the Sea,* with his music, was produced in 1937).

His musicality is one of Synge's strong links with Maeterlinck, who according to Maurice Bourgeois was his favourite author. He may not speak of him much, but then, as Yeats remarked, he seldom spoke of authors he admired: references he does make are always significant and those to Maeterlinck occur throughout his life. In 1898 he praised *Wisdom and Destiny* as an example of the growing 'spirituality of art', one of the few books of 'pure and perfect conception': Villiers de l'Isle Adam took a lower place among those who 'unite the highest endeavour with lower morbid sympathy'.[7] A production of *The Shadowy Waters* which he saw in 1903 reminded him of *Aglavaine and Selysette* (1896), an interesting indication of how he tended to think of a play first in terms of its rhythm, music and atmosphere, for the two works have only those things in common: plots and character groupings are totally dissimilar. And towards the end of his life, musing in his notebook about the difficulty of realising the poet's dream of beauty in the theatre, he thought of *Pelléas and Mélisande,* presumably as a striking exception: '. . . there is always the poet's dream which makes itself a sort of world. When it is kept a dream is this possible on the stage? I think not. Maeterlinck, Pelleas and Melisande? Is the drama—as a beautiful thing a lost art?'[8]

Deirdre of the Sorrows which was his next work, approaches Maeterlinck's play more nearly than any of his others, both in its situation—the young girl turning from her middle-aged 'official' lover to an unofficial young one who dies at the hands of his rival—and in its legendary setting. For the first time Synge had a cast of kings and queens rather than peasants; and had great trouble, in fact, trying to imagine how his 'saga people' would speak and think and lie down for the night. An early scenario of *Deirdre* includes musical motifs which

---

[7] 'La Sagesse et la Destinée.' Review in *The Daily Express* (Dublin), 17 December 1898.

[8] *Collected Works,* iv, 394.

seem to point to *Pelléas* and perhaps also to *Tristan and Isolde*. In the first act Deirdre goes off to dress herself to the sound of a huntsman's horn announcing Conchubor's arrival and later she sits spinning and singing like a true opera heroine; the spinning music of *Pelléas* would not be out of place. The final version drops these effects, but many of the great speeches, including Deirdre's lament over Naisi's grave, function like arias; the movement of plot is suspended to allow a lyrical outpouring of feeling in which pain is taken up into melody and beauty.

On the visual side too, Synge had strong affinities with Maeterlinck, Yeats and the French 'static' school. 'His power of visualisation was perfect', said William Fay. He was certainly clear what he wanted his stage to look like, though content to leave it to Yeats and his designers to fill in the detail; artists like Charles Ricketts, Jack Yeats, Robert Gregory were all well able to do that. The effects he aimed at often sound Maeterlinckian. When, for instance, William Fay pleaded for more variety in *The Well of the Saints*—he was afraid that what he saw as the universal bad temper on the stage would infect the audience —Synge used a painterly image to explain the tone he was after: it was to be 'like a monochrome painting, all in shades of the one colour'.[9] Just such a subtle monotony, as we saw, was what Maeterlinck admired in the symbolist painters and Symons admired in Maeterlinck. For Yeats it was natural to think of Synge and the 'static' French theatre together, as when he drew a contrast for Frank Fay's benefit, between the realistic school of Antoine and the 'immobile' Racinian acting style, illustrating the latter by an allusion to William Fay's performance in *The Well of the Saints*: 'Your brother understands, for instance, that in the first act of *The Well of the Saints* there must be long, quiet periods, a suggestion of dreams, of indolence' (*Letters*, p. 441). The scenery for *The Well of the Saints* was designed to emphasise and capture the 'monotone' impression Synge wanted: 'decorative scenery, mountains in one or two flat colours and without detail, ash-trees and red salleys with something of recurring pattern in their woven boughs'.[10]

There might be a Japanese formalism about the trees—it was in pondering designs for Synge that Yeats was first struck by the idea of using Japanese prints as models—and in every way the stage was to

[9] Fay and Carswell, op. cit., pp. 167–8.
[10] W. B. Yeats, Preface to first edition of *The Well of the Saints*, *Collected Works of J. M. Synge*, iii, 68.

serve the inwardness of Synge's play, 'to express what no eye has ever seen'.

Monotony and stillness, those two essentials of the Maeterlinckian drama, were supremely realised, for Yeats, in *The Well of the Saints*. Always he stresses its stillness, the 'leisure' that Synge created in the dialogue with spaces, pauses, slowing down 'even in the midst of passion'. It was a day of triumph, he proclaimed, when the audience was held by the first act of *The Well of the Saints* 'though the two chief persons sat side by side under a stone cross from start to finish'.[11] This is rather a Yeatsian exaggeration, since the first act includes the sensational event of the Saint curing the Douls of their blindness, but there is a real truth in it, all the same; for an audaciously long time there is nothing happening except a statuesque conversation between the two blind people followed by the hardly less static scene when they talk to Timmy the Smith.

Synge is never closer to Maeterlinck than in his stress on solitariness. It asserts itself even in the midst of his crowded scenes: through them all runs the terrible realisation that 'I was born lonesome, and I'll be lonesome always'. In the shebeen or at the village cross, the focus is on beings who are as alien in the world about them as Mélisande in the dark castle where she can never feel at home. In Synge's world too a new, modern importance is given to the loneliness of men without gods or even hope of gods, and to the simple, cruel facts of physical life; not the exceptional events, but the 'ordinary' ones of sickness, ageing, death. 'There's one sorrow has no end surely, that's being old and lonesome', is a recurring threnody. Nora in *The Shadow of the Glen* (1905) is haunted by thoughts of once free and admired souls fallen into decay; the great Patch d'Arcy who went 'queer in the head'; Peggy Cavanagh, the girl with a light hand at milking, now 'sitting in a dirty old house, with no teeth in her mouth, and no sense'. Even when she is being wooed by a young lover, her old husband seemingly dead, she cannot get thoughts of ageing out of her mind:

> Why would I marry you, Mike Dara? You'll be getting old, and I'll be getting old, and in a little while, I'm telling you, you'll be sitting up in your bed—the way himself was sitting—with a shake in your face, and your teeth falling, and the white hair sticking out round you like an old bush where sheep do be leaping a gap.

The corpse instantly provides a grotesque visual illustration—

[11] 'An Introduction for my Plays' in *Essays and Introductions*, p. 528.

sitting up from under the sheet where he was stretched out pretending to be dead, in queer, white clothes, his white hair sticking out round his head, while she continues unseeing; 'It's a pitiful thing to be getting old, but it's a queer thing surely. . .' It is a queer thing, and Synge makes us focus on it in a way that the pre-Maeterlinckian drama was not interested in doing. The shadow that falls upon the glen is the shadow felt in all the plays, anxiety at the thought of approaching age and death. Nothing can assuage that anxiety in *The Shadow of the Glen*, not the love making, not even the promise of the free, natural life the tramp offers Nora: always in the background is the memory of that other free roaming man, Patch d'Arcy, who ended up in the asylum, and whose spirit, with the pressure of death in it, is an ambiguous and palpable presence in the play. In his ability to make such an active force of these grim negatives, Synge comes very close to Maeterlinck. *Riders to the Sea* is akin to *The Intruder* in the simplicity of its structuring as a play about waiting for death: there is nothing for Maurya to do but sit and wait for the sea to strike again, then again, till she has lost all her sons. Death is heavy in *Deirdre* from start to last—as a girl of twenty Deirdre is already envisaging the form of her death—and even in that play so bursting with life, *The Playboy of the Western World* (1907), age and death get in through the often dark farce and the grotesque threnodies which only just keep this side of the line between humour and horror. 'Did you never hear tell of the skulls they have in the city of Dublin, ranged out like blue jugs in a cabin of Connaught?', says Jimmy, slightly drunk at the beginning of Act III, 'White skulls and black skulls and yellow skulls, and some with full teeth and some haven't only but one'. The humour of that does certainly separate Synge from Maeterlinck but the obsessive dwelling on macabre and gruesome detail keeps them close; of them both it could be said, 'Death fills all the spaces of the poem'.

These large affinities are often supported by striking resemblances of situation and detail. *The Well of the Saints*, for instance, though so Irish in flavour, has much in common with *The Sightless*. Both plays are set in a remote place—an ancient forest, a lonely mountainous region—in a far-away time ('one or more centuries ago' in Synge's play). In both the sense of time and place is further eroded by the blindness of the central characters; the rhythm of life is slowed down till our scale of values is drastically altered; we are ruthlessly drawn into the viewpoint of the blind ones, discover strange modes of perception and the terrifying power of imagination to create a world out of shadows and hints from the depths of the mind. In this sense both plays can be described as 'drama of the interior'.

The fluidity of their characters is another striking point of resemblance. Maeterlinck's, as we noticed, often convey the impression of living only in part of themselves; they may feel cut off from their own centre—like Pelléas and Mélisande watching their shadows embracing far from them—or, like the Old Man in *Interior*, be exceptionally aware of the self as a multiple, nebulous thing, capable of dissolving and re-forming in mysterious ways. Maeterlinck's characters often seem 'helpless before the contents of their own minds', to borrow a phrase Yeats used elsewhere. Here Synge diverges, for he is above all interested in the use his characters make of their alarming fluidity. Within the shadow of what cannot be changed (age will come and death is certain), they assiduously change themselves, improvising their self-dramas out of the materials they have to hand, sometimes finding ready collaborators, sometimes having to battle to establish their private view.

It could never be said of Synge's characters as Eliot said of Maeterlinck's that 'they take no conscious delight in their role'. On the contrary, an intensely dramatic sense of themselves is what marks out his leading characters: it is their greatest asset and also their doom, committing them to the endless story-telling through which they communicate their dangerous, golden inner landscapes and amazingly impose them on the given world of actuality. Their inner drama needs a stage audience, even an audience of one, to establish itself. We are not yet in the world of Beckett where a single character can hold the stage with his story of himself, but we are getting very near it.

I want now to look more closely at the technique of self-dramatising which makes Synge's drama (against all the odds) so forward-looking, taking my illustrations from the play which shows most clearly his affinities with Maeterlinck and Beckett and comes closest to being, in Yeats's terms, a 'drama of the interior'.

The Well of the Saints is Synge's most grotesque treatment of the self-dramatising process; of all the plays it pushes the hardest towards incongruity and absurdity, forcing us into uneasy relation with its dreamers and non-dreamers alike. We are made to see clearly the formidable obstacles in the way of the dream; the poverty of the physical materials it is built from and the lack of real support from the bleakly literal-minded villagers. Synge exposes this physical poverty to our view for a long, slow spell; in the static opening scene that so impressed Yeats there is nothing to look at but the weatherbeaten, blind beggar of fifty and his ugly, blind wife, sitting under a stone cross, ludicrously talking about her yellow hair and fine white skin and the jealousy she arouses in the young women. It is a sculptural scene, a grotesquely comic version of the statuesque grouping of the blind figures in *The Sightless,* we might assume, for Maeterlinck is strongly echoed elsewhere in the play; his beautiful blind girl with her marvellous pre-Raphaelite hair is surely in the background of the Douls' final vision of themselves:

> . . . a face would be a great wonder when it'll have soft white hair falling around it, the way when I'm an old woman there won't be the like of me surely in the seven counties of the east.
> . . . a beautiful, long, white, silken, streamy beard, you wouldn't see the like of in the eastern world.

Maeterlinck of course keeps us confined to the viewpoint of the blind, but Synge characteristically pushes the action to prickly and in the end violent oppositions between the modes of perception experienced by the sighted and the sightless. He holds the balance between them with a ruthless impartiality that cuts out any danger of sentimentality. Immediately after the cure, when Martin goes looking for his wife among the prettiest girls and the villagers mock him, our sympathy must be with the blind pair, and yet they repel pity, partly by their unattractive lack of pity for each other, but, more importantly, by the disdain which they are able to feel for their tormentors. It is not just a defensive reflex but a real disdain for the 'seeing' world which is so bounded by the facts of the flesh. 'Ah, you're thinking you're a fine lot', he says, 'with your giggling, weeping eyes, a fine lot to be making game of myself, and the woman I've heard called the great wonder of the west . . .'. The fearful appropriateness of that image, the 'giggling, weeping eye', attacks us as well as the stage audience. We have laughed and felt pity, looked in fact with the same eye as the villagers, and now we are told that this eye is an inferior one, unable to look into the rich inner world the sightless ones inhabited at the beginning of the play, and to which they return at the end.

Synge takes trouble to establish that the Douls are neither monsters nor simpletons; they are not unaware of facts nor free from doubts; at the beginning Martin is hankering after the sweet voices of the girls he cannot see and questioning whether Mary with her cracked tones can really be a beauty. His acceptance of the Saint's cure can be seen as a momentary faltering of his will, a weariness with holding up by the force of imagination the golden landscape he and Mary inhabit. He relaxes, as it were, into ordinary seeing, but it turns out a bitter experience; for the whole of the second act he is occupied in drawing contrasts between the two ways of perception, always to the disadvantage of the visible world. Now he seems able to see only ugly things; raw, beastly days, grey clouds, people with red noses, and, always, those weeping and watering eyes; 'the like of your eyes, God help you, Timmy the Smith'. In a way it is easy to dismiss this as sour grapes; the first disillusionment, forcing him to see himself as others see him, was a terrible blow, not easy to surmount. It may be true too, as the Saint suggests (and critics have often agreed with him), that the Douls suffer because they are so self-centred and aesthetically narrow; they should be turning their minds outwards, forgetting about 'the faces of men' and learning to look at nature and the splendour of the spirit of God 'till you'll be living the way the great saints do be living, with little but old sacks, and skin covering their bones'.

The Saint, however, has small grip on ordinary reality himself. He too is busy converting raw nature into material for a glorious vision and he can often seem naïvely unaware of simple facts, as Mary observes when she is told of his idea that young girls are best fitted to carry the holy water, being 'the cleanest holy people you'd see walking the world'. 'Well', she says, sitting down and laughing to herself, 'the Saint's a simple fellow, and it's no lie'. She finds him absurd as the villagers find the Douls absurd and indeed the sensible, laughing attitude to vision and imagination is very strong and persuasive throughout the play. Synge piles up the odds against the chance of our taking the Douls' vision seriously: there is their physical grotesqueness, often exuberantly comic, as in the scene where their bodies stick out behind bushes while they think themselves out of view; the incongruity of their overweening self-assurance; their cruelty towards each other. It is important to the whole effect that we, like the villagers, should see them as comic, sometimes pitiable, sometimes unsympathetic and remote. Only then can we appreciate the full force of the extraordinary power they have to make a self-contained, inner world of rich possibilities in contrast to which the factual world of the sighted, sensible people is intolerably narrow and constrained.

Because the odds against them are so enormous, it is peculiarly perturbing when their inner world forces itself into a position of superior reality. It happens first when Martin, earning his living by tedious chores for Timmy the Smith, courts Timmy's sweetheart, Molly Byrne, and actually succeeds in moving the hard, unimaginative beauty from her first contemptuous indifference to interest and even a kind of fascination: Synge describes her as 'half-mesmerised'. The romance is on the edge of bathos, as Synge makes plain; Molly is cruelly pleased, even when he is praising her charms, to remind him of his own physical shabbiness and the shock it gave him. And yet, even with so cool an audience, Martin is able not only to charm, but to invest his rhetoric with troubling implications for those who put their faith entirely in the visible world. He uses images of sight and blindness with increasing mastery. What does a woman want, he cries in a last passionate appeal, but to be seen by a man who can truly 'see' her:

> You'd do right, I'm saying, not to marry a man is after looking out a long while on the bad days of the world, for what way would the like of him have fit eyes to look on yourself, when you rise up in the morning and come out of the little door you have above in the lane, the time it'd be a fine thing if a man would be seeing, and losing his sight, the way he'd have your two eyes facing him, and he going the roads, and shining above him, and he looking in the sky, and springing up from the earth, the time he'd lower his head, in place of the muck that seeing men do meet all roads spread on the world.

Synge's strange language is at its least life-like here: the queer, bony structure, the intricately linked phrases, the alien word order, which one can well believe the Abbey actors had trouble mastering, almost defy us to take it as the ordinary speech of common men. And it is appropriate in that way, for Martin is by no means a common man, but one of extraordinary gifts; with so much against him, he can still make an impression on coarse-fibred Molly, while later, in the scene when he is preparing to reject a second cure, he momentarily persuades one of the incredulous and angry villagers that there is something in his account of what ordinary seeing is: 'He's right, maybe, it's lonesome living when the days are dark'. The word 'dark', normally in the play (as in Irish usage) a synonym for 'blind', has more the sense here of dull or drear, and implies support for Martin's view, that without imagination there is nothing to the world and its sights. A Maeterlinckian equation between sight and insight develops. Martin connects

Molly's villainy with her enjoyment of physical sight, and she, reversing the meanings, calls on the Saint to leave the obdurate tramp to his darkness: 'If it's that is best fitting to the blackness of his heart'. A violent opposition between these views comes to a violent climax when Martin asserts the supremacy of the inner eye by the act which so astounds and affronts the villagers and the Saint, his deliberate refusal of the second, permanent cure for his physical blindness:

> SAINT (*coming close to Martin Doul and putting his hand on his shoulder*) Did you never set eyes on the summer and the fine spring in the places where the holy men of Ireland have built up churches to the Lord, that you'd wish to be closed up and seeing no sight of the glittering seas, and the furze is opening above, will soon have the hills shining as if it was fine creels of gold they were, rising to the sky?
>
> PATCH RUADH That's it, holy father.
>
> MAT SIMON What have you now to say, Martin Doul?
>
> MARTIN DOUL (*fiercely*) Isn't it finer sights ourselves had a while since and we sitting dark smelling the sweet beautiful smells do be rising in the warm nights and hearing the swift flying things racing in the air (*Saint draws back from him*), till we'd be looking up in our own minds into a grand sky, and seeing lakes, and broadening rivers, and hills are waiting for the spade and plough.

Martin has taken the word 'dark' in the sense used by the others and transformed it to his own. The saint draws back, we might notice, at the phrase 'swift flying things racing in the air', as though he had scented black magic. And it *is* a kind of black magic the blind man has effected: he has almost persuaded at least one or two of the sighted that it is they who might be living in the real dark and disturbed us into thinking hard about this idea by the extraordinarily aggressive act of refusing the healing water. He refuses it for his wife too—in the later part of the play she is a more passive figure, willing to follow the strongest persuasion—and this tyranny no doubt sets up in us, as in the stage audience, some hostility towards him. It is certainly not possible, at this fierce ending, to patronise the sightless ones: our position as sighted beings has been too seriously undermined by the

powerful words that have reduced the faculty of sight to an image of
'giggling, weeping eyes'.

There is also a call on our admiration, for at the other pole his
words have power to extend, enlarge, enrich. Indeed Synge puts his
weight behind the rightness of the final choice, which includes the
forcing of Mary, by showing how with the return of the physical
blindness, a kind of inner light is restored. After all the bitter recrimi-
nations, the almost total estrangement of husband and wife during
their period of sight, affection and tenderness return:

> MARTIN DOUL (*throwing himself down on the ground clinging to
> Mary Doul*) I'll not come, I'm saying, and
> let you take his holy water to cure the blackness
> of your souls today.
>
> MARY DOUL (*putting her arm round him*) Leave him easy, holy
> father, when I'd liefer live dark all times beside
> him, than be seeing in new troubles now.

The play ends with a piece of striking visual symbolism: the Douls
groping their way out, to the 'south' of their imagining—which to
Timmy the Smith's mind is likely to be their death by drowning—and
the others lining up for the wedding procession of Molly and Timmy,
to the sound of the Saint's bell. Two ways of life, and we are left
divided between them, far from knowing clearly where our sympathies
lie, critical of the Douls as of the villagers, sure of one thing only,
that the inner eye has a terrifying power to create its own reality.

The well which gives the play its title and which has so haunted the
imagination of Yeats and Beckett, is a well never to be seen with
mortal eye. Synge makes it seem infinitely distant in Timmy's opening
account, a green and ferny well on an island, where there is a grave of
four beautiful saints; a drop of its water is 'enough to cure the dying,
or to make the blind see as clear as the grey hawks do be high up, on
a still day, sailing the sky'. A powerful image of vision that clearly
fastened in Yeats's mind to surface some years after in *At the Hawk's
Well*. Yeats got his well on to the stage as a square of blue cloth,
having by then acquired a technique for representing inner landscape
in terms of scenic symbolism. Synge did not have this, and in any case
it is characteristic that he should prefer to work through totally
ordinary and commonplace visible objects. There *is* a well in *The
Well of the Saints* but it is quite prosaic, simply part of the setting of
the second act, a village roadside with a forge, broken wheels lying

about and 'a well near centre, with board above it, and room to pass behind it'. Insidiously this contrast between the ordinary visible well and the magical world we hear of serves to remind us that the holy water and the well and all that goes with it are things of the mind and indeed that everything is; the characters are in a way blind by their own will.

At the far end of the shadowy road the Douls go out on at the end of the play, one seems to see coming to meet them the pathetic and alarming figure of Lucky, his long white hair falling round him, leading the blind Pozzo, or the Rooneys, that strange old married pair, clumping along, the blind man's stick tapping, listening to the country sounds which they sardonically enumerate. Synge said he didn't know whether his plays were typically Irish, but his method was. What is this method and what in it links it to the method of Yeats, O'Casey, Beckett? I have been trying to indicate answers to that question in the course of this chapter. In closing, I want now to draw together some of the threads and consider what there is in this 'Irish' method as it is used by Synge that has recommended it to the European theatre, made Synge's drama, indeed, one of the most influential forces in that theatre, despite its in some ways old fashioned, nineteenth-century airs.

A place where it seems natural to begin in thinking of what is especially modern and influential in Synge is that bare roadside scene in *The Well of the Saints*. Scenes like these are naturalistic enough and it is obviously possible in production to stress the naturalism: this is indeed what is most often done. But his landscapes should not be made too real; they have a local habitation and a name—County Mayo, the Wicklow hills, the Aran islands—but little particularity; the direction in *The Well of the Saints* is typical: 'Some lonely mountainous district on the east of Ireland, one or more centuries ago'. There should never be a realistic clutter on Synge's stage: even in the convivial opening scene in the shebeen of *The Playboy*, attention is always being directed to those desolate open spaces outside, where queer sounds in a ditch raise nightmarish thoughts. One could imagine a production where the shebeen was portrayed as a pathetically narrow 'interior' surrounded by mystical darkness, a vast and threatening exterior universe. Bareness, emptiness dominate: the few objects should stand out with an almost supernatural sharpness; the boots, the suit of clothes, the mirror in *The Playboy*, the fire of sticks burning in the ditch in *The Tinker's Wedding* (1907), the newly dug grave at the back of the shabby tent in *Deirdre*. The tramp in *The Shadow of the*

Glen wonders that Nora is not afraid to open the door on a dark night in a place as lonesome as her place, 'where there aren't two living souls would see the little light you have shining from the glass'. As Nicholas Greene points out,[12] there is substance in the charge levelled at Synge in his own time (by critics like Daniel Corkery) that he gave a misleading picture of the Aran islanders by almost leaving out of count altogether their Catholic piety. It is true that Synge by-passes that aspect of realism to focus on what interests him more, men in a world essentially without God. Old Mary in *The Tinker's Wedding* sets a characteristic perspective early in the play when she is trying to deflect Sarah from the 'queer' thought she has of marrying Michael:

SARAH (*angrily*)   Let you not be destroying us with your talk when I've as good a right to a decent marriage as any speckled female does be sleeping in the black hovels above, would choke a mule.

MARY (*soothingly*)   It's as good a right you have surely, Sarah Casey, but what good will it do? Is it putting that ring on your finger will keep you from getting an aged woman and losing the fine face you have, or be easing your pains. . . ?

The farcical action, which ends with the priest being completely gulled by the tinkers and Sarah abandoning her marriage plans with relief and exuberance, bears out Mary's notion that marriage for them is a total irrelevance. Morality and religion in Synge's world are ironically viewed as part of man's effort to protect himself from his awareness of living in a 'void', a world of exhilarating beauty and frightening indifference. No wonder there were riots, really, over the first production in the Abbey Theatre. That reaction was a truer response to what Yeats so accurately called the 'unclassifiable, uncontrollable, capricious, uncompromising genius of Synge' than the cosier enjoyment of the comedy which came in later times, after the Abbey company had begun to stress the realism and quaintness of the play.

Obviously Synge's realism exists and as I said at the start is a marvellous thing that no one would want to be without. Who could care to give up the Widow Quin, a character who came late into the fable and worked her way further in, one would say by sheer force of

[12] *Synge: a Critical Study of the Plays* (1975).

personality? There is a whole area of warmth and colloquial realism round her that is highly amusing and pleasurable in itself. But the art of producing Synge must be to strike on the stage the fine balance he himself maintains between that full-blooded, solid reality and the equally powerful impression that life is some kind of fantastic illusion, a conjuring trick performed in a dark space. A high degree of stylisation is needed; certainly it is essential if a production is to accommodate and make us take seriously grotesque incidents like the scene in *The Well of the Saints* when the Douls shelter in the briars, their behinds sticking out, convinced they can't be seen, spinning the images of their future.

It is hardly more than a step from those non-stop fantasisers to Hamm ensconced in his wheelchair telling out to the reluctant audience in the dustbins the story that keeps him going. Life as a stage dream, a theatrical process of self-creation and self-production; the modern theatre has wholeheartedly embraced this principle of Synge's drama, even going back to look at Shakespeare in this light, for instance, in John Barton's production of *Richard II*, where Richard and Boling-broke are represented as actors playing the role of King in turn. Synge is in the mainstream here: so too in his preference for comedy and farce as the vehicle of his lonely, nihilistic, ironic, iconoclastic view of the universe. It seems significant that the only play considered uncontroversial in his time, and instantly anthologised, was *Riders to the Sea*: as Yeats said, it was 'a comfort to those who do not like to deny altogether the genius they cannot understand'.[13] Certainly it is easier to place than the other plays, simpler in mood, closer to traditional forms—it has commonly been described as a tragedy in one act—and it is of course a moving and splendid piece. But a knife-edge balance of the comical and the sombre is much more characteristic of Synge. His use of farce is, as he says, 'Irish', in the style of Boucicault[14] before him: farce with a grim edge, violent laughter, tragic gaiety. It is exhilarating in the traditional way for its sheer fun, its zestful sense of life's eccentricities and incongruities, but it has another function, which gives it a more modern look: it becomes a way of confronting without despair the really bad jokes of life; physical afflictions, ugliness,

---

[13] 'Synge and the Ireland of his Time' in *Essays and Introductions*, p. 337.

[14] In reviewing a Dublin production of *The Shaughraun* in 1904, Synge pointed to the 'interesting comparison between the methods of the early Irish melodrama and those of the Irish National Theatre Society'. *Collected Works*, ii, 397–8.

old age, death. Synge's characters are haunted by those unavoidable jokes; Deirdre can't face the thought of getting old and losing her teeth; the Douls run from their reflections in the bleak world of fact. But Synge himself does not run. 'Squeamishness is a disease', he once said: his plays are blasts against that debilitation. He draws his subjects with aggressive anti-romanticism from the most unpromising places, taking a peculiarly keen interest in battered, unprepossessing tramps and nomads and old people, the deprived and afflicted, and tapping in them springs of humour, imagination, passion for life. He might have described his aim in Beckettian terms, for he is certainly one who does not shun subjects that others have shunned, such as impotence and ignorance; he too is an excavator, going by way of the derelict and lonely down into the depths and wonders of the human mind. This is the most important sense in which he fulfilled Yeats's advice to 'express a life that has never found expression'.

Synge's language is as much an artefact as the stories his characters tell themselves. Like those it has roots in observed reality: its lifeblood clearly is derived from the Gaelic he loved listening to, but it is a 'synthetic' dialect, a theatrical music appropriate only to actors on a stage: Yeats was surely right in saying, 'I can't imagine anyone getting his peculiar rhythm without being personally instructed in it'. Nicholas Greene's analysis of Synge's language shows convincingly how ruthlessly selective he was in his handling of peasant speech, by-passing common structures like Lady Gregory's famed 'Kiltartan infinitive', preferring at times an English structure or an archaic word to Irish usage and varying the style from one play to another, not in order to record real life regional differences (for Kerry speech turns up in the Mayo world, Wicklow peasants inappropriately use Gaelic constructions) but to achieve rhythmical, musical and dramatic decorum.

We are not intended to overlook but to register sharply the synthetic or 'made-up' quality of this strange, alluring, often comical language: it is a vital aspect of the great improvisation, the structuring and projecting of themselves in which the characters are engaged. To think of Synge is first of all to hear a lilting voice holding sway, telling endless stories, rewriting its own history and edging life forward into the future. Naturalism was as far from Synge's mind as was any pious, nationalist notion of Gaelic as a language due for revival. He did indeed feel a peculiar hostility to that notion. Despite his love of the melody and colour in the old language, he knew it was dying; perhaps it was only in the supremely artificial form of the theatre that it could live; the paradox, indeed, of the Grecian urn. He connected the Gaelic League's clamour for the revival of Gaelic with their parochialism, asking: 'Was there ever a sight so piteous as an old and respectable people setting up the ideals of Fee-Gee because, with their eyes glued on John Bull's navel, they dare not be Europeans for fear the huckster across the street might call them English'.[15]

But this wouldn't last. He imagined a future when some young man would appear and 'teach Ireland again that she is part of Europe'. He would sweep away what was narrow and parochial in the 'credo of mouthing gibberish', but with 'the pity that is due to the poor stammerers who mean so well though they are stripping the nakedness of Ireland in the face of her own sons'. It is tempting to fill in the features of this young man who was to teach Ireland that she was part of Europe; for in the world of art two indeed have appeared who might be thought of as fulfilling Synge's prophecy: both certainly have affinities with him as a playwright. Joyce was the first: he carried the torch for Ibsen at a time when it seemed that Ireland might be in danger of missing that great European experience and his one play, *Exiles,* was a delicately Irish flavoured exploration in modes derived from Ibsen and Chekhov. Synge's early unproduced play, *When the Moon Has Set,* most unusually for him, also looks towards Ibsen in many ways; in its contemporary middle-class setting, the strand of plain contemporary usage in its language, its cosmopolitan, intellectually torn hero, restlessly returned from Paris, like Richard Rowan and Ibsen's Oswald, to a narrow provincial society which he has to come to terms with. It becomes very Ibsenite in its combative ending, with Eileen stripping off her nun's habit and asserting her right to the 'joy of life' with Colum; perhaps, as some have thought, Ibsen was in Synge's mind when he wondered whether the play might not have some stage success 'with a certain kind of very modern audience'.

Beyond Joyce, however, steps Beckett, and it is to that further off figure that Synge especially reaches out. Synge's career remarkably anticipates Beckett's: he moved from Ireland to Paris, studied French, used French methods on Irish material, almost became a Frenchman, so his mother said when his hair was affected by his illness and he took to wearing a black wig and a soft hat in French style. Their drama is still closer: Beckett's masterful handling of loneliness is shadowed in

[15] 'Can We Go Back Into Our Mother's Womb?' in *Collected Works,* ii, 400.

Synge's theatre of bareness and austerity where, as Yeats pointed out, time runs slowly and there is little outer movement to distract attention from the powerful fantasies of the violently imaginative, comical, afflicted beings at the centre, who amuse and appal and impose on us with enormous élan and strength of personality their interior drama.

Synge picked up from the French, from the symbolists, from Maeterlinck, and then let his imagination loose on a rich Irish material which he made in the process European. His 'Irish' method has inspired Yeats, O'Casey and now Beckett, through whom it has become familiar far beyond Europe. I have been trying to distinguish the features of this method and to show how, despite all that is of the nineteenth century in his style and technique, Synge is in a way one of the most modern of the moderns. He claims that place by the use he makes of his sardonic humour and by his subtle handling of the self-conscious theatricality that seems so natural to his characters, but in the end persuades us it represents a mysterious, universal process of the human mind, the endless self-creation of 'men who are dark a long while and thinking over queer thoughts in their heads'.

6 ～ Yeats, Maeterlinck and Synge

In Yeats's early writing Maeterlinck figures as one of the priesthood through whom a new art, or Art—for it was in the nature of a religion —might spread and become 'the Art of the People'. He reviewed *The Treasure of the Humble* with enthusiasm, seeing Maeterlinck as a kind of Jacobin taking over the 'red bonnet' from Villiers de l'Isle Adam (amusingly incongruous thought) and leading the great modern insurrection against 'everything which assumes that the external and material are the only fixed things, the only standards of reality'.[1] Maeterlinck was the representative of Belgium in an European assembly of the spiritual and intellectual elect, along with Mallarmé, Wagner and others who entered importantly into Yeats's development as a playwright. Ibsen gets on to the list with an honourable mention only, though elsewhere he is linked with Maeterlinck in Yeats's thinking, for instance when he reflects on 'emotion of multitude', the shadowy extension of theme which the Greeks drew from the Chorus and Shakespeare from the sub-plot, but the modern drama was disastrously without: Ibsen and Maeterlinck however had devised a new method for invoking this vital emotion in their 'vague symbols that set the mind wandering from idea to idea, emotion to emotion'.[2] This, we might notice, is not unlike Maeterlinck's description of the 'atmosphere of the soul' in *The Master Builder*. When writing of Synge too it came naturally to Yeats to refer to Maeterlinck, as someone who had achieved distance and 'time for reverie' by taking for his characters 'persons who are as faint as a breath upon a looking-glass, symbols who can speak a language slow and heavy with dreams because their own life is but a dream' (*Essays and Introductions*, p. 334).

He also spoke up for Maeterlinck publicly. He was one of the signatories to a letter protesting against the Lord Chamberlain's ban on *Monna Vanna* and emphasising Maeterlinck's distinction and the 'singular nobility of his attitude towards moral questions'.[3] And

---

[1] *The Bookman*, July 1897. In *Uncollected Prose*, ed. J. P. Frayne and C. Johnson (1975), ii, 45–7. See also Yeats's review of *Aglavaine and Selysette*, pp. 51–4.

[2] 'Emotion of Multitude' in *Essays and Introductions*, p. 216.

[3] Letter to *The Times* of 20 June 1902. The signatories also included Arthur

occasionally he makes explicit references to the influence of Maeterlinck on his own work, as when he speaks (*Autobiographies*, p. 193) of Symons returning to the Rhymers from Paris with stories of Verhaeren and Maeterlinck which confirmed his own thought and encouraged him 'to announce a poetry like that of the Sufis'. In those days, though he had his reservations, he might not have minded people join'ng his name with Maeterlinck's, as they so often did. Symons especially discerned affinities between them, significantly in the places where their art now looks most modern. His account of Yeats's silences, for instance, could apply with equal force to Maeterlinck—and with allowance for their difference of tone, to Beckett and Pinter too: 'The silences of these plays are like the pauses of music, we have the consciousness, under all the beauty and clearness and precision of the words we hear, of something unsaid, something which the soul broods over in silence . . . they speak to one another not out of the heart or out of the mind, but out of a deeper consciousness than either heart or mind, which is perhaps what we call the soul'.[4] Symons went further than most in connecting Yeats and Maeterlinck but he was not alone among contemporary critics in doing so. Sturge Moore, who was close to Yeats as poet and friend as well as designer for his stage, found *Deirdre* a Maeterlinckian play which he imagined producing the effect of 'a religious mystery' in production: it impressed him by its atmosphere, 'and the way it is all of one fineness, I think far beyond anything I have ever read of Maeterlinck's, and in a similar kind of excellence'.[5] Gordon Craig was attracted by both playwrights and had thoughts of producing Maeterlinck's plays with puppets, taking up literally the implications in 'Plays for marionettes'. It was with some quiet satisfaction, one suspects, that Yeats recorded his giving up the idea in favour of a production of *Where there is Nothing* 'with elaborate scenery'. How interesting those productions would have been and how one regrets that in the event neither was carried out.

Critics of the time were struck by a general likeness of style between the Irish players and plays and the Maeterlinckian drama. C. E. Montague was reminded of the remote, still quality of *Interior* by the grave movements of the Irish company playing Synge; their delicate gestures, their austerely rhythmical speech had a quality he

Symons and Laurence Alma-Tadema, Maeterlinck's translator. I am indebted to Dr John Kelly for this information.

[4] *Studies in Prose and Verse*, 1904, pp. 238–41.
[5] *W. B. Yeats and T. Sturge Moore: Their Correspondence 1901–1937*, p. 11.

found 'equally strange and simple' as Maeterlinck's, though he observed they had not his mournful tenderness. This was certainly a likeness Yeats courted for, as we saw, French actors were his first model for a 'static' acting style, and *Interior* was a play that gave the style its fullest scope. It clearly interested him, since it was performed at the Abbey in 1907: perhaps if the theatre's repertoire had been more open to non-Irish drama, more of Maeterlinck would have got in, along with the Molière which did break through the barrier of Irishness that hardened as time went on. And yet Yeats might still have hesitated; for despite all his affinities with Maeterlinck, and the admiration—sometimes quite extravagant—he expressed for his work in early days, his attitude to his Belgian contemporary was highly ambivalent.

This was so even in the period of his greatest enthusiasm. Writing to Olivia Shakespear in 1895 (*Letters*, p. 255), he has much to say about Maeterlinck, looks forward to discussing him with her, praises *The Sightless*: 'His play about the blind people and the dead priest in the snow is delightful'—a warm, if oddly chosen, epithet. Then an abrupt switch and he is reporting a somewhat catty conversation in Paris of the year before, when he had enquired of Verlaine, 'Does not Maeterlinck touch the nerves sometimes when he should touch the heart?' and Verlaine had confirmed the doubt with a vengeance: 'Ah yes, . . . He is a good dear fellow, and my very good friend, but a little bit of a mountebank'. Poor Maeterlinck, one feels like saying, to have Verlaine for his very dear friend! Yeats's relish of this quotation suggests some personal animus, as do other casual remarks reported by himself or others: he was inclined to be rude about Georgette Leblanc, Maeterlinck's 'little bit', as he ungallantly called her; she was to be seen at performances dressed in red, looking, so he said, like Messalina. And Monk Gibbon records how in conversation once when he was tactless enough to speak of Maeterlinck as a possible Nobel prize-winner, Yeats registered very clearly his distaste for the idea, and so it seemed, for the author.

Behind these small episodes lay an apparent uneasiness about the quality of Maeterlinck's imagination. In that early letter to Olivia Shakespear he identified one of its defects as lack of 'that ceaseless revery about life which we call wisdom' and drew a contrast with the 'old dramatists, Greek and English, who think wonderful, and rather mournful, things about their puppets'. So far, so Maeterlinckian, one might say, but no; Maeterlinck has neither their 'revery' nor their capacity to 'utter their thoughts in a sudden line or embody them in some unforeseen action'. The argument is obscure, indeed contradicts what he says elsewhere about Maeterlinck's ability to create 'time for reverie'. As if recognising this and pulling himself up, Yeats ends with a compliment: 'He is however of immense value as a force helping people to understand a more ideal drama'. Always this to and fro of feeling, this impression of Maeterlinck as a kind of fallen angel. Yeats does actually use the expression 'angelic person' in the course of a later reflection on the subject of dramatic energy, the other quality he found Maeterlinck deficient in. Why did both he and Ibsen lack this essential force, he asked; was it to do with their immersion in vitiating city life?

> Is it the mob that has robbed these angelic persons of the energy of their souls? Will not our next art be rather of the country, of great open spaces, of the soul rejoicing in itself? (*Explorations*, p. 169)

Of course in a sense, Maeterlinck's later drama really was 'fallen'. There is no difficulty in following Yeats's hostile criticism when it is turned on plays like *Monna Vanna:*

> . . . The rhetoric of d'Annunzio, the melodrama and spectacle of the later Maeterlinck, are the insincerities of subjectives, who being very able men have learned to hold an audience. . . To be intelligible they are compelled to harden, to externalise and to deform. (*Explorations*, p. 259)

It is not surprising, highly understandable, indeed, that he went to see *Monna Vanna* when it came to London less for the sake of the play, so he told Lady Gregory, than from interest in the acting style of Lugné-Poë's company.

But his ambivalent attitude to the earlier work and to Maeterlinck as a figure in the modern drama is more complex and perplexing. It suggests to me that he may have felt some embarrassment, whether consciously or not, at the closeness between them. For they were extremely close in so many ways, in their ideas on theatre and their fascination with the occult, their feeling for the 'inexpressible', their distrust of what Yeats called 'that modish curiosity, psychology', their experimental techniques. Titles, key words and phrases often attest to the striking likeness of their thoughts. Maeterlinck treats mystical themes in a work called *The Buried Temple* (1902), Yeats in

The Trembling of the Veil (1926);[6] Maeterlinck talks of the 'drama of the interior', Yeats of a drama of the 'most interior being', both use the word 'soul' continually in a theatrical as well as a metaphysical context.

Maeterlinck was often, chronologically at least, a step ahead; and he had some advantages Yeats lacked, a company of actors trained in the style of Racine, for instance, and such a musician as Debussy to interpret and adorn his visions; he was obviously in closer touch with the French symbolists, especially Mallarmé, who thought his drama the realisation of the symbolist dream. There may have been times when he seemed rather in the way, despite his enormous use as a model, times too, as I suggested in speaking of Wilde, when he may have seemed to reflect or even parody qualities Yeats was dubious of and trying to check in his own drama—vagueness, abstraction, romantic melancholy. For Maeterlinck's intensity is often just on the brink of the absurd—in the old derogatory sense, as well as the admired modern one. Max Beerbohm, himself responsive to its charm, tells of audiences tittering during the romantic scene in *Pelléas and Mélisande* when Mélisande shakes her hair out over her tower; probably such awkward moments were not uncommon, especially in the over-elaborate, rather heavy productions the plays were so often and wrongly given. Maeterlinck's way of saying things Yeats fundamentally agreed with—for instance that the 'soul' exists in a dimension apart from ordinary morality—was sometimes marked by that enervating, sentimental quality which above all estranged Yeats from him. Some of the accidental likenesses between the two often bring out their closeness at their weakest point; it is certainly an odd coincidence that the two leading exponents of a musical drama should have been more or less tone deaf, as is reported of Maeterlinck by Granville Barker among others, and of Yeats by himself: 'I am, from the musician's point of view, without music. I can only understand it in association with words' (*Letters*, p. 888). Their shared taste for a certain kind of acting is also an interesting, and perhaps from Yeats's point of view, a potentially damaging link: Mrs Patrick Campbell was his ideal Deirdre; he may not have cared to think of her being equally at home with Mélisande.

And yet they did have so much in common. Their staging innovations I have already spoken of, and now I want to consider briefly how

[6] Behind both lies Mallarmé's saying that his epoch was troubled by the trembling of the veil of the Temple.

Maeterlinckian elements were fed into Yeats's own drama. Crucially Maeterlinck offered him a technique for exploring the elemental, hidden, neglected powers and drives of the human personality, 'the destiny or fatality that we are conscious of within us, though by what tokens none can tell'. The techniques Maeterlinck devised to bring this impersonal fatality into the foreground 'and send the actors farther off', gave Yeats important hints. I think there are signs that Maeterlinck stayed in his mind from the time when he was attending performances of his plays in the London theatre of the nineties to the time when almost everyone else seemed to have forgotten them. Maeterlinckian influence showed in his first play, *The Shadowy Waters* and is surely acknowledged in his last, *The Death of Cuchulain,* where he pays the characteristically ambiguous tribute of a distorted echo. The Old Man who speaks the prologue works himself into a frenzy thinking of the ballet dancers painted by Degas—a link here with all that old symbolist rage against the externality of European art—and finally explodes in a great shout—'I spit!' three times repeated; a comic-sardonic echo of the terrible climax to *The Death of Tintagiles* when Ygraine shouts 'I spit' as a last gesture of defiance against the invisible figure behind the great door. It is appropriate that a great Maeterlinckian moment should be recalled in this play, for Yeats's Old Man is the last in a long line of crabbed old men who are curiously and significantly related to the more melancholy and passive old ones on Maeterlinck's stage; the blind grandfather in *Pelléas,* the old man at the window in *Interior,* the other blind grandfather in *The Intruder.* Though so different in temperament, Yeats's choleric, histrionic old men share with those others a stage situation—of frustration, impotence, deprivation—which forces them into difficult modes of perception and self-scrutiny. They epitomise the process both playwrights sought to bring to the stage, the 'stilling and slowing which turns the imagination in upon itself'.

The self-aware Old Man is perhaps the most important archetype Yeats developed from the Maeterlinckian mode and in his turn handed on to Beckett. Another important legacy was Maeterlinck's modern transformations of fairy- and folk-tale material. His fairy-tale plays are usually sprinkled with strange little songs whose function is to communicate feelings too oblique, or obscure or intense for expression in ordinary speech; the mermaid-like song of inarticulate Mélisande—'Thirty years I've sought my sisters, / Far his hiding-place'; the distracted song of old King Ablamore in *Alladine and Palomides*—

'Unhappiness had three keys of gold'. This last one, sung by an old man prowling the gloomy corridors of his castle, swinging the keys he will soon use to lock up the doomed lovers, has a maniacal quality, much more alarming, one suspects, than Maeterlinck could have given him without the aid of music.

Yeats certainly took hints from these suggestive songs and from Maeterlinck's whole technique for representing the primitive drives of the unconscious through childish motifs, nursery rhymes and so on. Austin Clarke observed that one of Maeterlinck's plays was in the background of the 'anachronistic lyric' in *Deirdre* (1907):

> 'Why is it', Queen Edain said,
> 'If I do but climb the stair
> To the tower overhead,
> When the winds are calling there,
> Or the gannets calling out
> In waste places of the sky,
> There's so much to think about
> That I cry, that I cry?'

It is not really 'anachronistic', I think, for *Deirdre* does not have to be performed as a heroic/realistic piece; it could also be done in the more stylised manner of the dance plays, so emphasising the play's inwardness and making the lyric seem perfectly appropriate.

The violent strangeness of Maeterlinck's fairy-tale world has many reverberations in Yeats's drama. Imagery recurs, especially of the sea: in the Cuchulain plays, as in *The Sightless* or *The Death of Tintagiles,* there is always the sense of vast surrounding ocean, whether as a surface the characters venture on in brave boats or depths out of which fantastic creatures emerge to trouble the dreaming mind. *Pelléas and Mélisande* is a particularly haunting presence on Yeats's stage. *The King of the Great Clock Tower* (1935), indeed, might be seen as a *Pelléas* fantastically shrunk from five acts to a half hour 'moment' of manic symbolic intensity, with the king as a Golaud figure, desperately trying to draw some response from a Queen who, like Mélisande, has been plucked out of a mysterious void:

> I ask your country, name and family,
> And not for the first time. Why sit you there
> Dumb as an image made of wood or metal,
> A screen between the living and the dead?
> All persons here assembled, and because

They think that silence unendurable,
Fix eyes upon you.

She remains silent, though not with the passive, helpless silence of Mélisande; this is more like a refusal, for she turns to the questioner a 'beautiful, impassive mask'; her silence is formidable.

When the Stroller appears, laying down his confident, arrogant demands—he must see the Queen, she must dance for him alone 'Till I grow grateful, and grown grateful sing'—the King reacts with a violence which is a channel for unspoken feelings of bewilderment and impotence: like Golaud dragging Mélisande by the hair, he seems to seize the chance it gives him to come closer to the Queen; anything is better than her remoteness; 'Do something, anything, I care not what / So that you move—but why those staring eyes?' At that point, when the order for the beheading is given, the play does move away from the Maeterlinckian pattern. In *Pelléas and Mélisande* the love affair is curiously off-stage, unconsummated; Yeats too wants to go off-stage, as it were, behind the physical, but it is the arousal and consummation rather than the thwarting of desire that he is interested in. The beheading of the Stroller—that aggressively erotic piece of symbolism—brings the Queen sexually alive. 'O, what may come / Into my womb?', she sings, and the King applauds 'Ah!—That is better / Let the voice ring out'. Still he has no idea of what drives her to the sexual dance, what force it is that speaks through the severed head, telling of immortal longings and the pressure of mortal time:

Clip and lip and long for more,
Mortal men our abstracts are;
What of the hands on the Great Clock face?

But he no longer needs to know: the kind of understanding sought at the beginning has by the end of the play become an irrelevance. Words fall away: what is happening can only be learnt from the ritual through which the characters mime the demands of the unconscious. To twelve strokes on the gong, the queen performs her dance for the severed head, kissing its lips on the last note, and then a deep silence settles on the scene: the King as well as the Queen has become dumb. Silently they take their places in a tableau rich in pre-Raphaelite/ symbolist associations and with obvious echoes of Wilde's *Salomé*. There is a long look between them—inscrutable, for she never removes her mask—and for a moment he stands in the posture of

Golaud, threatening her with his sword. Then he kneels and lays it at her feet; they remain looking at each other in an equivocal tableau which suggests that their sexual union is now possible. It is a tableau too which looks straight to Pinter and those silent groupings through which he so often expresses similarly tortuous sexual processes; at the close of *The Homecoming*, for instance, where a woman's sexual power is suggested through long-held silence while a man crawls to her feet desperately trying to force a response from her. And in its turn *The King of the Great Clock Tower* echoes *Pelléas and Mélisande* and Golaud's tormented questioning of Mélisande as she lies dying:

GOLAUD   You know it now! . . . It is time! It is time! Quick!
            Quick! . . . The truth! The truth! . . .
MELISANDE   The truth . . . the truth . . .

There is a modern element in Yeats's play, however, which is shared by neither Maeterlinck nor Pinter. I am referring to the framing of the action by the Attendants who open and close the curtains on the inner scene, watch intently as though it were done for their benefit and have the final word—a word which takes us spinning out into a dimension conceivable by neither King nor Queen, though prophetically announced to them in the Stroller's evocation of the god Aengus. Time itself dissolves as the Attendants react to the climax they have witnessed in the time-bound play with the ghostly lyric of the hawthorn tree:

> I have stood so long by a gap in the wall
> Maybe I shall not die at all.

The dream is suspended, the dramatic illusion broken, to allow us a more complex view of it, a fuller air. In the companion piece, *A Full Moon in March*, the same technique is varied, as we saw, to bring out a subtle irony, a shift of power between the two Attendants corresponding to and counterpointing the shift of power between Queen and Stranger in the inner play.

Maeterlinck's drama lacks this dimension. He never breaks the illusion so drastically—the watcher in *Interior* is himself inside the action—and though he is not without irony, it is of a kind that can easily be overlooked or swamped by his more sombre notes. In *The Death of Tintagiles*, for instance, when Ygraine is rallying her supporters to defend the little brother from the monstrous Queen, her line 'Let us wait on our knees as we did before', should be spoken, so the original stage direction instructs, 'in an ironic voice'. Granville Barker commented that to omit the direction, as the English translator did, was 'to omit much meaning'. And yet it does seem that Maeterlinck was putting rather too heavy a burden on the actor by expecting him to convey so much in his intonation—nothing less, really, than a challenge to the idea of there being a God in the world.

For Yeats, certainly, such effects were too muted. His stage 'interior' was to be closer to that complex structure, the real mind: more of the daylight world with its air and space, its comedy and scepticism had to be in, and also the element of self-conscious theatricality which for him was an essential feature of the imagining process. Maeterlinck does not give us that; Eliot's idea that his characters 'take no conscious delight in their role' seems right on the whole (though I would disagree with him that this necessarily makes them, as he says, sentimental). It was to Synge that Yeats had to turn for those missing perspectives. He was the perfect model, a Maeterlinckian with a sense of humour, who could express an intense inner life entirely through the forms of the external world. When Yeats plucked him out of Paris and sent him to Aran to 'express a life that has never found expression', he meant the remark, no doubt, in the way it is usually taken, to refer to the 'real' life of the Aran islanders in all its colourful externality. But it was another kind of life that Yeats himself was seeking to express on the stage, and no one was better able than he to recognise that the process in Synge's drama was essentially the same inward process I have been tracing, the shaping of a highly coloured, solid looking outer envelope by the incessant workings of imagination and the creation of a 'new language behind language'. The phrase is C. E. Montague's; it occurs in the course of an essay on Synge in which he registers the Maeterlinckian likenesses but observes too the crucial difference, the 'minute admixture of something stingingly sane and hard—not sourness, but just an antiseptic against sugariness and the "sweetly pretty"'.[7] It was that 'something stingingly sane and hard' —'astringent joy and harshness' in Yeatsian phrase—that Yeats sought to combine in his own drama with the still, Maeterlinckian quality that so fascinated him in *The Well of the Saints*. Of course other influences were at work; we know how much he learned from Lady Gregory about the making of comedies. But the most important lesson had to come from the one who had gone as far as he had into the shadowy, solitary region where the self wove its own shape and

[7] *Dramatic Values*, p. 12.

lived its intensest life. For in aiming at something like Synge's violent laughter Yeats was reaching out to the opposite pole from the zone of quietness he thought the natural condition for an interior drama. He could scarcely have envisaged his new direction in the nineties when *Ubu Roi* drew from him the agitated prophecy: 'After us the Savage God' (*Autobiographies*, p. 349).

'A deep of the mind can only be approached through what is most human, most delicate'. 'Human' in his later drama has to take in violence, comedy, scepticism, and he developed a whole new range of theatrical devices for this purpose; these in their turn stimulated a fuller flow of Rabelaisian humour and an ever more complex theatrical perspective. We can see the instinct already at work in *Where there is Nothing* (1902), where the hero's effort to break out of the narrow mode of conventional thought is expressed as a compulsion to let a violent Nietszchean laughter loose in the world. And there were interesting attempts early on to introduce a comic perspective through prologues spoken by 'characters' outside the play. One of these seems to have been intended for *The Shadowy Waters*. The editors of *Druid Craft* suggest that it was possibly to have been spoken by the 'Black Jester' (Ricketts designed a costume for this character, who never got into a cast list) and that it may have been performed at the theosophical production of the play in 1905.[8] The speaker of the prologue tells the audience that he is going to make them experience a vision involving the characters he carries in a bottle around his neck—a strange collection of dogs, flowers, birds, and the supernatural lovers, Angus and Edaine. Yeats remarkably anticipates here John Arden's Bagman who also carries round with him (in a bag, not a bottle) 'little people' who come to life when they are shaken out in front of an audience. Yeats's prologue remained a shadow, however, like another, written for *The King's Threshold* (1904), which Austin Clarke amusingly recalled hearing at the Abbey, though as no one else seemed able to remember it, he began to wonder if it had not been an hallucination. Yet he had a particularly vivid memory of the unusual opening to the play. An old man, 'in a white night-gown with a peaked night-cap' (red, in the text), tottered in through the audience with a lighted candle in his hand, climbed laboriously on to the stage by specially built-up steps and delivered the prologue in confidential tones.[9] The story had a

[8] For the Ms transcript and an account of its history, see *Druid Craft*, pp. 302–4.

[9] For this and other comments on Yeats's plays, see his *The Celtic Twilight and the Nineties* (Dublin 1969).

truly Pirandellian twist, for the prologue was printed (in the *United Irishman*, 9 September 1903) before the production, as a kind of advertisement, the Old Man introducing himself as the uncle of one of the actors and explaining that he had been called on to speak the prologue because the company could not spare an actor to do it. Then it happened that there was *not* an actor to do it, and the prologue was dropped from the play after the short ghostly life Austin Clarke has recorded.

Spoken or unspoken, the prologue is full of interest as an indication of Yeats's drive to get his heroic machinery—the stilted boys, the burnished chariots—into a parodic frame, under the light of a saturnine humour. The Old Man is a great deflator of heroic attitudes, fussing about the draught through the curtain, sniffing at the play, reminding the audience in advance how big a gulf there is between their world and the characters, 'all of them as high up in themselves with the pride of their youth and their strength and their fine clothes as if there was no such thing in the world as cold in the shoulders, and speckled shins, and the pains in the bones and the stiffness in the joints that make an old man that has the whole load of the world on him ready for his bed'. On that note, with a last dig at 'play-acting', he stumps off stage and we move into a world that is remote indeed from the world of rheumatism and old bones, a world taken up with a heroical and abstract issue: will a poet be allowed to starve himself to death defending the right of poets to a place in the King's council? Yeats had intense difficulty in deciding what kind of answer that question should have, a happy or a sad one. At the time the prologue was written, he was still seeing the play as comedy; one of the Old Man's tasks is to justify the happy ending; 'if he that is in the story but a shadow and an image of poetry had not risen up from the death that threatened him, the ending would not have been true and joyful enough to be put into the voices of players'.

Yeats didn't quite manage to convince himself with that argument, the ending turned tragic in later versions and so remains. But he also built up the burlesque element, adding low comedy parts to provide parodies of the heroic action, as in the Mayor's rehearsal of his big speech—' "Chief poet, Ireland, townsman, grazing land", those are the words I have to keep in mind'—and the cripples' chatter about the queerness of poets and of miracles performed at a holy well by a 'little holy fish . . . and it rising up out of the blessed well to cure the crippled'.

The bizarre touch of Synge in this is a reminder that *The King's*

Threshold was performed by the Irish National Theatre Society in 1903, the year when first they produced a play of Synge's (*The Shadow of the Glen*). In (perhaps unconsciously) parodying him, it is as if Yeats were already aware that he would eventually need to go even beyond Synge in iconoclastic laughter. That certainly does not happen in *The King's Threshold* where the comedy is relatively tame, though there are some droll cacophonies, 'As if the farmyard and the rookeries / Had all been emptied!' as the Lord Chamberlain says, appearing at one point to impose a decorous censorship. There was one whiff of modernity in the play which Yeats was rather proud of. Seanchan's hunger strike, which ends in his death and the capitulation of the King, was, he pointed out, in advance of political reality, for at the time the play was written, 'neither patriots nor suffragettes had adopted the hunger strike, nor had the hunger strike been used anywhere, so far as I know, as a political weapon'.

Yet of course, despite all this, *The King's Threshold* could never be thought of as 'modern' as a totally non-realistic play like *At the Hawk's Well* now seems to be. There is in a way more modernity in *On Baile's Strand* (final version, 1904), for though there is nothing to match the Old Man's prologue, the element of black farce is much stronger. The tragic revelation that Cuchulain has killed his own son comes about in a tableau of disturbing visual absurdity, the great hero sitting on a bench between Fool and Blind Man, wiping blood from his sword with feathers from the same heap as the Fool is drawing on, plucking feathers to stick into his hair; a grotesque, silent parody of Cuchulain's image of himself as a proud hawk. The Fool lets out the terrible information that comes too late with a naïveté that is grimly comic, and when Cuchulain rushes into the sea to fight madly with the waves, he describes for the Blind Man's benefit what is happening— 'Now he is up, now he is down'—like a commentator reporting the racing in *The Playboy of the Western World*. The play ends with an aggressive anticlimax, the Blind Man's mundane exploitation of the tragic situation: 'There will be nobody in the houses. Come this way; come quickly! The ovens will be full. We will put our hands into the ovens'.

The Fool and Blind Man owe their comic freedom, their obstinately untragic perspective, no doubt in part to the 'grotesque and extravagant' masks Craig designed for them. All Yeats's early masks—those worn by the Fool and Blind Man in *On Baile's Strand* (1904), the Fool in *The Hour-Glass* (1914), the Old Men in *The Player Queen*

(1922)—were of that type. Curiously, the playwright who was devoted to the 'theatre of beauty' took a long time to realise that masks could be beautiful; not till he saw a music-hall dancer doing, as he said, 'imitations of Ito' did he become fascinated by the 'temporary beauty' the mask could give. Up to then, he said, he had only realised its grotesque possibilities. This is a good indication of how strong his impulse was towards farce, burlesque and comic effects generally.

That impulse became a driving force of his drama as soon as he had acquired the stage means to let him express it freely. The close relationship between total theatre techniques and the move to comic freedom is strikingly seen in *The Green Helmet* (1910), where it seems as if he were deliberately taking a Maeterlinckian dream interior and jazzing it up, drawing it into the modern sphere of surrealist farce. He was certainly mapping out the ground for later more serious explorations in the realm of the unconscious—as if he had to test his method by first exposing it to a bracing, satirical perspective. Some of the symbolic apparatus of the dance plays—the supernatural visitant emerging from the sea, the severed head—make their first appearance on Yeats's stage in the jovial, rough and tumble context of *The Green Helmet*. Everything in this play is designed to shock and surprise; the 'intentionally violent and startling colour scheme', the noisy sound effects, heroes, servants and wives all bawling at each other, running round the stage blowing great horns, the bouncy, rollicking verse, all coming to a head in the first surrealist explosion when three black hands come through the windows (an effect Yeats understandably expected to find difficulty in staging) and plunge the scene into total darkness into which a sea green light slowly filters, revealing the visitors from the sea, the Red Man and his cat-headed band. The jazzy stage scene and sound were meant to act on the audience fundamentally in the same way as the music and colours of *The Shadowy Waters*, lifting them out of time and place, taking them 'nearer to fairyland'. The difference is in the nature of the fairyland; now it is both more humorous and more threatening, a child's half-nightmare of men with cats' heads, horned giants and a head that is struck off and lies laughing on the ground till the Red Man picks it up and charges back into the sea again. An anarchical fluidity is suggested by these beheadings and the absurd nursery school battles triggered off by the Red Man; all is ridiculous and yet Yeats claims seriousness for it too. When the Red Man claims a head for a head, a darkening of mood is indicated by the darkening of the scene; the monstrous figures who take over the stage are bathed in an eerie green light, giving them a power they did not have in daylight and allowing Cuchulain, the only character who faces the horrors of the dark, to be a real hero after all. 'Quick', he says, to the Red Man, offering his head with comic panache, 'to your work, old Radish, you will fade when the cocks have crowed.' He is rewarded with the green helmet and the praise of the creature from the depths. It is a wish fulfilment—'The uncrowned king is actually crowned', as T. R. Moore says—and that was a potentially dangerous situation for Yeats as playwright. His fascination with heroes is, after all, one of the characteristics that might seem most likely to cut him off from modern audiences. It does not, because he knows himself so well; his own self-consciousness is the true subject. In all the Cuchulain plays he is careful to use distancing techniques, generally to show up dark spots in the heroic moon. Here there are no dark spots; but instead the wholesale correction of farce, which allows us to enjoy, as Yeats so clearly does himself, the exuberant rush of all that heroic energy, and yet preserve a sceptical Brechtian perspective on it. *The Green Helmet* was his first full-scale venture in the modern looking form he called 'heroic farce'. In its prose form as *The Golden Helmet* it was produced at the Abbey in 1908 and in the same year he began another play, *The Player Queen,* which he also tried for a time to get into tragic form, suffering as a result more than his usual agony with the 'dreadful opening work' on the first scenarios. The time he spent trying to write it as tragedy he later came to see as wasted. By 1910 although still committed in his mind to tragic form, he had been given Craig's masks and screens and had experimented with them in *The Hour-Glass,* in the process, as we saw, radically changing the form of that play. Something very similar happened with *The Player Queen* (performed by the Stage Society in 1919), where again there is a clear relation between the use of masks and the freeing of the comic spirit. The play opens with a scene of extravagant visual comedy; the heads and shoulders of two old men in grotesque masks silhouetted against a lighted wall, looking down the street, straining to see and hear, complementing each other's deficiencies in their eagerness to get a full view:

FIRST OLD MAN   Can you see the Queen's castle? You have better sight than I.

SECOND OLD MAN   I can just see it rising over the tops of the houses yonder on its great rocky hill.

FIRST OLD MAN	Is the dawn breaking? Is it touching the tower?
SECOND OLD MAN	It is beginning to break upon the tower, but these narrow streets will be dark for a long while (*A pause*). Do you hear anything? You have better hearing than I.
FIRST OLD MAN	No, all is quiet.
SECOND OLD MAN	At least fifty passed by an hour since, a crowd of fifty men walking rapidly. . . The young are at some mischief,—the young and the middle-aged.
FIRST OLD MAN	Why can't they stay in their beds, and they can sleep too—seven hours, eight hours? I mind the time when I could sleep ten hours. They will know the value of sleep when they are near upon ninety years.
SECOND OLD MAN	They will never live so long. They have not the health and strength that we had. They wear themselves out. They are always in a passion about something or other.

Still more in this play than in *The Green Helmet* Yeats seems to have Maeterlinck in mind. No doubt about there being an element of parody in that last scene, where the Maeterlinckian world of towers and queens and castles glimmers faintly through an alien, sardonic context. Symons said of *Ubu Roi* that it was 'a sort of comic antithesis to Maeterlinck', having the kind of relation to his drama that the Greek satyr play had to the tragedy which it followed and reflected. Rather amusingly when his initial reaction to *Ubu Roi* is recalled, Yeats seems, in the burlesque of *The Player Queen*, to be taking up Jarry's role. He also takes a decided step towards O'Casey, whose sardonic double turns are anticipated in his crusty old men with their complementary afflictions. Again as in O'Casey's plays, the most fantastic and ribald moments in Yeats's play are some of the most serious. One of them features yet another old man, the Old Beggar, who parodies the romantic poet and actor, Septimus, by also receiving inspiration—of a particularly grotesque kind. When he is possessed, he goes through a ludicrous ritual, rolling on the ground and braying like a donkey to announce the coming of a new reign. He is absurd, but his intuitions are not. 'Do those who are dead, old man, make love', Decima asks him, 'And do they find good lovers?' A chill wind falls with his answer; 'People talk, but I have never known of anything to come from there but an old jackass. Maybe there is nothing else. Who knows but he has the whole place to himself?' A Beckettian phrase, that last, and like one of Beckett's sceptical actors, the Old Beggar continues to play his part which looks so solitary and futile but is vital because bound up with the parts of all the rest; the Queen can't die till he has rolled and brayed; only the donkey knows, by some mysterious dispensation, 'when there is to be a new King or a new Queen'.

By the end of the play, the theatrical mode has become universal; there are no non-actors, only different degrees of skill and self-consciousness in performance, notably between the 'real' Queen, and the professional, Decima, the Player Queen. The use of masks also becomes self-conscious. The mask of Noah's wife which is on one level a perfectly ordinary object in the actor's stock, to be handed from one to another or dropped carelessly into a property basket, is shown becoming fearful in its power to fix an actor in a role he may not want to play: so Decima is threatened when her rival presses it on her with the slighting words, 'Low comedy is what you are fit for'. She fights back, wins for herself the role she knows is hers, the Queen's, which is the most dangerous part in the world of the play, only to be acted in a heroic spirit. We are getting very close to the world of Genet's *The Balcony* in the scene where the Queen and Decima change roles, one removing her gold dress and slippers, the other putting them on, each at once becoming what the costume says they are. But as always Yeats puts the emphasis less on fixing than on flexibility. Dizzy vistas of change open up when Decima in the persona of the Queen separates herself from her lover, the other actors and her old self; that 'woman player' is no longer to exist for them. She is Queen, but in the moment of attaining the much-wanted role she prepares to overlay it with a new one; as the play closes she is calling for someone to help her put on the despised mask of Noah's wife; she will hide behind this face, a face that can be seen as 'modest' or as 'foolish, smiling'; everything is in the point of view.

We are given an alarming but also exhilarating freedom to choose our own perspective. The play has tilted in all directions, to the absurd, the heroic, the erotically violent, to leave us in this state of precarious equilibrium; sure only of one thing, the seemingly infinite potentiality for change in the elusive, histrionic human personality. The play was started shortly after *The Playboy of the Western World* had its first performance at the Abbey and it bears clear marks of Synge, above all in its pervasive theatricality and 'conscious delight' in role playing. Yet the influence of Synge did not displace Maeterlinck. In a much later piece, *The King of the Great Clock Tower*, Yeats was, as we saw, still quarrying in the Maeterlinckian vein. Never indeed was the 'interior' more dream-like than in that play or in the still later *The Herne's Egg* (1938), yet never was the absurd given a freer range, or the detachment more assured. By that time Yeats had acquired full mastery over the two styles he had inherited from Maeterlinck and Synge; through their fusion he was able to express the whole of himself on the stage.

7 ⌒ Yeats's Drama of the Interior: a Technique for the Modern Theatre

Yeats's plays have been rising in critical esteem for some time now; studies like Peter Ure's admirable *Yeats the Playwright* (1963) have stressed their dramatic subtlety and there is increasing respect for their theatrical effectiveness, as Reg Skene's *The Cuchulain Plays of W. B. Yeats* (1974) vividly demonstrates. It is still rather difficult to discuss them in the same way as other people's plays, Beckett's, say, or Pinter's, since productions remain infrequent, but it is that kind of discussion I want to attempt, drawing on what experience I have had of seeing or being involved with the plays in production and thinking of them always in that way.

I am not suggesting, of course, that one approach should be universal: that would be an absurd notion in relation to any playwright, but above all to Yeats. My thesis indeed is that his plays are exceptionally open to interpretation. He assumed that symbols had the power to change our mode of thinking by luring us to 'the threshold of sleep' and evoking 'indefinable and yet precise emotions'. This is certainly what can happen when the plays are well performed; the audience may feel perplexed, even lost or anxious about 'understanding', yet in my experience, especially of student audiences, they are also held, haunted by the music, ritual and strange imagery, moved and stirred, though they may not be able to say why. Each will have his own distinct response, but it is fascinating to find common impressions emerging, even among people who may have known nothing about Yeats or his plays: perhaps, as he suggested, we do on these occasions—which can be occasions of great theatrical intensity—make unusual contact with other minds, even, as he thought, with the 'great mind and great memory . . . the memory of Nature herself'.

There is no need, really, for the rather widespread feeling that his plays cannot be appreciated without a great deal of special knowledge. In a teasing phrase Yeats once spoke of different levels of meaning in his work, for the Boy and for the Sage. This could be taken as endorsement of the esoteric view of his drama, but it does not have to be, for in a way it is true of all drama of any richness; we receive from it according to the mental store we bring to it. In that sense, certainly, Yeats's plays call for preparedness, but he writes in the first place, as all good playwrights do, for the Boy, for the open imagination, responsive to what is *there*, not daunted by surprise, but eager for it, wanting the experience, not the explanation of it. I want to take up that Boy's viewpoint, not arbitrarily shutting out knowledge when it would be natural to bring it in, but equally not feeling the need to bring it in nor to continually test my own responses on other critical interpretations, but rather to register my view of the plays in a context of the theatre of Beckett, Maeterlinck, O'Casey, as part of a great modern repertoire.

'Modern' may seem an odd word for the 'antiquated romantic stuff' as the Old Man sardonically calls it, out of which Yeats made his plays. How can anything be modern that is always looking backwards to Irish history and ancient legends, and if it takes the present for its theme, as in *The Dreaming of the Bones*, does so only to show it being invaded by a ghostly past? But it is not in the Irishness or in the ritual shaping of old legend and mythology that the heart of the drama lies, or so I am suggesting. All that is the 'stuff'. What Yeats fashioned from it is something different, a self-delighting theatrical process which continually reminds us of its theatricality, and in doing so subtly implies an analogy with the inner processes of the mind itself. It is a drama of the interior, which may use names like Cuchulain rather than Ygraine or Estragon, but has the same sense of timelessness as the plays of Maeterlinck and Beckett, and like theirs can be grasped intuitively, without benefit of book.

It is always clear in the dance plays that the stage is a kind of 'No-place', like the bare room in *Endgame* which is both strangely unfamiliar and instantly recognisable as the other world in the head, the 'obscure theatre of the soul'. The scene is an empty space with perhaps one or two symbolic objects to serve as obsessive focal points —a well, a lighted window, a cross, a withered tree—and into this space comes a drama conjured up by 'agents' who themselves cannot explain it: they improvise but have no control over the action once it is set in motion. Sometimes, indeed, we have the illusion of penetrating beyond the secondary agents, the musicians, to the real initiator—the Old Man in *The Death of Cuchulain*, for instance, opens the play by claiming to have invented everything we are going to see—but the great question here is always, how can the amazing drama which acquires such autonomy be related to the inadequate being who launches it? Presenting to each other masks which they may change but cannot abandon, under the spell of forces they are hardly aware of —there is no contact between them and the musicians—the actors perform their fated rituals. The fatalism is strong; the suggestion of a mechanism that, wound up, cannot be stopped is one of the most powerful effects of this drama. Yet it is undermined, even to an extent contradicted by the opposite impression of unknown, uncontrollable energies welling up from watery depths, promising or threatening change. A change in thinking or feeling, a movement of the mind so faint sometimes that it is scarcely discernible, is, it seems to me, the outcome of all these improvisations.

I want now to illustrate the variety Yeats achieves within his seemingly narrow form, starting with the plays he himself grouped together in *Four Plays for Dancers* (1921) and going on to three later pieces, *The Cat and the Moon* (1926), *Purgatory* (the only one not in the dance convention) and *The Death of Cuchulain* (both 1939). In each a 'moment of intense life' is dramatised, in each an austere convention is strictly observed. Yet always the mental landscape is varied, the mood and atmosphere utterly distinctive. The movement of mind may be, as in *The Dreaming of the Bones* (1919), a tremor of conscience hardly experienced before it is retracted, or, as in *Purgatory*, the violent culmination of a trauma. The emphasis may be on the ability of the mind to stand apart and examine its own dream, as the Old Man does in *The Death of Cuchulain*, or on the unselfconscious pursuit of a dream, as in *At the Hawk's Well* (1917). Solitariness may be explored, or an unlikely communion between two seemingly alienated minds such as we are shown in *The Only Jealousy of Emer* (1919). It is not easy to analyse the fine shades of difference in mood between one play and another and yet always, from the first beat of the opening verse, each has its unique music; the mournful remoteness of *The Dreaming of the Bones* is not that of *Calvary* (1929), though like; the irony in *At the Hawk's Well*, though dark, is less sombre than in *Purgatory*. While *The Cat and the Moon* is in a mood all its own; comical, lilting, touched with only the gentlest poignancy.

I referred earlier to *At the Hawk's Well* as the model for Yeats's new theatrical syntax. I return to it with my leading question in mind; what is this drama likely to convey to an audience that knows nothing of 'the old epics and Mr Yeats' plays'? The question is especially appropriate to this much interpreted piece; it would be easy to be daunted by the massive commentary on the possible 'meanings' of the well and the water of life and wonder whether the play could be appreciated without a key to its symbols, or even whether it was actable. Yet in fact this is one of the plays most often seen in performance, and when it is seen, the problem of 'meaning' tends to evaporate; it is so clear from its continual clash and counterpoint of views that there is no such thing as one meaning to suit all characters. Divergence is the theme, the strikingly different responses of the figures on the stage to the mystery they conjure up among them, the haunting concept of a supernatural extension to life: 'He who drinks, they say, / Of that miraculous water lives for ever'. To the Young Man the water of life and its Guardian are glamour and ecstasy, to the Musicians, although they are the agents of the evocation, a thing of terror. Most complex of all are the feelings of the Old Man; in his response there is a dour realism, a hard familiarity with the routine workings of the magical event he always misses, which still does not stop him desiring it and continuing to *wait* even as he slowly withers.

If we set out to discuss the play in terms of 'character' the Old Man would be the most interesting figure, as indeed he often appears in stage performance; it seemed right, for instance, in the televised version of the production given by the Yeats Theatre Company in 1973,[1] that the screen should be filled at the end by his grotesque and compelling mask, this be the image we took away with us. The irony which is the prevailing mood of the play strikes more subtle notes from his bitter knowledge than from the Young Man's brash ignorance. But does the play allow us to think of the characters in purely realistic terms as totally separate self-standing individuals? Yeats raises a question about this, while at the same time ruling out any simple answer. The two masks are kept in a most delicate balance, so that at times they do seem like separate characters and at other times create an overwhelming impression that the separation between them is no more than the gulf between the youth and age of one being.

They make contact, these two, in a world out of time, where opposites meet, as the Musicians hint at the start:

> The heart would be always awake,
> The heart would turn to its rest.

---

[1] Production by Niema Ash with the Yeats Theatre Company at the Howff Theatre Café, Regents Park, London, in 1973. Televised by the University of London Audio Visual Centre.

Both are nameless: it is surely very significant that in this first dance play on the Cuchulain motif, Cuchulain should not be named in the cast list, but kept anonymous like a Maeterlinckian character. For those who do happen to know the story there is indeed a sardonic joke, when the Young Man tells his name and the Old Man does not know it: 'I have never heard that name'. But whether we get the joke or not, we are given a hint in the flat, measured tone that there is something significant here; retrospectively we can appreciate an uncanny irony, as if the older self, in a dream, confronted with his youthful image, had failed to recognise it.

Lack of recognition is certainly stressed. They are strangers and opposites, old-young; nervous-brave; bitter-dashingly confident. But underneath the differences runs a deep likeness. Both wear the full mask, move like marionettes, echo and shadow each other's words and stories, think of themselves as being—or having been—'lucky':

OLD MAN	I came like you
	When young in body and in mind, and blown
	By what had seemed to me a lucky sail.
	The well was dry, I sat upon its edge,
	I waited the miraculous flood, I waited
	While the years passed and withered me away.
	I have snared the birds for food and eaten grass
	And drunk the rain, and neither in dark nor shine
	Wandered too far away to have heard the plash,
	And yet the dancers have deceived me. Thrice
	I have awakened from a sudden sleep
	To find the stones were wet.
YOUNG MAN	My luck is strong,
	It will not leave me waiting, nor will they
	That dance among the stones put me asleep;
	If I grow drowsy I can pierce my foot.
OLD MAN	No, do not pierce it, for the foot is tender,
	It feels pain much. But find your sail again
	And leave the well to me, for it belongs
	To all that's old and withered.
YOUNG MAN	No, I stay.

'Waiting' and 'luck': the repetition of those two motifs brings out how much Old and Young Man have in common at the very centre of their being. They are both subjected to the same irony, for they act in ignorance and call it luck. One of them knows better now, but they cannot learn from each other; the Young Man's belief in his luck is not affected by the perspective the Old Man offers, and still more ironically the Old Man himself is not deterred by his disillusionments from his waiting. The most affecting moments of the play, it seems to me, are those when the Old and Young Man appear locked in a mysteriously close relationship, strangers who have nevertheless somehow shared a life, felt lucky in the same way, wanted the same thing, been 'absent' from their imagined centre. The withered Old Man, doubled up with age like the thorn trees, stands there almost as a parody of the 'living for ever' the Young Man desires, reminding us of the Musicians' troubled brooding at the play's opening on long life and old age:

> A mother that saw her son
> Doubled over a speckled shin,
> Cross-grained with ninety years,
> Would cry, 'How little worth
> Were all my hopes and fears
> And the hard pain of his birth'.

When he pleads with the Young Man not to leave him alone at the end, there is an uncanny sense of two poles miraculously touching. Something of that sort was movingly suggested in the final tableau of the Open University production in 1975 when the quicksilver dancing figure of the Young Man appeared behind the old one in a lightning contrast—as if a whole life were being unrolled and the inevitability of its 'choices' glimpsed in a moment of piercing intuition.

One of the strangest things in this dream theatre is the self-containment of the actors and their inability to see outside their own parts. The Musicians direct, but they cannot enter into the other roles, especially cannot understand the fascination of the dancer, that ambiguous, mute figure. For us, the audience, it is different: if the dance is effectively done—and the dance convention must assume this —we do understand why it is that the Young Man is drawn to follow her. And yet we may shrink with the Old Man (it would only be natural) from the pain the Young Man's role entails—piercing the foot, perhaps, to fight off the sleep that blots out the transcendental experience. And we can equally understand the Musicians' aversion from the Old Man's role; fifty years of waiting for something, some miracle, some revelation; a waiting that has not fed him but left him dry, a creaking marionette.

So for us the play is about the shifting and jostling among all these roles and points of view. The action ends with the Musicians' refusal of sympathy, the assertion of their preference:

> Folly alone I cherish,
> I choose it for my share;
> Being but a mouthful of air,
> I am content to perish;
> I am but a mouthful of sweet air.

They try to call up another landscape altogether:

> 'The man that I praise',
> Cries out the empty well,
> 'Lives all his days
> Where a hand on the bell
> Can call the milch cows
> To the comfortable door of his house.
> Who but an idiot would praise
> Dry stones in a well?'

But that landscape cannot establish itself, the Musicians' view must remain partial for an audience who have responded with the Young Man to the erotic excitement of the dance and been affected by the Old Man's tenacity, his refusal to say 'I am content to perish'.

The process of the play, it seems, has been the building up of tension among the contrary impulses in a mind at a fatal moment of choice which is in a way no choice at all, for it is determined by the dumb actor who cannot be known or argued with, the dancer. In one of his many pronouncements on masks, Yeats once said:

> all happiness depends on the energy to assume the mask of some other life, on a re-birth as something not one's self, something created in a moment and perpetually renewed; in playing a game like that of a child where one loses the infinite pain of self-realisation, in a grotesque or solemn painted face put on that one may hide from the terror of judgment. . . (*Mythologies*, p. 334)

At the Hawk's Well does not deal with the 'infinite pain of self-realisation', nor with the creative joy of putting on a mask. The revelation in this play is for the audience rather than the characters; it is deeply ironic, with a near Maeterlinckian emphasis on fatality and the darkly absurd side of our failure to know our own inner compulsions, our 'shadows'. The Young Man in his ignorance is absurd to the Old Man and the Old Man is absurd to the Musicians because, knowing as much as he does, he goes on waiting: 'Who but an idiot would praise / A withered tree?'. But there is also a distinctive un-Maeterlinckian note of delight in the illusion and its intricacy, above all in the mysterious extension of possibility suggested by the silent dancing figure, the shadow who is capable of playing an unknown number of parts.

The Young Man leaves the stage to the sound of battle and women's voices, going to the tragic fate the Old Man has prophetically envisaged. He is 'no longer as if in a dream', so the stage directions say; it is to the daylight world he returns, to encounter a woman of flesh and blood. But his fate was decided in the world of shadows where he moved spell-bound under the direction of Musicians and mute dancer.

Transitions between the worlds of daylight and dream—the mind awake and the mind in trance—are a characteristic feature of the earlier plays. They are especially striking in *The Only Jealousy of Emer* and *The Dreaming of the Bones,* two plays which separate themselves from the others in *Four Plays for Dancers* by their much greater realism, a realism curiously contained within the customary dream-like and ritualistic context of the dance convention. That is indeed the special sense they create; the solid world of externality is penetrated for a fleeting moment to allow a glimpse of the hidden region where the 'real' action takes place.

The Only Jealousy of Emer begins with a cryptic allusion to the ruling dream of the play in the Musicians' melancholy opening lyric:

> A woman's beauty is like a white
> Frail bird, like a white sea-bird alone
> At daybreak after stormy night
> Between two furrows upon the ploughed land. . .

Then they transport us to a scene rare in Yeats's drama, a domestic interior, focusing like a camera eye on homely details—the fisherman's cottage with its cross-beams darkened by smoke, the oar against the wall—introducing the characters almost as if preparing us for a conventional, triangular love drama. There is Cuchulain, the husband, the 'amorous, violent man', lying in a trance on the bed; his wife watching, his young mistress coming to the bedside at the wife's summons 'on hesitating feet', to try to do what the wife cannot, draw him back to life. Realism is strong in the encounter between wife and embarrassed mistress, and throughout the play the mistress, Eithne

Inguba, remains in a separate mode from the rest. Once the dream convention asserts itself she has to leave the stage; she never looks into the man's dream as the wife does. When at the end she returns to woo Cuchulain back to life, it is as though she had never been away; his recovery seems to her an immediate response to her entreaty: 'And it is I that won him from the sea, / That brought him back to life'. She is in a different time scale, in the other, more realistic play that hovers on the fringe of this one, an external world in which the moment of revelation cannot occur.

Some of the solid realism attaches to the wife too. She is outside the dream, though signals pass between her and the man who is so nearly drowned in it. Throughout she stands on one side of the stage watching and we are surely interested in her, the viewer, at least as much as in the ghostly shapes which reveal Cuchulain's mind. His role here is as her husband; it is essentially a play about marriage and the wordless communication achieved at the deepest levels of consciousness between two people who in their outer lives seem estranged and ignorant of each other's feelings. We need to see the play to receive the full force of this complex communion, for visual effects are crucial in it, above all, the masks, here used to suggest not fixity of personality, as in *At the Hawk's Well*, but, rather, its precarious fluidity, the multiplicity of selves within this one man, Cuchulain. The play was written, Yeats said, to find 'what dramatic effects one could get out of a mask, changed while the player remains on the stage, to suggest a change of personality'. There are problems here which he may not altogether have solved, for it is clearly a risk to have so much depending on a visual effect which the audience in a theatre might have difficulty in following: television in some ways offers a better medium, with its capacity for focusing on significant detail. Yet it should not be too difficult for the modern theatre to find its own means—back projection of the masks, for instance—to represent the shocking personality change; first, the heroic mask—the mistress never sees anything but that—and then the monstrous, distorted mask of the Figure, so unrecognisable as Cuchulain that it calls for another name. Bricriu, the name of a Celtic god of discord, was what Yeats settled on, but in an earlier draft he used the more generalised expression, 'Evil Genius', to designate the thing out of the sea depths which takes over the person of Cuchulain.

When Eithne cannot face that hostile mask and leaves the stage, the Figure gives Emer a wounding explanation: 'I show my face and

everything he loves / Must fly away'. But who is 'he'? Is it the Cuchulain who wears the heroic mask or the Figure of Cuchulain in the
distorted mask or—for there is a third—the Ghost of Cuchulain
which crouches on the floor, unseeing and unhearing? The wife has
the painful privilege barred to the mistress of seeing all these faces of
the man she loves. The Ghost is the part of him that is farthest from
her, almost unreachable. Only by way of the Figure can she get
access to that remote self: when he touches her—with his left hand,
the unwithered one—the veil drops, she is able to perceive what we,
in our godlike position, already see, the crouching Ghost. He is, it
seems, totally cut off from her; one of the strongest visual impressions
the play makes is of his remoteness, his absolute immersion in his
dream and his perilous closeness to the sea, those terrible depths his
body was dragged from before the play began. The off-stage sea is
kept in mind continually, by the open door, the Musicians' song
comparing woman's beauty to a sea shell, and overwhelmingly by the
appearance of the Woman of the Sidhe who has swum up out of the
waves, so the distorted Figure tells us, to catch the Ghost like a fish
in her net as he sits there, head on knees, in foetal posture, as if he were
still at the bottom of the sea, or—the analogy insidiously suggests
itself—in some Maeterlinckian limbo between modes of consciousness.

And yet, though he looks so totally cut off from human intercourse,
his wife can get access to him: she has sunk some way into his depths
by facing the dark self with the withered arm, which is pressing her
to give up the hope that sustains her life, the hope that she will regain
the love of the sunlit heroic self. The distorted Figure suffers from the
thought of that hope, tries to make her see its impossibility, and in
doing so opens her eyes, reveals what is happening in the man's
inmost imagination. She sees, and we see with her, the creature that
comes through the open doors to the sea, the Country under the
Wave, as it is hauntingly called. The dancer who enters must suggest a
being of unearthly, moon-like beauty, so strange and fantastical that
the Ghost is hardly sure he knows her:

> Who is it stands before me there
> Shedding such light from limb and hair
> As when the moon, complete at last
> With every labouring crescent past,
> And lonely with extreme delight,
> Flings out upon the fifteenth night?'

She is also metallic, an artefact, as Yeats stresses in his stage direction:

> *Her mask and clothes must suggest gold or bronze or brass or silver,*
> *so that she seems more an idol than a human being. This suggestion*
> *may be repeated in her movements. Her hair, too, must keep the*
> *metallic suggestion.*

This is one of the suggestions that producers ignore at their peril: it would be fatally easy to reduce the dance to a commonplace allurement, as in those Salomé dances which Yeats despised so much. Everything must be done to keep the dancer inhuman, alien; by using electronic music for her dance, for instance (although Yeats had in mind strings and his usual flute and drum), or having a male dancer, to preserve the ambiguity and other-worldliness of the visitant. The exquisite, hard, indestructible beauty enters the scene as a kind of desperate answer to the poignant thought the Musician opened the play with:

> A woman's beauty is like a white
> Frail bird, like a white sea-bird alone. . . A strange,
> > unserviceable thing,
> A fragile, exquisite, pale shell. . .

That pathetically fragile beauty has been projected into a form that looks perfect, finished. But it is not finished: somehow the dancer needs him to complete her; 'Because I long I am not complete'. The marvellous artefact, the almost unimaginable beauty is his, then, has been evoked from some infinitely far-off place of the imagination to which he in his turn is almost irresistibly drawn.

The audience in the theatre must feel the drawing power of the dancer and the hypnotic attraction of her dance but not be totally hypnotised. For we have also to watch the man watching and, on the other side of the stage, those other watchers, the wife and the Figure with the withered arm. The complicated visual reactions that are called for by this stage configuration involve us very directly in the complex state of consciousness the play is exploring, and in the curious subliminal communication that occurs between man and wife.

For at the moment when it seems that the Ghost must follow the glittering idol out to the sea, a sense seems to strike him of the human woman so near, watching so intently. A memory breaks through of the wife as she once was; a young bride, a frail bird, a fragile sea shell which time's cruel tide has carried from him:

> O Emer, Emer, there we stand;
> Side by side and hand in hand
> Tread the threshold of the house
> As when our parents married us.

A poignant moment, joining the two who seem so separate, giving the wife something to set against the isolation she has been made so acutely aware of. It is only a moment; the inhuman voice of the Woman tauntingly reminds him of his imperfect marriage, mocked by a hundred infidelities, a thought seemingly he cannot bear. The voice tells him he should not have to bear it, should be free from those cramps of the mind:

> But what could make you fit to wive
> With flesh and blood, being born to live
> Where no one speaks of broken troth,
> For all have washed out of their eyes
> Wind-blown dirt of their memories
> To improve their sight?

He follows her, calling for her mouth, the kiss that will free him from memory, sever the painful human bond. A fine sense of chill here, for we must surely feel that the freedom she offers, this hard, clear vision unhampered by the 'dirt' of memories is a threat to his human identity. Then the other side of the stage—or mind—springs into life; the self that is the opposite of perfect, the dark self speaks and it forces the wife to accept a dark truth. Her only way of drawing the Ghost back from the 'death' he seeks in the sea is by renouncing her hope that the hero's love will some day return to her, the thought that seems to press so intolerably on Figure and Ghost, mixed up as it is with memory and remorse. When she makes the heroic act of will—'I renounce Cuchulain's love for ever'—the left-handed self has done its work; it can sink back on the bed and allow the self that had seemed dead to sit up and turn its impassive, heroic mask towards us; life is taken up at the point where it was suspended; the distorted Figure was, after all, a life force. It is an uncanny moment in the theatre, when the heroic self shows that he knows nothing of the crisis he has survived, credits his young love, not his wife with recalling him to life, has only the shadow of a memory: 'I have been in some strange place and am afraid'.

His ignorance is a 'bitter reward', in the Musicians' phrase, for the understanding wife: we must feel the bitterness, and also, as Peter Ure suggests, the heroism of Emer's renunciation. Certainly, it is a painful privilege the wife has, to know the whole man better than he knows himself. But still it is a privilege. The unique achievement of this play is to take us into the process by which people know each other in deep wordless intuitions and to register the faint, barely perceptible tremors of communication between a husband and wife; she seeing further into his nature, its divisions and contradictions; he, though seeming so remote, nevertheless responding to the movement of her feeling and being saved thereby from sinking too far into the depths where human affection has no place.

A peculiarly fine, tentative movement of mind is registered in *The Only Jealousy of Emer*. So too in *The Dreaming of the Bones*, but here the experience is intensely solitary, on every level, including the realistic, 'daylight' one, which is never lost sight of (one of the play's great charms indeed is its vivid evocation of a real mountain climb from its start at the flat-topped stone fouled by the drinking cattle, up past the thorn tree line to the Abbey ruins and the summit). The Young Man who is making his escape after the Easter Rising is terribly alone on this so-real mountain. The landscape the Musicians conjure up in their melancholy music is absolutely empty: 'Even the sunlight can be lonely here, / Even hot noon is lonely'. It is exquisitely beautiful, but hard, full of broken objects, unroofed houses, tombs and ruins everywhere. The hills themselves, as the Musicians sing, are hard and gem-like; enclosing the scene and the actors in a faintly sinister way:

> . . . and all about the hills
> Are like a circle of agate or of jade,
> Somewhere among great rocks on the scarce grass
> Birds cry, they cry their loneliness.

The image of circularity is taken up into the physical movements of the actors, the slow, ritualistic circling of the stage three times by the Young Man and the two strangers he meets at the start of his journey. In the dance convention it is a natural means of representing the climb to the summit, but in this play it is much more than that. Circularity becomes the sad symbol of the inner action, for the play ends with the Young Man unable to break out of the closed circle of his thoughts; he goes away as he came, set and solitary.

Masks have a different role again in this play, being one more means of stressing the distinctive loneliness. The Musicians, as always, have a mask-like make-up, the Stranger and the Young Girl are in heroic masks, but the Young Man is unmasked. He is the only figure in the landscape with a vulnerable human face,[2] one of the clear indications that for all its rich reference to a daylight, contemporary world, this is as much as any of the other plays a drama of the interior: he is alone with his shadows. Yeats's lighting hints reinforce this impression. The strangers come on him out of the dark; they are there fitfully, glimpsed one moment by the glow of his lantern, 'a pair of heads against the sky', then gone, then taking shape again to let us see the Young Girl, as with a sudden shocking movement, she blows out his lantern. 'I have to put myself into your hands', he says, 'Now that my candle's out.' The simple phrase has subtle reverberations: putting himself in their hands means, on the face of it, relying on them to guide him up the mountain; but from the moment when the lantern is so mischievously put out, we must suspect that the journey is to be inward, into his own dark; a drastic rerouting of his thought and feeling from the familiar and habitual view of things to a strange, new one— 'dizzy' is the word the Musicians proffer in their opening lyric:

> Have not old writers said
> That dizzy dreams can spring
> From the dry bones of the dead?

A shadowy world begins to superimpose itself on the external scene; sights and sounds take on a different colour, become muted, shadowy, like the sound of the horse which suggests to the Young Man a human rider in purposeful pursuit of him, but to the Stranger something lost and ruminative; 'An old horse gone astray. / He has been wandering on the road all night'.

'Wandering'—'night-wandering', in the Musicians' phrase—is the right word for the process we now follow; the wandering of a mind in unaccustomed freedom which it finds at once frightening and seductive. We go behind the simple words of the Young Man, his open, unmasked face, to the ghostly landscape of the interior where contradictory impulses war and can be painful and sweet at the same time. His dialogue with the Stranger and the Young Girl is a dialogue of one, so we are delicately persuaded at every turn by the light falling on the inhuman masks of the ghosts, by the dream-like effect of the

---

[2] A point that came out strongly in the television recording of my production of the play with a student company (made by the University of London Audio Visual Centre and directed for television by Martin Hayden).

ritual circlings, by the lyrics which continually remind us that this is
an interlude—daylight will return—by the repetition of motifs; the
ghosts are the loneliest of all the shadows on the mountain side. The
Stranger is well named; as the three dreamily climb and talk, to the
accompaniment of lyrics which always hint at division (the bones
dream, the cock crows), he comes to seem the materialisation of some
unacknowledged element in the Young Man's thought. We can see
how the two presences might have been pieced together from a medley
of images; the sights and sounds of the journey, especially the ruins
and the graveyard; memories of his grandmother's stories of ghosts
doing penance for their sins; and other thoughts that lie so far back he
does not know he has them till the shadows draw them out.

The Young Man's self-ignorance is obliquely communicated through
his unawareness of so much else. Everything indeed depends on his
not knowing who his guides are. The anonymity of the dance
convention is crucial here, and the heroic masks, which allow Yeats
to hint at their identity to the audience without betraying it to the
Young Man. The lovers they tell of must be nameless too, only then
can he allow himself sympathy with them—and he is sympathetic,
generously shocked by the hardness of the penance they are said to be
enduring. An important part of his nature seems to find release in the
emotional identification he is able to make with the legendary lovers
who for such an age of time have been frustrated in their longing for
consummation by 'the memory of a crime'. We see soft feelings gain
on the harsh, impersonal mood which was uppermost at the beginning
of the climb, especially when his eye lighted on objects that reminded
him of the betrayal of Ireland. Then the anonymity is shattered. With
a shock effect equal to the dowsing of the lantern, two names explode
into the calm like pistol shots: he 'remembers' the whole story:

YOUNG MAN   You speak of Diarmuid and Dervorgilla
               Who brought the Norman in?
YOUNG GIRL   Yes, yes, I spoke
               Of that most miserable, most accursed pair
               Who sold their country into slavery; and yet
               They were not wholly miserable and accursed
               If somebody of their race at last would say,
               'I have forgiven them'.
YOUNG MAN   O, never, never
               Shall Diarmuid and Dervorgilla be forgiven.

All the gentler, tolerant impulses are swept away; he pulls back his wandering thoughts, re-directs them under the influence of that one implacable memory 'of a crime', binds them with a remorseless refrain: 'O, never, never / Shall Diarmuid and Dervorgilla be forgiven'. He tells himself the Young Girl's dangerously persuasive tale was no more than a passing fantasy:

> I could not help but fall into the mood
> And for a while believe that it was true,
> Or half believe.

They have reached the summit, and now, when he looks at the land-scape, he can see nothing but its ruins, the crimes of history. But still the impulse of sympathy is alive; the dream of love will not be suppressed but breaks out more desperately and directly in the dance of the Stranger and Young Girl which silently enacts the tale they told him. It is his tale too, we may feel, for he understands it so well; though we can see it for ourselves, he still acts as our interpreter, reading the language of the dance for us with close sensibility. When the dancers cover their eyes it suggests to him that their hearts have suddenly broken, when they stretch their arms up it is 'as though to snatch the sleep / That lingers always in the abyss of the sky / Though they can never reach it'. He teaches us how to respond to the strangeness and sweetness of the dancers' movements towards and away from each other, how to see in the meeting of their eyes love's power to transcend the crimes of time:

YOUNG MAN   All the ruin,
> All, all their handiwork is blown away
> As though the mountain air had blown it away
> Because their eyes have met.

And yet he turns away, refuses forgiveness, puts it behind him as a 'temptation':

> I had almost yielded and forgiven it all—
> Terrible the temptation and the place!

We have seen so far into the wandering mind through his dialogue with the shadows out of his dark, we must surely feel that in obliterating the dancers he is killing something in himself, giving himself over to the hard, unforgiving mood which matches the stony landscape and to the sad inversion of values which makes forgiveness seem like a temptation to do wrong.

The shades vanish, the Young Man leaves the stage and the Musicians fold up the cloth as if they were folding up the night and his dream, singing of loss—the 'music of a lost kingdom'—and of the bitterness mixed with the sweetness in that 'wandering airy music':

> Dry bones that dream are bitter,
> They dream and darken our sun.

There is no feeling of judgement; these Musicians have no marked persona of their own, they seem to be singing for the Young Man, not about him, expressing in their neutral swing between opposing moods the divisions in his nature he himself is not consciously aware of. Noncommittally, they take their song from night to day, from complexity and tentativeness to single-minded confidence:

> But now the night is gone.
> I have heard from far below
> The strong March birds a-crow.
> Stretch neck and clap the wing,
> Red cocks, and crow!

We are bound to feel the exuberant lift of this, but the melancholy, airy music cannot be so easily dissipated by the robust cock-crow. The sense of loss remains; the beauty of the dance is still in our minds; the sadness of its rejection hangs about the Young Man like a misty aura, as he goes into his clear, hard, daylight world.

Yeats has brilliantly captured an almost imperceptible movement of mind in this most delicate of all the dance plays; there seems no other way we could know of that moment of doubt for it has no outcome nor is it understood by the one who experiences it. Yet it is no less real for that; indeed, Yeats is in this sense a most searching realist.

In the remaining play of this group, *Calvary,* there are none of these transitions between daylight and dream; from start to last we are in a strange place out of time; there is nothing but the dream. Whose dream, it is not so easy to say. The chief character, Christ, carries it as he carries his cross, but its form was laid down, so he says, 'When the foundations of the world were laid' by a being outside the play whom he calls God and also 'my Father'. It has become anonymous, a work of collaboration kept going, from one Good Friday to another, by the willingness of actors and audiences to enter into the re-enactment. Whether characters or audience can refuse their parts is the question Yeats probes, anticipating, in his modernist emphasis on role playing and existentialist choices, a whole world of modern drama from Pirandello to Sartre and Genet. In *Calvary* for the first time, indeed, he exploits to the full the opportunities the dance convention gives for self-conscious play with the theatrical illusion.

The audience cannot help but collaborate; this is something we are made to realise with disturbing clarity. We come to a play called *Calvary* with the plot already clear in our minds, 'real' in the way that perhaps no other plot is, complete with pictures—from Masaccio, Tintoretto, Perugino—to set the stage by. It is particularly important here that it should be quite bare in actuality, for we are continually reminded that we are engaged in constructing a world out of nothing. It is the easiest of evocations; the Musicians need do no more than drop a laconic phrase or two—'the road to Calvary', 'Good Friday's come'—for us to fill in the scene, see the sad hill, the climbing figure with the cross, surrounded by mocking or grieving faces. Then a peculiar doubleness develops; the reality we so readily attach to the event is stripped from it when the Musicians remind us that the actor who comes on, in the mask of Christ, is there to act, or 'dream' his passion through; the cross is only there because he dreams it. Yet it is so clearly there, and yes, they say, the unreal cross has the power to shorten the breath and wear away the strength of the man who carries it. And we believe it, as we believe in the invisible crowds the Musicians sketch in for us, climbing on each other's shoulders to get a better view, shouting:

> Call on your father now before your bones
> Have been picked bare by the great desert birds.

Objects and characters have acquired the terrible reality of things in a play; unchanging, fixed. Yet they are also—as the Musicians' interventions continually remind us—fluid, easily made to come and go. In our role as audience we are drawn deep into this paradox, and the other on which the dance convention rests: the play pretends to be an improvisation, yet seems to deny that improvisation is possible; the plot is fixed, variations must always lead back into the main event. The characteristic impression the dance plays make of a machine that has been wound up and cannot stop is particularly strong and painful in *Calvary*. We are made to feel the pain both of the one character, Christ, who is totally committed to his role, and of Lazarus and Judas who resent theirs and desperately try to force through their own improvisations. Yeats contrives the most delicate balance of sympathy between these responses. Christ's calm dignity, his quiet acceptance of his fearful part is impressive and poignant. Yet there is a pull towards Lazarus and Judas and their need to break free of the Calvary play into an action they can think of as their own, where there might be a free play of chance and the unexpected.

Unexpectedness was the note first struck in the Musicians' song for the unfolding of the cloth. Before they evoked the Christ scene, they sang of an alien world like the far side of the moon where a white heron stood up to his feathers in the stream, hypnotised by his own moon-lit reflection, in danger of starving to death if it were not that there *must* be change:

> But that the full is shortly gone
> And after that is crescent moon,
> It's certain that the moon-crazed heron
> Would be but fishes' diet soon.

It is an image of wild and terrifying self-sufficiency, so much we can perceive in the first moments of hearing; also that there is a curious negative connection between this scene and the one we expected to see, for three times we hear the refrain: 'God has not died for the white heron'. Music is important here. The Musicians sing of the white heron to the sound of flute, zither and drum, Yeats suggested. The instruments could be varied, but there must be a flute. The Musicians keep the image, its high plaintive sound going through the play like a Wagnerian leit-motif, reminding us always of the heron's lunar domain, as the Musicians remind us of it, immediately after they have established the Calvary scene:

> O but the mockers' cry
> Makes my heart afraid,
> As though a flute of bone
> Taken from a heron's thigh,
> A heron crazed by the moon,
> Were cleverly, softly played.

From then on, whenever flute notes are heard, the image of the moon-struck heron swims into mind. Lazarus enters to the dying strain of the flute song and the lunar landscape pushes further into the play. He is like the heron, we can tell, self-absorbed, solitary; half-crazed too, we might think, as he broods on what he lost when Christ drew

him out of the tomb; a terrible privacy in the desert, or some corner
where he could chuckle to himself 'mere ghost, a solitary thing'.
Yeats thought of Lazarus and Judas as types of intellectual despair
outside the aegis of Christ's sympathy; that comes to us very directly
in the bleak darkening of the bird landscape when Lazarus evokes it:

> Make way for Lazarus that must go search
> Among the desert places where there is nothing
> But howling wind and solitary birds.

Yet, as the Musicians hinted at the start, there is promise as well as
terror in that emptiness, where some great change is awaited. So with
Lazarus: he speaks of longing for death and wears a deathly mask, but
'death' is not extinction; he can imagine, though so bleakly, a mode of
existence outside the Christ play, and he moves, the Musicians point
out, with youthful energy. He should leave the stage as he entered it
with springy step, 'Like a young foal that sees the hunt go by / And
races in the field'.

The lonely, self-contained figure leaves and the Musicians banish
the alien landscape, returning us to Calvary and a familiar tableau.
They tell of the devoted women 'That live but in his love'; they are
clustering round, weeping, wiping Christ's feet with their hair. We
see nothing, but inevitably we collaborate, people the stage from our
own mental store with well-known figures, a Mary in a blue cloak, a
Mary with unbound hair. Then there is a peculiarly disorientating
effect; Christ expresses shock as the stage is suddenly cleared of the
characters who were never there:

> . . . why have they fled?
> Why has the street grown empty of a sudden?

This virtuoso emptying of an empty stage (curiously anticipating the
stage crowded with invisible characters in Ionesco's *The Chairs*)
creates a chilling aura of absolute loneliness for the entry of the loneliest
of all the characters—Judas. In the brief sequence of his dialogue with
Christ, Yeats takes us into an existentialist hell more profoundly
sombre than any of Sartre's. Judas's tortured efforts to claim his
traitor's act as his own—on this very day, Good Friday, when its
fearful fruit is shown—are horrifying; but still, his agony is real, as
Christ's is and through it we feel again the rising tide of alien thought
that cannot be contained in the Calvary play. In his writhing and twist-
ing to be free of Christ's calm certainties, he conveys a sense of horror

we could even share, the nightmare thought that there is no free will:

> CHRIST But my betrayal was decreed that hour
> When the foundations of the world were laid.
>
> JUDAS It was decreed that somebody betray you—
> I'd thought of that—but not that I should do it,
> I the man Judas, born on such a day,
> In such a village, such and such his parents;

Like Lazarus, he both draws and alienates sympathy by the suggestion of madness in his feverish imaginings of freedom. He improvises his part to make it his own with the sinister and absurd relish of the villain in a melodrama; nobody would have guessed how he would play it, how he would wear his old coat when he went to sell Christ, how he would chuckle to himself 'as people chuckle when alone'. There is a kind of madness too in his final exultation:

> I did it,
> I, Judas, and no other man, and now
> You cannot even save me.

Christ seems to accept this statement with his 'Begone from me'. But he has no power to send Judas out of the play; the three Roman soldiers who form the final chorus return the resentful actor to his appointed role: 'He has been chosen to hold up the cross'. An unorthodox crucifixion tableau is set up, with Judas standing behind Christ, holding the cross so that they seem both to be stretched out on it, Judas as Christ's shadow, pinned down with him in the rigid frame of Calvary that gives them both inescapable, perpetual life.

It is not on that note of fixity, however, that the play ends. Everything opens up again with the new perspective the three Roman soldiers introduce. Unconcernedly, they take over the stage, talking to Christ with a friendly indifference which is both theatrical relief— after the intensity of feeling that has gone before—and an affront:

> They say you're good and that you made the world,
> But it's no matter.

Nothing matters, they say, but chance, the luck of the game; they are going to dice for Christ's cloak, but don't care who wins:

> Whatever happens is the best, we say,
> So that it's unexpected.

They move into a dance which is one of the most arresting and complex in all the plays. The dance of the dice-throwers represents gamblers falling out, settling the quarrel by throwing dice, and then, reconciled by chance, taking hands and wheeling about the cross. The configuration of the stage forms a silent language: on one hand, the rigidity of the cross, on the other, the choral revolutions, a spectacular dancing out of the image of change and chance with which the play began. Two truths are there: Christ and Judas can never change, but there must be change; the full moon must give way to crescent, everything must become new.

There is an intricate division of sympathy at this point. Though Christ was only dreaming or acting his passion, he has raised all the feelings appropriate to the great drama: it is a deeply poignant conclusion. We have also experienced the terrible oppression that torments Lazarus and Judas. The 'comic' dance is in a way, then, a release and yet through it we go out into the cold, so to speak; out of the domain of the familiar, terrible, loved or resented story of Christ into a new, unknown cycle which promises nothing but what pleases the indifferent dice-throwers—chance and the unexpected. It is a dread moment. We must surely feel a pang on our own behalf when Christ calls out the line that has to be said:

> My Father, why hast Thou forsaken Me?

We have been detached from our familiarity with Calvary, made to see it as a mental landscape we build up for ourselves. When the Musicians step forward for the folding of the cloth and the white heron tune returns for the last time, we know its meaning now on our pulses. The lonely birds celebrated in each stanza of the closing song—sea-bird, ger-eagle, swan—are images we easily recognise of the lonely souls (they might include our own) that cannot live in the domain of the Calvary play, but must go out, like Lazarus, to build up their own world from the emptiness that Christ has not filled for them:

> God has not appeared to the birds.

It is on the myth-making processes of our own minds that the light falls in *Calvary*: we take a step into an empty space where Estragon and Vladimir are waiting, looking out for a Godot who doesn't come, and Hamm brings his prayer session to an end with—'The bastard, he doesn't exist', Clov adding, 'Not yet'.

I want now to look at three plays that were not grouped together by Yeats as the pieces in *Four Plays for Dancers* were. They have special interest because one is that rare thing in his drama, an out and out comedy, and the others are the last plays he wrote, when he was in his old age and at the height of his powers; we can feel behind them what Frank Kermode, speaking of the poems, has called 'the pressure of a passionate life which gives them special grace'. *The Cat and the Moon*, uniquely among the plays I have been discussing, is in prose, framed by lyrics sung in the usual way by three Musicians. It stands out too as the play that most clearly offers a way into a popular dance or music drama on something like the lines struck out by John Arden. It has always been one of the most popular and accessible of Yeats's plays, understandably, because it so easily and naturally combines ritualistic, magical effects with colloquial, homely talk and characterisation. Throughout there is an Irish lilt and humour which is very endearing. It is a great irony that this play should have so much weighty and erudite commentary attached to it, that Yeats indeed should have set an example to his critics in this respect, with his elaborate use of phrases like Antithetical and Primary Tincture: as so often, if we were to pore too long on the exegesis, we might conclude that the play would be unactable.

The reality is different, though what is so satisfying is just the way the charming simplicity of the play in the theatre leads easily and naturally into reflections such as Yeats recorded about it. It is obvious (when it is seen as well as when it is read) that it can be taken on many levels, but it offers itself happily in the first place as the simplest of folk tales; a Lame Beggar is riding on a Blind Beggar's back to a holy well where a Saint offers them a choice of being cured or blessed, and the outcome is happy for both; the Blind Beggar gets his sight back, the Lame Beggar chooses to stay lame and be blessed but ends up dancing, with the Saint instead of the Blind Man on his back. Such is the story, but there is also a great deal of character in the piece, rather more than in the usual folk tale. The two beggars emerge as decided personalities: despite their grotesque masks which pin them down as simply 'blind' and 'lame', each has his own distinctive tone of voice and characteristics; the Blind Beggar is practical, thrusting, masterful; the Lame Beggar fanciful, tentative and unreliable. The Blind Beggar has to depend on the lame one for facts, including his location in time and space, but he soon makes himself master of them and continually corrects the lame one's views. He finds him almost unbelievably flighty and shortsighted, as indeed he is, for he keeps protesting that the sheepskin he is wearing is white, even after the cure when the Blind Beggar is able to see for himself that it is black, which means that it has been stolen by his friend. 'Are you that flighty?', says the Blind Beggar: 'I am that flighty'.

Being flighty means telling lies that are bound to be found out, but it also means putting a higher value on something remote and visionary —having one's name in the book of the blessed—than on the material satisfaction of being able to walk. It means being able to see the Saint up in the ash-tree when the Blind Beggar, for all the freshness of his restored sight, sees nothing at all. Neither do we, the audience: we only hear the voice of the Saint putting his question, 'Will you be cured or will you be blessed?'. We can see that the First Musician is speaking for him, so it might be thought the Saint has even less reality for us. Yet of course that is not so; the absence of realism makes it easier to believe; we can take the invisible Saint on the same terms as the invisible well and ash tree, and may indeed end by seeing a face and sharing the Lame Beggar's surprise when the weight on his back turns out to be no heavier than a grasshopper's.

We are brought in fact to the point the dance plays always bring us to, where everything turns out to be shaped by the inner eye. We see more than either of the beggars, for presumably we understand the reactions both of the Blind Beggar, whose first use of sight is to administer a ritualistic beating to the friend who cheated him, and of the Lame Beggar who finds, despite the beating, despite the seeming fixity of his affliction, that he can make his leg move when the invisible Saint is on his back. It is a touching moment in the theatre when he responds to the voice from the unknown source telling him to dance and makes a rapturous discovery of the faculty of movement, from the first clumsy efforts, through a slow easing of the limbs to the throwing away of the stick and an ever more confident dancing to the clash of cymbals and perhaps the sound of an Irish jig. It would be hard not to like this play or be unaffected by its sense of the wonder in human capacities and perceptions. Unlike the other plays I have been discussing, it all seems to take place in broad daylight, appropriate to the 'ordinary' miracles it celebrates, yet its fresh, open air scene is permeated with intimations of some other, more mysterious dimension. Though so individualistic, Lame and Blind Beggar are masked; it was a thrilling moment in the Yeats Theatre Company's production in 1973 when the two ragged figures who emerged from among the audience scattered at tables in the Café theatre, turned their backs on us and suddenly whipped round to show their formidable and beautiful masks. We knew then that the play was going to take us beyond the veil into some inner region, though the daylight world rushed cheerfully back when they began chatting in their easy style, counting the paces to the well, telling droll anecdotes about the holy man of Laban and his curious friendship with the old lecher from County Mayo. For those who recognised it, realism certainly came closer with that last allusion, in which Yeats reaches right out of the folk tale to take a sly dig at two real people, George Moore and Edward Martyn. But, as always, that knowledge is an extra; we need have no idea who the originals were to receive from the story about the unlikely pair told by one of another unlikely pair a sense of seemingly infinite recession, making the pull of opposites seem the force on which everything depends. 'Maybe it is converting him he is', says the Lame Beggar, when the Blind Beggar tells how the holy man tries not to listen to the old lecher's tales. No, says the blind man, laughing; he wouldn't have him any different, 'not if he was to get all Ireland. If he was different, what would they find to talk about, will you answer me that now?'. And the Lame Beggar— 'we have great wisdom between us, that's certain'.

This is surely what we are feeling ourselves: together Lame and Blind Beggars, like the holy man and the lecher, make up a whole life; indeed, from the first moment of their entry, one riding on the other's back, the idea of what Beckett calls a pseudo couple is with us. They are so totally dependent on each other, such perfect opposites, so neatly complementing each other in their assets and afflictions. Despite their individualism it seems at times as if they must be thought of as elements in one psyche: it is hard to imagine how they could survive separation. And yet they do: the Saint's entry into the scene effects the change and it is this that gives the play its specially exhilarating quality. What seemed fixed turns out not to be so: the Blind Beggar goes his way and the Lame Beggar, abandoned and still lame, finds an extraordinary new strength in the conviction that he is blessed:

LAME BEGGAR	But how can I dance? Ain't I a lame man?
FIRST MUSICIAN	Aren't you blessed?
LAME BEGGAR	Maybe so.
FIRST MUSICIAN	Aren't you a miracle?
LAME BEGGAR	I am, Holy Man.
FIRST MUSICIAN	Then dance, and that'll be a miracle.

The play can almost be thought of as a comic version of *Calvary*, with this time a creative tension between the two opposites who are locked together by their needs. It also begins and ends with a lyric celebrating the inevitability of change in imagery of the moon and the creatures under its influence—not a bird here, but a charming cat:

> Minnaloushe creeps through the grass
> Alone, important and wise,
> And lifts to the changing moon
> His changing eyes.

The Cat and the Moon was designed as a 'kiogen', a slight piece coming as a relaxation of tension between two more demanding ones. It has that special value among the dance plays and a popular quality which, as I have been suggesting, connects Yeats with writers like Sean O'Casey and John Arden. I want now to turn to a very different kind of play, in dark and tragic mood. *Purgatory* has been one of the most influential of Yeats's plays, as we need look no further than Beckett's *Play* to realise. It is not in the dance convention, though its naturalism is only on the surface and gives way, so to speak, under the relentless pressure of a mind absorbed in its dream. It could not be a dance play; no musicians can enter here; no music,[3] no relief from the obsessive sights and sounds which express the Old Man's purgatory. There are two solid objects, the bare tree and the ruined house. Everything else must seem spectral, though sadly it is not always so in production; some too too solid ghosts have been seen (especially, perhaps, on the Abbey stage)[4] and at the other extreme, no ghosts at all, hence no ambiguity. When the balance is right we should receive an oppressive sense of the outer world being invaded and distorted by an inner drama, which means, of course, that the external reality must be well established to start with. The character of the Boy is important here: in his ignorance and sturdy, coarse common sense, he seems at first totally immune from his father's maniacal fantasies.

We too start in the Boy's position, outside the dream, watching from a safe distance a strange, wild old man pouring out to his son the lurid tale of the degradation that came on the Old Man's mother, her house, and above all on himself, when she married the drunken groom,

---

[3] Transference to a totally musical form has, however, been attempted in Gordon Crosse's operatic *Purgatory*, New Opera Company, 1966.

[4] Austin Clarke (*The Celtic Twilight*, p. 98) mentions one 'very substantial ghost' which drank from 'a real bottle of Power's or Jameson's'.

his hated father. Then Yeats draws us deeper into the poisoned dream, establishing a hypnotic focus on the two objects that stand out with ominous clarity on the otherwise empty stage; the ruined house where 'somebody' is waiting and the bare tree that so oddly brings out the old man's life-loathing. When he looks at it, he sees the tree of fifty years before, covered with leaves; 'Fat, greasy life' is his alarming phrase. Nothing else can get into the scene except those skeleton objects and one terrible sound; the hoof beats, getting realistically louder as if on a gravelled avenue, though, as the Old Man dreamily reminds his son, the place where they are standing is all overgrown with soft grass. Then suddenly everything snaps into life; as if a light had been switched on in the mind, the light goes up on a window in the ruin to show a young girl standing, waiting—so the Old Man says —for the man riding to her on that relentless horse. 'Beat! Beat!' It is the very sound of a pulse in the brain, part memory—when the hoof beats begin he is telling the story of how he killed his father and left him in the burning house—but part anticipation too, a thought that can't be quietened, a thought of 'what I did or may do'. Madness perhaps, and yet the scene is so vividly there, for us as for the Old Man, that we can no longer identify with the boy who sees nothing 'but an empty gap in the wall'.

The light fades, goes up again—vividly suggesting a mind's flickering impulses—and now the Boy's mind too is invaded; the murderous hate that possesses the Old Man comes up tentatively in him as a question: 'What if I killed you? You killed my grand-dad, / because you were young and he was old. / Now I am young and you are old'. They are struggling over the money-bag, the Boy's chance of freedom from the tyrannical father, and that is the moment when the window lights up again to show a second ghostly figure, a man standing at the window pouring whiskey into a glass. The Old Man can do nothing but look, totally hypnotised: the narrative must unroll, although he had tried so grotesquely to stop it, calling out to his mother not to conceive—a fantastic attempt to cancel out the past and his own life. The self-loathing, the fearful resentment of the father and grief for the mother make a mood so intense and uncontrollable that it draws the Boy in. For the first time he sees: 'A body that was a bundle of old bones / Before I was born. Horrible! Horrible!' The scene has become as real as that, and yet it is totally unreal, and the Old Man knows it, knows that the ghostly figures must remain oblivious, whatever he says or does: 'That beast there would know nothing, being nothing, / If I should kill a man under the window / He would not even turn his head'.

He does kill a man under the window, his own son, using the same knife he killed his father with, the knife he cuts his dinner with; a third object is added to the nightmare furniture of the stage; we might imagine the light focusing on that thing so perverted from its proper domestic use. Sounds too convey the sense of perversion. The Old Man unnervingly breaks into a lullaby after he has stabbed his son and ended, as he thinks, the torment he imagines his mother enduring:

> Hush-a-bye baby, thy father's a knight,
> Thy mother a lady, lovely and bright.

The familiar lines drop into the desolate silence with a truly ghostly effect, as if he had managed to give the dumb phantom a voice as well as a dim shape. With the lullaby, the evocation is complete; such is the Old Man's power as a medium we may even have been persuaded to suspend our disbelief in the possibility of there being a presence there, a spirit suffering in a purgatory of its own making. Perhaps we need to do this, to have sympathy with the Old Man, for it is only in his care and grief for his mother that he shows any human kindness. The concern is wild, excessive, Oedipal; we must feel too, that he is projecting on to her his sense of his own degradation, his own purgatory. Yet it is touching as well as monstrous when he calls out to her that he has released her soul from its misery by stamping out the line of generation:

> Dear mother, the window is dark again,
> But you are in the light because
> I finished all that consequence.

The balance of feeling is tremulous indeed at this point. We cannot after all forget the poor Boy who said no more than the truth when he attributed his own ignorance and uncouthness to his father's treatment of him—'What education have you given me?' It cannot have seemed so perverse to us as to the Old Man when he tried to free himself from this terrible father by taking some of his money. It is the Old Man who is outrageous, monstrous. Maybe we can only find sympathy for him by thinking of him as mad, the victim of his own crooked brain, with its inhuman logic—he never seems madder than when he is at his most scholastic, trying to work out, with the aid of Tertullian, the proportion of pain to pleasure in the purgatorial renewal of the sexual act to which he has condemned his mother because he hates his life so much. His ruined cleverness has some pathos, but is alienating: he seems so far from human reach when he tries to exorcise the curse in the blood by murdering his son, not seeing the irony so obvious to us, that he is only demonstrating its grip on him.

Yet despite all this, we cannot escape any more than he can, the pressure of the vision, the evidence forced on our senses by the stage scene: in some way we cannot account for, the dead do still live, so why not, then, in purgatory?

> Re-live
> Their transgressions, and that not once
> But many times; they know at last
> The consequence of those transgressions
> Whether upon others or upon themselves;

To entertain that fearful thought is to come dangerously close to the madness which exploded in those meaningless murders: in that way it is a relief for us too when the window goes dark and the violence subsides and the bare tree, picked out in the light, stands there, as he says, 'like a purified soul, / All cold, sweet, glistening light'. And a terror for us too when the sound returns, the thud of the hoof beats; now more than ever like a pulse hammering in an obsessed mind, a mind that sees the irony at last, sees it may never be able to break out of its closed circle, though still it cannot admit the purgatory as its own, must project everything on to the loved and hated cause of its suffering:

> Twice a murderer and all for nothing,
> And she must animate that dead night
> Not once but many times!

There is a terrible threat of hopelessness in this ending: the interior drama has engulfed everything; no light of day, it seems, can reach this 'deep of the mind'. And yet, as always in Yeats's drama, something stirs, even in the most deadly impasse. There is an effort to struggle out of the pit, for a new element comes in with the invocation that closes the play:

> O God,
> Release my mother's soul from its dream!
> Mankind can do no more. Appease
> The misery of the living and the remorse of the dead.

In the nightmare context, that anguished prayer represents an effort of will so immense that it does, I believe, lift us from the morass where we are in danger of drowning with him. The circle is not totally filled: the mightier spirit invoked might find its way in through the chink the Old Man manages to prise open at the end.

Still, the overwhelming impression left by *Purgatory* is of a fearfully claustrophobic inner world. It is easy to see how the play has served as model for those playwrights from Eliot to Pinter who have wanted to explore dark involutions of mind; obsessive anxieties, disabling guilt, murderous drives turned inward. *The Death of Cuchulain* is a model at the opposite pole; a private dream here becomes a public one; it reflects a personal life but in a form so strange it seems hardly to belong to the dreamer. Yeats gets brilliant distancing effects in this play by now withholding, now exposing the performing elements, beginning with a flamboyantly anti-illusionist device, a prologue spoken by a comically irascible Old Man, a caricature of playwright Yeats, as Yeats indicates by grotesque exaggeration of some of his own familiar attitudes:

> I wanted an audience of fifty or a hundred, and if there are more, I beg them not to shuffle their feet or talk when the actors are speaking. . . On the present occasion they must know the old epics and Mr Yeats' plays about them. . .

It is certainly an odd irony that critics have sometimes missed the humour of this and given Yeats no credit for the sardonic self-criticism. No doubt it would be harder to miss it in the theatre. In Reg Skene's production, for instance, when the Old Man was made up to resemble Yeats, the effect must have been, as he says, to sharpen the irony in a startling way.[5] An interesting paradox develops. The Old Man is brutally interrupted just as he is getting a bit beyond himself by an outbreak of off-stage drum and pipe music. He seems a victim of some intervening power, but no; disconcertingly he tells us he arranged in advance to be checked: 'That's from the musicians; I asked them to do that if I was getting excited. If you were as old you would find it easy to get excited'. So the Old Man is distraught and slightly absurd in his arrogance and lack of control. But he is also providential, subtle, knowing his own weaknesses and capable of working out ways to check them.

[5] *The Cuchulain Plays of W. B. Yeats*, p. 123.

Then we go into the inner play and at once it is recognisable as the epic story he promised, which is also the summing up of many of Mr Yeats's plays. The material of a tumultuous life is crystallised in a dream précis where time is foreshortened and events move with a laconic, magical swiftness which keeps us wondering all the time how much of what we see is taking place in bodily reality, how much in the deep of a mind. Whose mind is the question? Cuchulain's no doubt, but that we know reflects the Old Man's and that in its turn sardonically reflects the mind of Mr Yeats—and behind him, what? The invisible hypnotist, perhaps, who hovers in the action of the inner play, drawing the characters somnambulistically after. Cuchulain is called on to the stage by his mistress, Eithne; but who speaks through her when she delivers the militant message: 'The scene is set and you must out and fight'? Emer, his wife, she says, and yet she is holding a letter from Emer which says exactly the opposite: Cuchulain is not to fight, the odds are too heavy against him. Like a sleepwalker, Eithne can only say that the message came to her in 'some place' where she thought she was with Emer. She is moved by a force she can only dimly sense, until suddenly it materialises for her and she sees a superhuman being standing between them, a woman with the head of a crow; Cuchulain cannot see it but he knows it—the spirit of war, the goddess, Morrigu. The creature touches Eithne with its black wing and the intuition deepens: she was put into a trance, given the false message that is really the true one by another of Cuchulain's women, his boyhood mistress, Maeve, who is now coming with an army to kill him; that old rival appeared in monstrous form as a woman with an eye in the middle of her forehead; a fantastic projection of her hidden thoughts, as Cuchulain derisively suggests. He is wrong in his guess at her motive—she is sending him into battle to die, he says, because she is ready for a younger lover—but the monstrous visions do seem to represent something in her mind, a flash of uncanny self-knowledge. The unwilled, undesired league with Maeve and the war goddess reveals the nature of her passion for Cuchulain: it is for the violent man, and he must not change but must die as he has lived, violently.

Cuchulain too, though he is not good at reading others or at looking into himself, is touched for a moment by self-knowledge: he broods on the idea of change:

> You thought that if you changed I'd kill you for it,
> When everything sublunary must change,

> And if I have not changed that goes to prove
> That I am monstrous.

He *is* changing, however, shaping the events of his story as he will have them, becoming his own producer. 'I make the truth!' he says, when a servant raises a question about Eithne's treachery. He is beginning to stand at a distance from his life, view it more clearly, respond on a deeper level. And Emer knows why: 'It is because you are about to die'. He knows it too, though he still tries to turn away from the knowledge:

> Spoken too loudly and too near the door;
> Speak low if you would speak about my death,
> Or not in that strange voice exulting in it.
> Who knows what ears listen behind the door?

Death has come very close, a Maeterlinckian presence, in the imagery of the door and the unwilled messages from the source that cannot be identified. With each sequence that follows, punctuated by pipe and drum music, the ghostliness increases; we move further away from external reality, further into the interior. First there is a bitterly poignant encounter between the mortally wounded Cuchulain and Aoife, the woman who gave him his greatest fulfilment and greatest tragedy—the son he killed in ignorance. There is still a line out here to the daylight world of the epic story, but the solid reality of Cuchulain's world—which was established with astonishing speed—is being faded out with the same speed; it has become no more than a façade through which we receive glimpses of another world, strangely more real, where the scene is set, the essential messages made up. There is an overpowering impression of being in some void out of time when Aoife calls to the dying man, 'Am I recognised, Cuchulain?', and instantly he is back in their youth, seeing her as she was; she has to recall him, remind him that her hair is white. For an instant—one of the most humanly moving in Yeats's drama—they share the tragedy of their lost son; are parents together mourning a boy of promise. And yet, though so human, the encounter is also insubstantial, like something which ought to have been, rather than what is. It is a happening at the threshold where the human is about to dissolve; the ghosts are gathering strength: Aoife has come to kill not to love: she winds him in her veil, fastens him to the stone where he has propped himself—a great visual moment this, when the emblem of beauty and desire is chillingly turned to soft fetters, a winding sheet. Her part is done then. Yeats supplies her with a not very convincing motive for leaving the stage—invention seems to falter here—but we must feel it is right that she should go; it is not for her to strike the death blow. Though so attenuated, she still has too much of the human about her and we are going behind the door now into the unimaginable region Yeats is going to imagine for us.

The figure who replaces her is well able to take us a step further away from the human—a Blind Man, impersonal, anonymous who makes ready to kill Cuchulain with no feeling either for or against him, simply to earn the reward of the twelve pennies offered for the hero's head. As he horribly feels his way up the dying man's body, seeking the place to let out his life, his casual indifference to high names and deeds brings into the play the authentic chill of death, with its levelling disregard for human complexity. When he cuts the last thread attaching Cuchulain to the life of human feeling, it seems like total annihilation; as soon as that unerring, trivial kitchen knife hits its mark, everything must go, even the memory of the veil which the Blind Man thrusts aside indifferently as 'womanish stuff'. But it is not to be pushed aside so easily: it is taken up into Cuchulain's thought where it merges with other images of feathery softness—women like birds, birds like women—materialising to his sight, though not to ours, as the shape of the soul that must be projected out of his life:

> There floats out there
> The shape that I shall take when I am dead,
> My soul's first shape, a soft feathery shape,
> And is not that a strange shape for the soul
> Of a great fighting-man?

He seems to be looking into the mirror of his life—which the play has been—and seeing there an image of his essential self, for whom women have been a source of supernatural delight and freedom. The moment of death is a moment of utmost creativity; he can almost hear now, as well as see, the shape he has conjured for himself:

> I say it is about to sing.

And then, it seems, he is blotted out: the Blind Man is heard calling out, the stage darkens, there is a momentary illusion of finality; Cuchulain has died, his drama has ended. But it all begins again. When the lights go up, we have moved into a new phase where it is hard to recognise the human components; the bare stage is possessed by the crow-headed goddess and the seven deadly, abstract objects she presides over; seven black parallelograms, one in her hand, six ranged behind her. She explains their meaning—they are the severed heads of Cuchulain and his killers—with a still, remote gravity that makes her seem to be indeed, as she says she is, speaking to the dead; we have gone beyond the door. Yet what she is telling us will happen has a strangely familiar air: it is surely with a shock of recognition that we hear her calm closing line, 'I arranged the dance', and see Emer appear to perform her dance of rage against the six and of 'adoration or triumph' for the abstract shape that now represents Cuchulain. For this is what we were promised at the beginning by that Old Man whom we have probably forgotten if the illusion has done its work. He must return to mind now, and that frenetic prologue of his: 'Before the night ends you will meet the music. There is a singer, a piper, and a drummer . . . I promise a dance . . . Emer must dance, there must be severed heads. . .' Everything was there, already then, in his head, all the elements, yet from them came something we could never have expected from the distraught prelude, a dramatic illusion so coherent, controlled and powerful that we have ceased to think of it as illusion; it has become much more real than the Old Man, though it has moved so much further from the light of common day. A goddess has taken over his role, is saying his lines: 'I arranged the dance'. Perhaps from the first feathery touch on Emer's shoulder, the action was under her wing. It is certainly with a sound from her world that the dance of human mourning ends and another kind of life seems to be asserting itself. We hear at last the music Cuchulain said we would hear, listen with Emer in the intense silence that grips the stage to faint, far-off bird noises, recall, surely, his prophecy, 'I say it is about to sing', with its implications of a mysteriously continuing existence.

Again the stage darkens—the hypnotic alternations of light and dark are a powerful means of evoking the 'chimeras that haunt the edge of trance' (*Essays and Introductions*, p. 243)—and then with a violent physical shock we are jerked from the ethereal quiet to a noisy, brilliantly lit scene and another kind of music, like nothing else in the play, the rollicking music of an Irish fair.[6] We are in modern times; the illusion has been abruptly broken, the theatrical elements exposed once more. The Old Man does not reappear, but we see at last the

[6] Austin Clarke used the band of the Transport Workers' Union to play a rollicking jig.

three Musicians who have been kept out of sight throughout; a significant variation on the visual pattern of the dance plays, which allows the inner play an appearance of greater autonomy—until it is suddenly broken down and we are launched into a dizzying series of adjustments to our sense of reality. The Musicians offer a glimpse into the machinery but they are also at work building up a new illusion; in their ragged clothes they are acting street singers who are acting a harlot singing to a beggar man about Cuchulain. He is as real to them as Easter 1916 and Pearse and Connolly, the flesh and blood men who shared in that event. There is a statue to prove it by Oliver Sheppard; a sardonic, Brechtian footnote, this, which in seeming to stab at the illusion in fact gives it an extraordinary extension of life. The figure of Cuchulain is taking over the stage, but where did it come from, have we not seen it put together out of bits and pieces, music, dance, abstract shapes? Yes, the Singer reminds us; Cuchulain was 'thought' by an Old Man:

> No body like his body
> Has modern woman borne,
> But an old man looking back on life
> Imagines it in scorn.

Then suddenly the harlot too, with her song of Easter 1916, recedes into the past, along with Cuchulain and Pearse and Connolly. We are returned to our present, the room with actors, and reminded—with a chill gravity that is like nothing so much as the dismissal of the warm lovers to their far-off legend at the close of *The Eve of St Agnes*—that it was no more than a fable.

So we are back where we started, with the Old Man; but the circle is not a closed one. Just the reverse; the mood is expansive, exhilarating; out of the shifting realities of the theatrical process something has come alive that goes on attracting more life; the illusion is loose in the world, for good or ill. The Old Man has called up creatures from nowhere he can explain and they have gone far beyond him; whether he invented them or they used him we cannot tell; the relationship between him and the goddess, the unknowable being who takes over his lines, remains a mystery.

Yeats turns the light on the interior of his own mind in *The Death of Cuchulain*, bringing his dramatic opus to a close with the same uncanny appropriateness that distinguishes the ordering of his final poems. He never knew the dream so deep, he said, and we can surely agree with him, for it is that insoluble mystery, the creative process itself, that is the subject of this last play. It seems an appropriate stopping place for a discussion which has been seeking to show the potentialities and flexibility of the dramatic form he evolved and its suggestiveness for the modern theatre. In getting so much of himself into this subtly autobiographical play—absurdly irascible Old Man as well as amorous Cuchulain—and confronting the audience so directly with the back-stage of the drama those two make between them with the aid of the goddess, he had created a new kind of dramatic mirror, as complex as any the novel or poetry could offer, to reflect complex modern states of self-consciousness. After *Purgatory* and *The Death of Cuchulain* everything became possible; *Play* could follow, and *The Homecoming*, *The Family Reunion* and *Footfalls*; the theatre was able at last to catch up with the modern movement in the arts.

8 ~ The Vitality of the Yeatsian Theatre

The theatre we have today is much nearer the theatre Yeats aimed to bring into being, where all the arts were one Art. It is characteristic that in the seventies the English Music Theatre should have emerged as an off-shoot from the English Opera Group founded by Benjamin Britten and Peter Pears; that Robert Cohan has successfully established his Contemporary Dance Theatre in London; that Lindsay Kemp should draw on material from Genet and make a dance version of Wilde's *Salomé*, that this extraordinary mime should be inspired by Baudelaire. Ritual is no longer alien to the modern theatre; Peter Brook and others have restored it to its central role, and there have been interesting experiments along Yeats's line such as Barrie Edwards's *Ritual Theatre* (I.C.A. 11 September 1973) which aimed at subliminal communication through ritualistic movement and music played by three musicians (on instruments that included a tin flute).

As far back as 1970 the ballet critic, Oleg Kerensky, felt that the border lines between ballet and its sister arts were becoming indistinct: a revolution was occurring in which the pure dance elements were being weakened and a new synthesis being sought: 'part dance, part mime, part circus, part art display, part happening'.[1] Dance is being taken nearer all the time to drama in pieces such as the Contemporary Dance Theatre's closely plotted *Hunter of Angels* (1967) and Lindsay Kemp's *Flowers* (1970) (which takes up Genet's suggestion that his 'divine saga' should be 'danced, and mimed with subtle directions'). Both these dance dramas use physical movements interestingly to suggest psychic movement; much balancing on different levels creates an extraordinary sense of an action reverberating in several dimensions. In the 1974 production of *Flowers* the acrobatic effects—strange masked dancers sweeping down from ladders—against all the odds brought into the gross, homosexual prison world the suggestion of mysterious angelic intervention, a strangely Yeatsian effect. Methods of total theatre, violent strobe lighting and electronic sound, were exploited to convey an essentially inward experience, the sexual fantasies of imprisonment. When Kemp at the end tore the masks off

[1] O. Kerensky, *Ballet Scene* (1970), p. 79.

the faces of his fellow actors, the sensational, noisy, scenes we had been witnessing seemed to be dissolved and revealed as the projection of one man's inner landscape. In the Contemporary Dance Theatre's complex *Hunter of Angels* a ladder again figured as an important visual symbol; placed flat on the ground at the start, it suggested an imprisoning structure Jacob and his angel twin inhabited, a womb they had to fight their way out of, competing to be the elder; later the cryptic rivalry was danced out in imagery of wrestling and in a thrilling ascent and descent of the ladder which was now propped upright, the dancers alternately reaching the lofty dominating position. To follow the whole of the elaborate drama, audiences would no doubt require the aid of a programme note, but this grappling on the ground and in the air vividly evoked without words the sense of psychic interplay and a striving towards a higher form of being.

Perhaps these dance dramas are able to achieve such complex effects because a tradition has been building up over the years, with strong encouragement from the playwrights, Yeats himself, Cocteau and Eliot chief among them. Cocteau's *Parade* (Théâtre du Chatelet, Paris, 18 May 1917) has been an influential model. It was the supreme collaboration of the arts, with music by Satie, designs by Picasso, choreography by Massine: so completely indeed did the collaborators take over Cocteau's original idea that his name actually disappeared from the credits in Apollinaire's programme note. A very uncomfortable realisation of Symons's idea that in the total theatre of the future the playwright might have no more role than that of prompter! The structure of *Parade* anticipated the self-conscious theatricalism of the modern movement: it was presented as a sideshow performed for a stage audience who insisted on watching it rather than accept that the 'real' performance was 'on the inside'. Satie's score was circular, ending where it began, and there was a strong marionette element; the performers were under the direction of other performers known as 'managers' who were encased in eleven foot high cubist constructions. As a critic of Cocteau points out,[2] contemporary reviewers found it appropriate to apply to Cocteau's lively guignols that term so charged with meaning by Gordon Craig, 'super-marionettes'. The parodying or blurring of sexual distinctions for surrealist effect was also a feature of Cocteau's art, and in this indeed he often seems to provide a model for Lindsay Kemp: in *Le Boeuf sur le Toit* (1920), for instance, a Salomé-like figure appears dancing around a decapitated policeman;

[2] F. Brown, *An Impersonation of Angels* (1969).

the part was played by one of the Fratellini clowns. It was of course natural for Cocteau to take over a character from Wilde; in his frivolous way he is continually flirting with his ideas, as with those of Craig, Yeats and Maeterlinck.

A work like *Parade* was a sport in its time, playing to the élite only, as Apollinaire observed. He thought it, however, so successful and fascinating that it must be the advent of a new and more complete stage art which would eventually attract popular audiences. He was right: dance dramas in the tradition of *Parade* no longer play to minority audiences, to judge from the successful record of companies like the New York City Ballet: and actors increasingly show interest in balletic techniques and in the specialised training in mime and movement offered by centres such as James Roose Evans's Stage Two. A peculiarly modern theatrical form seems to have arisen, the dance drama which explores through physical movements the deep movements of the psyche. Its choreographers draw on myth, fables, biblical stories (as in Geoffrey Cauley's *In the Beginning* (1960) where the tale of Adam and Eve is danced to clarinet and oboe music of Poulenc), or literature (*Miss Julie* (1950), *Flowers*), or invent new mythic structures, as Martha Graham does in *Deaths and Entrances* (1943) or *Acrobats of God* (1960). Dance drama has taken up themes that preoccupied the early symbolist poets and painters; self-consciousness, self-absorption, divided and alienated states of being. Images and motifs which fascinated the *fin de siècle* artists reappear; Undine takes the stage as a dancer in Ashton's *Ondine* (1958); into the space left by Sarah Bernhardt and Mrs Patrick Campbell step Fonteyn and Nureyev as the new Pelléas and Mélisande. Maeterlinck seems indeed to be attracting the choreographers as once the composers; Gray Veredon's balletic version of *Pelléas and Mélisande* (1976) to Schoenberg's music made one reviewer reflect how appropriate the ballet form was to the 'symbolism and dream-like fantasy' of the play. And in his re-creation of *Afternoon of a Faun* (1953) to the original music of Debussy, Jerome Robbins has given brilliant definition to that half-formed image that so haunted Arthur Symons of the performer gazing at herself in the glass, ingeniously using the conventions of the medium to project an image of self-reflection; two dancers, man and girl, practising before an imagined mirror, and despite their growing awareness of each other, never able to break away from the solitary communion with the mirrored self.

If dance is moving closer to Wilde's 'meeting place of all the arts', so in its own way is opera. 'Music drama' is the term that increasingly comes to seem the right one, or 'Actions with Music', the description Bond and Henze apply to their work of collaboration, *We Come to the River* (Covent Garden, 12 July 1976). Some oblique dramatic effects well in key with symbolist doctrines are achieved in this piece. In the virtuoso percussion scenes, for instance, when the drummer held the stage alone, rushing in seemingly wild improvisation from one instrument to another, striking out melody as he ran from the gleaming, metallic backcloth, the panic of war was suggested, but also a remarkable artistic control which somehow was able to draw from the horror the stunningly unexpected music and visual beauty. *We Come to the River* made a drastic break with operatic convention by allowing movement out of the proscenium frame; the Covent Garden orchestra pit was boarded over, much reducing the separation customary between orchestra, singers and audience and at intervals great processions were made through the auditorium—a brass band, ladies of the chorus singing—an effect still new in the world of opera, if no longer in the 'legitimate' drama.

Many composers have explored the frontier territory between opera and drama since Schoenberg in the unfinished *Moses and Aaron* (composed 1931–2) represented Moses' inability to convey directly the full force of his vision by having him speak with orchestral accompaniment rather than sing like his brother. The balance between the speaking and the singing voice which Yeats tried for all his life has been attempted from the composer's end of the spectrum in works like Edward Harper's *Fanny Robin* (1976), a half-hour piece which distils the tragedy of Hardy's gentle heroine in a musical drama where speaking and singing voices have equal roles.

In other ways too the theatrical climate seems right now for Yeats. There is an emphasis very much like his on improvisation and performance in the round 'under the same light', the 'much prized one-room effect', as Irving Wardle calls it,[3] with all the works exposed, the performers' skills consciously presented. Since Artaud applied his shock to the French theatre of the thirties, the techniques he enunciated in *The Theatre and its Double* (1938) have passed into common practice. Grotowski and Peter Brook have companies devoted to what Brook calls 'holy theatre': ritual for them is not an esoteric but an essential experience for any audience. The modern taste for simplicity

[3] In a review describing the modification of the stage structure at Stratford-on-Avon 'to obliterate all lingering traces of the proscenium'. *The Times*, 2 April 1976.

and seeming spontaneity, especially in folk art, is also favourable to Yeats's drama. He was ahead of his own time in his fascination with the art of folk singing as he found it among the Irish country people and with such folk dancing as he encountered. 'We should take up all those old things and make them subtle and modern', he wrote to Florence Farr in 1908 (*Letters*, p. 508). The prescription has been whole-heartedly endorsed by the modern theatre.

I have dwelt so far on the upsurge of support for a Yeatsian style of drama in the theatre itself, among performers and directors, where naturally enough there has always been the strongest impetus towards a concrete theatre 'of all the arts' which might also be a theatre of revelation. Inspired practitioners—Gordon Craig, Copeau, Artaud—have steadily moved the theatre in the direction of more musical, rhythmic and intuitive forms, and there has been continuity in the movement. Oriental influences continued to flow through Artaud, as once through Yeats, though the source was no longer Japan but Bali. An especially powerful charge of energy came from Artaud for whom a non-verbal theatre was a desperate necessity. He suffered from a kind of allergy to words which made art forms like the Balinese dance drama, with its harmonious, musical communication of mystical truths, a release comparable to the restoration of speech to a dumb man. He was an admirer of Maeterlinck who took Maeterlinck's attack on words to a wild extreme. In the English theatre Peter Brook has taken up Artaud's ideas with a similar kind of hunger. He has been the most influential force in the creation of a theatrical context favourable to Yeats ever since in 1964 he launched the Theatre of Cruelty in London, splashing on his programme flamboyant lists of opposites; what he called the 'dead forms'—Plot, Construction, Elocution, Method, and so on—and the new, live ones—Collage, Revelation, Mobile, Gesture. . .

Pretty well all the influences I have been mentioning come together in Lindsay Kemp's *Salomé* (Roundhouse, 21 February 1977) a piece dedicated to Wilde which might well be taken as the symbolic realisation of his dream of a theatre of all the arts. It is a spectacular re-creation of the play in mime, dance and dialogue (a free mix of French and English), full of brilliant inventions—the severed head is suggested by the subtle deploying of a cloak—and totally removed from the commonplace by the audacity of Kemp's Salomé. A man no longer young, dancing Salomé as himself in the final sequence, denuded of all exotic aids, somehow, against all the odds in the world, conveyed the poignant frustration of the young virgin, Wilde's 'tragic daughter of passion'. Here indeed was a demonstration that *Salomé* is a 'soul' drama.

A striking illustration, too, of the continuity of the Irish/European tradition, for Kemp, though from so different a background, expresses in his *Salomé* the same aesthetic passion as Wilde and Yeats for French literature and art (Moreau is a favourite artist, as his stage scene shows) and for Japanese design.

Among the playwrights of the period there has been nothing to equal this steady build-up of pressure for a new kind of theatre. Yet although more slowly and erratically, writers have been moving in a similar direction. And Yeats has been a crucial influence. The two playwrights who most completely assimilated his inspiration and extended his form of drama were O'Casey and Beckett, as I will be attempting to show in the following chapters. The history of Yeats's influence on English playwrights generally would need a volume to itself, but I want to indicate briefly the kind of impact he had and the line of continuity there is from his drama through Eliot to present-day playwrights, Pinter in particular. For in this way too, a theatrical climate has been formed which should make it easier for modern audiences to appreciate Yeats's own drama.

From the start of his dramatic career Yeats fascinated the English poets who had theatrical ambitions. The attempt of the Georgian poets to create a drama in the Irish mode is an interesting story deserving fuller treatment than it has yet received. Masefield dedicated plays to Yeats and tried to move in his direction, using ritual and the rhythms of folk speech in plays like *The Tragedy of Nan* (first produced in 1908), which enjoyed a minor vogue in its day. Gordon Bottomley also experimented interestingly with myth and ritual and what he called 'lyric' and 'choric' plays, expounding his doctrine of alternative theatre in a manifesto with many Yeatsian echoes, *A Stage for Poetry: My Purposes with my Plays* (1948). Arthur Symons's dramatic experiments I have already mentioned, and another intimate of Yeats's circle, Sturge Moore, was also trying to change the climate of the English theatre. He was a leading figure in *The Masquers,* a company devoted to the idea of a 'Theatre of Beauty': in 1902 he was calling for the creation of a National Theatre to stage 'the simplest and most aesthetic plays . . . [to] the most cultivated audience that can be obtained'. His own play, *Niobe* (1920), is a radio play before its time: he tried to make silence a dynamic element by putting his players behind screens and focusing attention on the unseen, unheard Artemis.

A bare, open stage, free of the proscenium arch, a ritualistic style of acting, with music and silences playing a vital role, these requirements continually recur in the thinking and experimenting of the writers who followed Yeats. Their plays were often performed in rooms or small theatres in private houses: apart from Masefield, they did not often break through into the professional theatre. The nearest professional approach to the stage they were all seeking came about in the twenties when the Festival Theatre was started in Cambridge by an ardent Yeatsian, Terence Gray, cousin of Ninette de Valois who acted as his choreographer for dramas that ranged from Greek tragedies to *On Baile's Strand*. Gray took Yeatsian subjects like the stories of Deirdre and Cuchulain and tried to build round them a drama in Yeatsian mode where at moments of extreme emotion what he called the 'tyranny of the spoken word' would be replaced by 'movement, by the expressive power of light and mass and design and colour and human mime'. He was a follower of Maeterlinck and Craig, who aimed to capture what he called the 'utter yet charged silence' of the former and carry through the staging ideas of the latter. He was indeed the first director in control of a permanent English theatre and professional company to practise consistently an 'art of the stage' derived from Craig, using an open stage and creating his scene by the play of light on stylised arrangements of cubes, cylinders and so forth. From the theatre records and pictures that survive,[4] it seems that these stage effects—silhouettes against a background of empty sky, a semicircle of polished poles to suggest houses—were of a kind to have pleased his masters, though when he turned from composing stage pictures to dialogue the case was rather different: his scenarios are a medley of ersatz Synge, flapper's slang ('Oh, shut up', says his fifteen-year-old Deirdre) and Ibsenite aphorisms about the love life in the soul. Gray evidently knew this himself, for he said the words did not matter, anyone was welcome to change them.

The kind of imagination that can find the right words and also envisage the power of purely theatrical effects like dance or music is after all a rare one. The English playwright who came nearest Yeats in this respect was Eliot. His visual imagination was weak, but his feeling for the dramatic possibilities in music and rhythm very strong,

---

[4] See especially his own book, *Dance Drama* (1926), from which the above quotations are taken and *The Cambridge Festival Theatre*, a slide set with accompanying booklet, by Richard Cave, published by the Consortium for Drama and Media in Higher Education.

and the idea of a synthesis of all the arts was extremely potent for him.

Eliot was independently affected by many of the same influences that formed Yeats's theatrical style. As a young poet he looked in the first place to France ('the kind of poetry that I needed . . . was only to be found in French'). He too was a devotee of the symbolists and a Wagnerian. From the experimental use of musical quotation in his early poems—the 'Weialala leia/Wallala leialala' of the Rhine Maidens in *The Waste Land*—to the significantly named *Four Quartets* his poetry was marked by the symbolist yearning to make all the arts approximate more closely to music. He was also a lover of the dance and of music hall. He was brooding as early as 1920 on the possibility of turning the popular forms of entertainment into 'a form of art'.[5] And his memorial tribute to Marie Lloyd[6] conveys brilliantly in its brief space the concrete feel of her turn in the theatre, her droll way of rummaging among the objects in her bag as she sang 'One of the Ruins that Cromwell knocked Abaht a Bit', and above all the spontaneous collaboration she instigated between herself and her audience. In his longing for such a collaboration and his admiration for the improvising technique of performers like Marie Lloyd the modern side of Eliot's dramatic imagination shows very clearly. His love of the dance was equally strong; in the pages of *The Criterion* and elsewhere he continually praised the art of ballet, extolled the superior discipline of dancers to that of actors and asked Symons-like questions: 'If there is a future for drama, and particularly for poetic drama, will it not be in the direction indicated by the ballet?' (*Selected Essays*, p. 46). He constantly advocated a return to ritual; 'for the stage—not only in its remote origin, but always—is a ritual, and the failure of the contemporary stage to satisfy the craving for ritual is one of the reasons why it is not a living art'.

He seems also to have learned from some of Yeats's models, such as Symons and Maeterlinck. His acknowledgement of these sources of inspiration is seldom overt, but with Eliot meagre acknowledgement does not necessarily mean small interest; he makes such authoritative statements about writers he does want to distinguish that it is easy to overlook the possible importance in his imaginative life of others he refers to in a more sidelong way. Such a one is Maeterlinck. Eliot's many remarks about him are almost always dismissive. His drama was

[5] 'Our problem should be to take a form of entertainment, and subject it to the process which would leave it a form of art.' *The Sacred Wood*, 1920, p. 63.

[6] 'Marie Lloyd' (1923) in *Selected Essays*, 1932, pp. 418–21.

a hybrid, like Shaw's, which 'in failing to be dramatic, fails also to be poetic' (*Selected Essays*, p. 41); '. . . the plays in prose (so much admired in my youth, and now hardly even read) by Maeterlinck . . . to say that the characterisation in them is dim is an understatement' (*On Poetry and Poets*, p. 77). And more interestingly: 'His characters take no conscious delight in their rôle—they are sentimental' (*Selected Essays*, p. 42). Yet he keeps talking about him—and certainly seems to have had him in mind when he achieved one of his most spell-binding effects in *The Family Reunion* by a technique first used in *Interior*. He professed scepticism about Maeterlinck's special interest in 'the inexpressible': 'Perhaps the emotions are not significant enough to endure full daylight' (*Selected Essays*, p. 42). Yet he himself was to be a notable explorer in that same region, the 'fringe of indefinite extent, of feeling which we can only detect, so to speak, out of the corner of the eye and can never completely focus. . .' (*On Poetry and Poets*, p. 86). Maeterlinck's saying, 'Words can tell us scarcely anything of that which should be told', is continually echoed by Eliot's characters; Sweeney in his tabloid nightmare muttering to his uncom-prehending audience, 'I gotta use words when I talk to you'; Harry, on the point of breakdown, agonising, 'But how can I explain, how can I explain to *you?*'.

Eliot of course had another model in Yeats himself, and in the Irish drama. '. . . Yeats had nothing, and we have had Yeats', he proclaimed, in his celebrated memorial essay: 'I do not know where our debt to him as a dramatist ends—and in time, it will not end until that drama itself ends'.[7] He saw that Yeats's plays had in them the seed of the future and speculated that even the 'imperfect' early plays were 'probably more permanent literature than the plays of Shaw'. Characteristically, he says little in this essay and elsewhere about the practical possibilities they suggested to him for his own drama, partly because he concen-trates on language, and from that point of view the new Irish theatre was not very helpful to him: Synge's language was 'not available except for plays set among that same people'; Yeats's had not much to give a 'modern' verse drama, except for *Purgatory*, where he 'solved his problem of speech in verse, and laid all his successors under obligation to him' (*On Poetry and Poets*, p. 78). *Purgatory*, indeed, affected Eliot deeply, significantly by making him uncomfortable: 'not

[7] 'Yeats: The First annual Yeats Lecture, delivered to the Friends of the Irish Academy at the Abbey Theatre, Dublin, in 1940', reprinted in *On Poetry and Poets* (1957), pp. 252–62.

very pleasant' is his phrase. From all this, it might well seem that he had not taken up the hints offered by Yeats's experiments in total theatre. He has little to say about the dance plays and he pays a decidedly backhanded compliment to that early exploration in music drama, *The Shadowy Waters*. It was 'one of the most perfect expressions of the vague enchanted beauty of that [the pre-Raphaelite] school', and yet it was also 'the Western seas descried through the back window of a house in Kensington, an Irish myth for the Kelmscott Press' (*On Poetry and Poets*, p. 256).

But the dance plays did make their mark all the same. He was one of those who saw the first performance of *At the Hawk's Well* in Lady Cunard's drawing-room in 1916, and it seems to have made a great impact on him. He later told Arnold Bennett that he had in mind to write a 'drama of modern life' with 'certain things in it accentuated by drumbeats'.[8] The darkly expressive little masterpiece, *Sweeney Agonistes* (1926), was the outcome, with its strong jazz rhythms through which a dark, suppressed world of feeling finds outlet. He did not use actual drums, but when the play was produced in 1965 with music by John Dankworth[9] it seemed entirely natural that the highly syncopated verse (so cunningly disguised as colloquial talk) should be accentuated by instrumental jazz. Everything was in tune: the hypnotic and sinister rhythms of speaking voices, musicians and dead-pan music-hall choruses: we were in an interior world of obsessive anxieties where the most commonplace actions like the shrilling of a telephone were loaded with ominous force. Eliot's description of this piece as a 'fragment' has misled many of his readers. Seen on the stage it does not seem incomplete, but rather a self-contained and intensely theatrical event, a Yeatsian 'moment' which ends precisely where it has to, with Sweeney taken as far as it is possible for him to go, in his oblique confession:

> I knew a man once did a girl in.
> Any man might do a girl in.
> Any man has to, needs to, wants to
> Once in a lifetime, do a girl in.

The modernity of Eliot's technique has been sharply illuminated by some productions in recent years—Dankworth's of *Sweeney*, and in

[8] A. Bennett, *Journals* (1971 Penguin edn.), p. 482. Entry for September 1924.
[9] Produced by Peter Wood in the memorial programme, 'Homage to T. S. Eliot', Globe Theatre, 15 June 1965. A recording was produced by Vera Lindsay for E.M.I. Records.

1972 Terry Hands's production of *Murder in the Cathedral* (1935) at the Aldwych Theatre with an impressionistic set by Farrah, its pillars and arches tremulously fading in and out with each change in the stage light, its properties—white altar, huge cross—carried on by priests seeming to be deliberately setting a scene for a martyrdom. It created an exotic, insubstantial world which insidiously suggested itself, Genet style, as a creation of the troubled mind, a projection of an inner landscape which the male characters—the priests, and above all, Becket—needed desperately to establish as protection against a double terror. First a mysterious sexual nausea was brilliantly indicated by an athletic female chorus, dancing and miming the acts of sex and birth as an accompaniment to horrific images of animality—huge and ridiculous scaly wings, the taste of putrid flesh in the spoon. Then came the terrible vision of the 'void', hypnotically delivered by priests in a chillingly flat monotone:

> no objects, no tones,
> No colours, no forms to distract, to divert the soul
> From seeing itself, foully united for ever, nothing with nothing.

The play became a modern drama of self-consciousness in which the nausea and dread were related to troubling divisions in Becket's own nature. The temptation scene was, unusually, played in public, with the tempters emerging from the crowd and slipping back into it while Becket stood apart as the priests robed him, turning him from a vulnerable figure in a hair shirt into the Archbishop who had finally escaped from the horror of his own multiplicity. When the Fourth Tempter, who had been sitting with his back to the audience throughout the robing scene, turned round to reveal a mirror image of the Becket in the hair shirt, it was as if in abandoning this twin, Becket had committed a kind of self-murder. The achievement of the production was the remarkable distancing which gave the familiar Christian ritual an unfamiliar look and brought disturbing new notes into Becket's death, making it seem his only way of relief from the pain of a fragmented consciousness.

Murder in the Cathedral may only show its modern side in a production, like this one, which makes special efforts to reveal it, but *The Family Reunion* (1939) is clearly, in part at least, an experiment in the interior mode derived from *Interior* and *Purgatory*. Eliot projected the mode further into the future by brilliantly commandeering a 'modern' ritual of the most ordinary kind from the upper-class drawing-room and showing how it could be made to reveal the anguished activity of the secretive inner self. The characters 'freeze' into interior monologue, move towards each other as if in a dream in lyrical interludes which rely, like Yeats's, on the hypnotic effect of cadence, tone of voice, ritualistic movement. Such is the ritual Mary and Agatha perform at the close, moving round and round Amy's birthday cake after her death, blowing out a few candles 'at each revolution' so that their last words come out of the dark—an overwhelming physical image of the inner dark the play has plumbed:

MARY   Not in the day time
               And in the hither world
               Where we know what we are doing
               There is not its operation
                          Follow follow
AGATHA   But in the night time
               And in the nether world
               Where the meshes we have woven
               Bind us to each other
                          Follow follow

The dreamy movement, the unbroken flow of the verse (without punctuation, it goes round in a circle like the actors), take us far into the nether world. Eliot wanted to go even further, as far as Yeats had gone when he represented the dark drives of the unconscious in the 'presences' of the dance plays. Eliot's 'presences', the eyes at the window, seem to me a brilliant device for achieving a similar effect in a conventional, realistic setting. Something dumb, physical, inexplicable, forces its way into the dialogue, upsets the delicate flow of words between Harry and Mary, jerking him out of his healing trance by the nightmare sensation of 'eyes' on him—the terrible feeling he tried to convey to his family on his first entrance into the room:

HARRY   How can you sit in this blaze of light for all the world to look at?
          If you knew how you looked, when I saw you through the window!
          Do you like to be stared at by eyes through a window?

He 'sees', 'smells', senses the 'sleepless hunters' that will not let him sleep, but possess him in the 'instant of inattention'. What do we, the audience, see? Eliot had no ready answer to that question: the weakness of his visual imagination compared with Yeats's is certainly shown up in his account of the various methods tried in production and his dissatisfaction with them all. But the fact that he could not visualise them himself does not mean that it cannot be done or that he had not imagined a potent theatrical device for expressing the inexpressible. In Michael Elliot's production of the play in 1969 the Eumenides were very much there, vaguely tent-like shapes descending as the lights dimmed, appalling because so hard to place, so nearly shapeless like the worst horrors of the night. By the simple, brilliant device of placing the action in the round, so that the audience looked through a skeletal frame at the family interior, he was able to involve us in uneasy complicity with Harry's point of view; we too spied on the oblivious family, understood as they could not, his neurotic consciousness of being watched; were threatened when the scene darkened and the monstrous shapes descended between us and the interior giving enormous urgency to Harry's attempt to evade them:

> I tell you, it is not me you are looking at,
> Not me you are grinning at, not me your confidential looks
> Incriminate, but that other person, if person
> You thought I was.

In this same production the modulations from conversational speech into somnambulistic choruses and interchanges delicately conveyed an impression of 'unspoken' thoughts and feelings ranging from the banal (but no less private) ruminations of the aunts and uncles to the complex agonies of the mother-ridden, wife-loathing Harry. Eliot later repudiated these sequences as being too much like 'arias'—strangely, in view of his symbolist affinities. But his repudiation should not be taken too seriously. Looking back to *The Family Reunion* now, used as we are to the ritualistic handling of dialogue by Pinter and others, we can more easily appreciate what Eliot is doing with his changes of rhythm and cadence, stepping up the nervous charge in ordinary talk— 'Put on the lights. But leave the curtains undrawn. / Make up the fire. Will the spring never come? I am cold'—till we penetrate to a deeper level of consciousness where communication occurs without the characters' intention or understanding:

HARRY   What have we been saying? I think I was saying
             That it seemed as if I had been always here
             And you were someone who had come from a long distance.

Eliot's exceptional command of evocative rhythms gave him his equivalent for Maeterlinck's 'inarticulacies' and Yeats's unequivocally musical form. In the comedies from *The Cocktail Party* (1949) onwards, he filtered that music of the inner ear through more and more aggressively commonplace matter, taking over the bright, deadly, cocktail party ritual of Noel Coward's comedies and pointing up its sinister potentialities. The characters posture and play-act, present façades so impenetrable they might almost be real masks. Julia and Alex, those nightmarishly jovial eavesdroppers in *The Cocktail Party,* certainly use volubility as a kind of mask to conceal their true nature from the 'subjects' they manipulate and push to confessions that could not otherwise materialise. The central character, Edward, knows—without knowing that he knows—what these 'guardians' really are:

> The self that can say 'I want this—or want that'—
> The self that wills—he is a feeble creature;
> He has to come to terms in the end
> With the obstinate, the tougher self; who does not speak,
> Who never talks, who cannot argue;
> And who in some men may be the *Guardian*—

With that word, the 'guardian', Eliot calls up the dumb Guardian in *At the Hawk's Well,* the dance play that particularly impressed him by its 'internal' way of handling Irish myth (*On Poetry and Poets,* p. 260). 'Internal' is the word for *The Cocktail Party* too; its displays of noisy externality are no more than the mocking cover under which the guardian/intruders conduct their work of silent observation and the uncovering of what has been kept hidden. A double dialogue develops, with the spaces between words, the non-answers, the tangential jokes building up unwilled, resented revelations.

With *The Cocktail Party* and the later comedies, as with *The Family Reunion,* Eliot opened up a way for Pinter, who certainly comes riding in at this point. Pinter's is nothing if not a 'drama of the interior', as he occasionally hints himself in titles like *Landscape* (1969), *The Basement* (1967), *No Man's Land* (1975). He has taken over Eliot's convention of black comedy for very similar purposes; *The Birthday Party* (1960) and *The Homecoming* (1965) are both in their different ways new versions of *The Family Reunion,* and they have a family resemblance also to those shadowy prototypes, *Interior* and *The Intruder,* where another kind of domestic interior is invaded and penetrated by dark, intimidating forces. Pinter's technique of 'little words', pauses, silences, repetitions, hesitations, is the closest thing to Maeterlinck's art of the unexpressed that the English theatre has yet seen—though his 'inarticulacies' coexist with a terrible volubility that is more akin to the sinister flow of talk in *The Cocktail Party*. He too thinks of volubility as a defence against being known and his characters are virtuosi in the art: their interior world is not easy to get at; they have to be endlessly harassed by intruders. Pinter is rightly celebrated for his ingenuity in devising modes of harassment—opening doors, lights going on or off, insistent telephones, unexpected visitors —to give us glimpses behind the opaque veil that conceals the inner self of a Lenny or a Spooner. What we see is often no more than a recession of posturing shadows, raising the uneasy question whether there is any 'real' self at all. Pinter is greatly addicted to the imagery of blindness and dark and light which recurs so insistently in the interior drama from Maeterlinck to Beckett, but for him it is not so much a way of reaching the light as of bringing home to us how hopelessly we are all in the dark. A brutally physical dark, it is, as in the dread game of blind man's buff in *The Birthday Party* or the dead-pan self-mocking performance of turning out the light in *No Man's Land*:

> FOSTER   Listen. You know what it's like when you're in a room with the light on and then suddenly the light goes out? I'll show you. It's like this.

Of all the playwrights I have been discussing, Pinter is the most Maeterlinckian in certain aspects, above all in his emphasis on life as an enigma and on the universal fear of silence:

> I think that we communicate only too well, in our silence, in what is unsaid, and that what takes place is continual evasion, desperate rearguard attempts to keep ourselves to ourselves.

He is especially successful in dealing with unyielding, evasive silences, often veiled in pleasant blandness, like Ruth's at the close of *The Homecoming*, Stella's in *The Collection* (1963):

> JAMES   You didn't do anything, did you?
>   *Pause*
>   He wasn't in your room. You just talked about it, in the lounge.

> *Pause*
> That's the truth, isn't it?
> *Pause*
> You just sat and talked about what you would do if you went to your room.
> That's what you did.
> *Pause*
> Didn't you?
> *Pause*
> That's the truth . . . isn't it?

In that sequence, Pinter could almost be rewriting the inquisition scene in *Pelléas amd Mélisande* when Golaud torments Mélisande on her death-bed with his obsessive questions: '. . . And we must have the truth . . . we must at last have the truth, do you hear? Tell me all! Tell me all! . . .'.

Though it has a similar apparatus of inquisition—guardians, intruders, watching eyes—his drama is separated from Eliot's by its almost total lack of a sense of saving grace. His furies, far from turning into bright angels, are more apt to cart off their victims to some horrific sounding sanatorium for further treatment of the grim kind they have been meting out, stripping the self of its protective fantasies. And yet the echoes from Eliot in his plays have become if anything stronger as time has gone on; in *No Man's Land*, indeed, they come very close to being quotations, as in the scene where Hirst, the ruined alcoholic writer, so terribly goes down on all fours and crawls out of the room, while Spooner, the literary sponger he has picked up by chance on Hampstead Heath and who is supposedly a total stranger, is made to reflect, as if regurgitating *Prufrock*, 'I have known this before. The exit through the door, by way of belly and floor'. Pinter makes sure we catch the echo by a strong musical emphasis. The motif, 'I have known this before . . .', recurs three times, in a general pattern of stylised pauses and repetitions, accentuated by internal rhyming, which makes the dialogue more like a piece of chamber music than any thing he has yet written. His musicality relates him to the 'interior' tradition, as also his feeling for the visual symbolism of the stage. His settings are always 'composed' to suggest interior patterns, as in the fantastic changes of interior decoration which represent the characters' changing view of themselves in *The Basement*, or in the room with the dominating window of *No Man's*

Land: the National Theatre's production[10] of this last created a fearsomely claustrophobic impression of a mental trap when the heavy curtains were drawn across the great bay in daylight. And there are small affinities, like his fondness for windows and reflections, which comes out strongly on those rare occasions when he attempts the other kind of Maeterlinckian silence, not hostile but tender and gracious, promising communion and mystical awareness. So, in *Silence* (1969), Ellen walks into the region of the stage inhabited by Rumsey and with him gazes, tranced, out of the window to see there her own reflection in a new light:

RUMSEY	Look at your reflection.
ELLEN	Where?
RUMSEY	In the window.
ELLEN	It's very dark outside.
RUMSEY	It's high up.
ELLEN	Does it get darker the higher you get?
RUMSEY	No.

Silence

In these many ways, Pinter places himself clearly in the Yeats/Beckett tradition. Maeterlinck and, more overtly, Eliot, are inescapable 'presences' in his drama, and he has of course expressed publicly his passionate devotion to Beckett. Sometimes too he seems to look directly to Yeats. He is known to admire the dance plays and they are what come naturally to mind in those scenes of his when restraints break down and the characters enact their hidden feelings in demonic, wordless rituals. The convention becomes more completely musical; drum notes sound, hammering out obsessive inner rhythms: the fingers of husband and wife tap out erotic messages on the bongo drum in *The Lover* (1963); Stanley in *The Birthday Party* moves further towards breakdown when he snatches up the painfully suggestive present from Meg, the child's drum, and strides round the room, beating it in a growing frenzy: 'Halfway round the beat becomes erratic, uncontrolled. Meg expresses dismay. He arrives at her chair, banging the drum, his face and the drumbeat now savage and possessed'. The drum is put here to a purpose unlike Yeats's but one he would surely have recognised as belonging to the interior mode; it is certainly a

[10] 23 April 1975.

'deep of the mind' we go into in the nightmarish scenes that follow the beating of the drum when McCann and Goldberg reduce Stanley to a gibbering automaton. We might also say that the play realises Eliot's idea—which came to him after seeing *At the Hawk's Well*—for a 'drama of modern life, perhaps with certain things in it accentuated by drum-beats'.

The line from Yeats through Eliot to Pinter represents the interior drama at its most reserved and secret. Eliot was also a catalyst, however, in a more public domain. The methods he pioneered in *Murder in the Cathedral* (1935)—alienation techniques like the incongruous music-hall refrain of the Knights after the killing of Becket, talking out to the audience, the use of jazz rhythms for sinister, psychological effects—were taken further in the thirties by the more politically-minded poets who created the Group Theatre, notably Auden and Isherwood. *Sweeney Agonistes* (1926) too had an impact on these writers; when it was produced in 1936 by the Group Theatre, very appropriately Yeats was among the audience. Appropriately, because the Group Theatre aimed to realise his idea of a modern drama; they too dreamed of a theatre of all the arts; they drew on artists like Robert Medley, on choreographers, composers, dancers and singers. Benjamin Britten, Rupert Doone, Hedli Anderson; all the major performing arts were represented.

So far as one can tell, it was only an accident that they did not produce any of Yeats's dance plays:[11] they certainly had him in mind—most of the time, one would say. A dance often figures in the plays of Auden and Isherwood as an expression of obscure feeling; at the centre of *The Dance of Death* (1933), for instance, is the figure of the Dancer moving through Europe, bringing with him a lengthening shadow of war and social unease. And the surrealist scene on the mountain top at the end of *The Ascent of F6* (Group Theatre, 26 February 1937) contains a strange, semi-balletic performance by masked characters representing life-size chessmen. They answer questions from the stage audience (a bourgeois couple planted in the stage boxes), each removing his mask as he speaks, and then go through their moves in a silence accompanied by drum rolls. Ransom wins, his brother/opponent collapses, and he receives a final revelation when the Figure at the summit removes her veil to show the form of his mother

---

[11] A full account of the Group Theatre and Yeats's association with it is in preparation by M. Sidnell.

in her youth. He ends there; dying with his head in her lap, to the macabre music of her lullaby:

> Still the dark forest, quiet the deep,
> Softly the clock ticks, baby must sleep!

Can we help but hear behind this another ghostly sound, the lullaby the Old Man in *Purgatory* sings for the shade of *his* youthful mother?

That kind of musical effect is a reminder of how directly the Group Theatre continued the Yeatsian tradition. Music-hall, musical comedy, opera, melodrama were the admired modes of the Group playwrights. They certainly relied greatly on the music written for them by Benjamin Britten, which must have contributed enormously to the effectiveness of, for instance, the musical comedy caricatures in *The Dog Beneath the Skin* (1935) and the shifts of feeling in the political 'melodrama' (accurately named), *On the Frontier* (1938). That last piece was dedicated to Britten and includes a firm direction 'All the Chorus *must* be able to sing'.

Britten continued to write music for playwrights after the war in the late forties, and in Nō-inspired pieces like *Curlew River* moved ever closer to the Yeatsian style of music drama. So this particular Yeatsian thread has held firm from his own time through Eliot's variations right up to the present day. The heir to Yeats and Eliot in this context is John Arden who has taken the music-hall and musical techniques I have been describing into a region of his own, tragic in *Serjeant Musgrave's Dance* (1960), comic in *The Workhouse Donkey* (1964). Arden has himself acknowledged the influence on his work of 'the Irish people'. For him the emphasis is on Synge and O'Casey, as one might expect, though he also pays tribute to Yeats and—perhaps alone among present-day playwrights—to those earliest English plays inspired by Yeats, Masefield's *The Tragedy of Nan* and *The Tragedy of Pompey the Great* (1910). 'Little known, but marvellous', Arden says. He has also spoken of wanting in his early days to write a play on the life of Hitler in the style of *Sweeney Agonistes*. All these influences mix, of course, with others, but it is clear that for Arden the Irish have been important in forming a convention he can work with, a 'modern' tradition in which he finds it natural to include Yeats and Masefield, O'Casey and T. S. Eliot.

The tradition is so well established now that the most original English playwright of his generation, Edward Bond, can use techniques derived from Yeats without consciously taking Yeats as a model. He does not see himself in the Yeatsian tradition; indeed, his more obvious affinities are with very different writers, Chekhov, for instance, or Brecht. Yet always in his plays there is that powerful stratum of melodrama—the real melodrama of the folk, which Symons thought must be the basis for a new poetic drama. Always too a searching into the recesses of the spirit, often expressed in flashes of supernatural intensity; John Clare rambling in the ghostly spaces of his mind, encountering the emanations of memory; the young man in *The Sea* (1973) standing on the shore edge watching a mad man stab at a dead body that has become in a strange way his 'double'. This last is a grotesque and mysteriously touching realisation of the image the play sprang from, so Bond has said: 'I threw my mask into the sea'. We are very near Yeats there, as with so much on Bond's stage: the Japanese rituals in *Narrow Road to the Deep North* (1968), the customary Nō-like bareness of his scene; the telling silences—most unexpected and disturbing in his portrayal of Shakespeare in *Bingo* (1974)—the encounters with ghosts and döppelgangers; haunting 'moments', rich in the stillness that 'turns the imagination in upon itself'; in that way, more Yeatsian than anything being written for the English theatre.

I have said enough, I hope, to indicate how opportune for Yeats's plays the theatrical climate is now. What, then, of the place his plays have had so far in this modern theatre that looks as though it should be so ready to receive them. For some of Yeats's critics the answer to that question is a dusty one. Under the title 'A Challenge Unanswered' one speaker at the Yeats International Summer School at Sligo in 1975, Dr James Flannery, developed the idea that Yeats's drama had been by and large ignored by the theatre: he saw the setting up of a company devoted exclusively to the plays as the way they were most likely to become known and appreciated. It is an understandable view, but it seems to me that the evidence of interest in Yeats's drama is growing all the time, not just among critics but also in the theatre, especially in that region somewhere between professional and amateur which has become such an important sphere of action in late years, since the growth of university drama departments. James Flannery's own university (Ottawa) is one of several universities and colleges where a strong drive is being made by Yeats scholars to bring the plays before students in the only way they can be fully grasped, that is in performance: and his own productions have contributed much to this livelier appreciation. Similarly, the sense of

Reg Skene's involvement in production adds greatly to the interest of his interpretation of the Cuchulain plays. In my own experience alone, there has been a striking increase in availability of effective productions in the last few years. Several of the dance plays have been produced or video recorded (a development I will return to later) in the University of London; two of these, *At the Hawk's Well* and *The Cat and the Moon* were produced with the Yeats Theatre Company by Niema Ash, who is both an experienced choreographer and director and a student of the plays. A similar cross-fertilisation between theatrical and academic talents has been involved in many recent productions, in the student performances at Bedford College of *On Baile's Strand* and *The Only Jealousy of Emer* (both 1976), *The King of the Great Clock Tower* and *Calvary* (both 1977) directed by Richard Cave; at Royal Holloway College of *A Full Moon in March* (1975), which I directed, with Niema Ash as choreographer, and *The Dreaming of the Bones* (1977), and at the University College of North Wales, Bangor, where a professional theatre director, Sam Macready, was for a time a member of the drama department. He demonstrated the power of the plays to draw not only specialised but popular audiences when he took a repertoire of four pieces, including *The King of the Great Clock Tower*, on a tour of Ireland, staying in widely varying locales and finding that audiences in schools, colleges, private houses—even on the deck of their homeward bound ship—were gripped and enthusiastic.[12]

'Amateur', always a tricky word, becomes an especially difficult one where Yeats's plays are concerned. He himself often wrote after all, with amateurs in mind—the Abbey Theatre was for a time a semi-amateur venture—and although he acquired professional performers of very high standing as he went along, he always retained his sense of the plays as particularly open to performance by untrained people who loved poetry; 'Certainly those who care for my kind of poetry must be numerous enough, if I can bring them together, to pay half a dozen players who can bring all their properties in a cab and perform in their leisure moments'. He wrote this in a note on *At the Hawk's Well*, and as late as 1934 he was still taken with the notion that his plays might best be performed in the round (to use today's expression) by a group of students who could make a little money playing them 'and gradually elaborate a technique that would respect literature and music alike'. The plays clearly do have a future in this region of improvisation

[12] I am indebted to Sam Macready's unpublished thesis for his account of his Irish tour.

and adaptability. One of their special virtues is exactly this self-standing quality which Yeats implies in his vision of the players bringing all their properties in a cab and needing nothing else. There is an exhilarating sense in production of having the whole thing there, under one's hand, ready to leap into life the moment the musicians begin to play: they and the actors do it all; a laugh from a severed head can be a bizarre note on a guitar, off-stage events like Cuchulain's battle with the waves come to us through the sound of drum or flute. Even lighting effects are not a necessity. Yeats thought, with some reason, that the effect was more strange and satisfying if there were no separation between the audience and the masked actors. But, of course, the dance plays were also performed with quite elaborate lighting on the Abbey stage; *Fighting the Waves*, the pure dance play or ballet derived from *The Only Jealousy of Emer*, was one of his greatest successes, and for that lighting was important. Either method is legitimate and will have its own virtue. In Richard Cave's production of *The Only Jealousy of Emer*, the impression of a mind moving deeper to its centre and then outward again was created by a series of delicate colour changes which were reversed as the action moved back into the daylight world, and in my own production of *A Full Moon in March*, the play opened in darkness with a light slowly coming up on the emblematic disc which represented the moon, and music and light fading away together at the end till only the glowing disc was visible.

Another especial attraction of the plays for a group working together as an ensemble is the opportunity they give for improvisation and collaboration. We found, for instance, that our play did not begin to work for the actors till they had heard some music; a few notes on a flute were enough. The interest of the musicians attracted a composer, Dyl Bonner, and from his music came the dance; this was indeed collaboration so close that it would have been impossible to say which decided the form the dance eventually took. I have been speaking of isolated student productions, but of course, there has always been some professional interest. In Yeats's own time there were a few interesting productions outside Dublin, Robert Speaight's *The Resurrection*, for instance, and Terence Gray's balletic *On Baile's Strand* at the Festival Theatre, Cambridge. In the present day, the Abbey itself, and companies in Paris and New York, such as the Théâtre Oblique, the Open Eye Theatre and Café la Mama have done productions, and there has been a substantial attempt to build up a Yeatsian repertoire and a house style by Mary O'Malley at the Lyric Theatre, Belfast. Her productions of the dance plays have attracted much attention and stimulated a composer to write extensively for them.

It is true that, except for the experimental and fringe theatres, the professional theatre in London has shown indifference, yet there are murmurs that this state of things is about to change: we hear that Peter Brook, always so great an influence, uses the dance plays for the exercises his company practise in his theatre workshop in Paris; that Harold Pinter would like to produce a dance play, or perhaps *Purgatory*. The venturesome repertory planned by the National Theatre includes works like the *Oresteia* which calls for a full range of musical and dance or movement skills; there must be hope that these will be turned at some time to Yeats's drama; the Cottesloe Studio Theatre could provide an admirable milieu for such experiments. We have by now seen many stage scenes very much in his style in plays by other authors; the scene in *Marat Sade*, for instance, when Charlotte Corday circles round de Sade, 'whipping' him with her long hair and brilliantly suggesting erotic cruelty, conjures up for those who know *The Only Jealousy of Emer*, the Woman of the Sidhe, dancing round the crouching Ghost of Cuchulain and dropping her metallic hair on him, seductively and threateningly. So the theatre is catching up with Yeats; there are good grounds for thinking that his plays will be more often seen in the future than in the past.

Of course some nervousness about producing the dance plays is understandable; they seem to call for such a daunting variety of performing skills, especially in dance and movement. This is a real hurdle; the plays lose a great deal if the dance is not fully expressive and collapse altogether if it is badly done. That particular danger was met in the Open University production of *At the Hawk's Well* by a division of the roles into acting and dancing parts: all the lines were given to the Attendants to chant in song-speech or 'folk singing', while professional ballet dancers mimed and danced the action. There were gains here, notably the fey beauty Cuchulain's role acquired when performed by a brilliant male dancer from Covent Garden; there was a cost, however, in diminution of human interest and a loss of irony: the characters were too completely puppets for us to feel the force of their inconsistencies. There is a danger in separating the elements when the knitting up of personal and impersonal is so vital to the play as a whole.

That is a question of interpretation, but of course it is immensely valuable to have a video recording of this quality, not least because it helps to make possible something new in the study of Yeats's drama. A critical discussion based on different directors' interpretations of the play in performance is one of the surest signs that the plays are experiencing something of a renaissance. It also demonstrates how much more open to theatrical interpretation they are than has sometimes been thought. There is certainly a case for a company developing a house style and emphasising what the plays have in common. There might even be such a style as 'Irish Nō' in reality, although the expression has sometimes been used sardonically to indicate the absurdity of any such attempt. But though this would have its value, there must be room too for exactly the opposite approach, the producer feeling free to vary his style from one play to another or in different productions of the same play. There would be plenty of support for this free approach in Yeats's own practice. Sometimes, it is true, he sounds rather categorical about what should or should not be done; he did not want any variation from the stage directions to *A Full Moon in March,* for instance (though I am afraid we disobeyed him), and he was strict about giving permission for new music.[13] But more often his stage directions, comments and suggestions—to himself and others—are tentative and open, part of the work in progress in fact. He had wonderfully bold, clear ideas of the essential effects he wanted, but he was always ready to try out new means of getting them. He was willing to present a play in a studio setting, without artificial lighting, or on the Abbey stage; inspired by a sculptor's fine masks he would rewrite a play as a ballet; he was willing to have the dancers' parts taken by men or women, and would distribute the lines accordingly, rearranging sometimes—or offering to—in a most ruthless and surprising way. He was quite prepared to sacrifice a vital interaction in *The Dreaming of the Bones* if the dance had to be performed by a dancer who could not speak: her 'few' lines, he said, might be given to Dermot. Often it is possible to see Yeats feeling his way in his stage directions and commentaries, using words like 'perhaps' or 'may', waiting for a sight of actors on the stage before he can know just what he has to write. Is the Lame Man in *The Cat and the Moon* to remain on one knee after he gets off the Blind Man's back, 'or crouching until he

---

[13] I am indebted to Mr Warwick Gould for drawing to my attention a letter from Yeats to Macmillan (B.M. Add. Ms 55003f.37), announcing that he had appointed Mrs Dorothy Pound to be his 'musical agent' and that all settings of his works must be submitted to her for approval.

can pick up, as I have no doubt he does, the Blind Man's stick?' That 'as I have no doubt he does' charmingly suggests the rush of visual imagination becoming confident, after the first tentative glimpses. And Yeats was extraordinarily open to visual stimulus: we have seen how important Craig's screens and masks were in changing the whole direction of his drama.

Though so brief and stylised—and clearly functioning within limits which are very finely drawn—the plays nevertheless are rich enough to make possible a remarkable variety of stage interpretations. *The Only Jealousy of Emer*, for instance, I have seen in two productions which each worked well at opposite poles. Sam Macready's stressed the psychological realism which is a feature of the play: his Woman of the Sidhe took her tone from the human context, offering Cuchulain a pure, luminous but essential human beauty, while Richard Cave's in her fantastic Mardi Gras hat and streamers, was more distant and more strange. Neither was the metallic being of Yeats's imagination—that too one would much like to see. The plays call out, in fact, for as many interpretations as there are imaginations to respond to them.

One modern development which offers the dance plays a whole new projection is television. True, we must lose on the screen the special excitement that comes, as Yeats said, from being in the same room and under the same light as the actors, with no barrier between, so that we are intensely aware of them conjuring up the illusion from their own resources. But after all, the plays are not always produced, even in the theatre, with that absolute purity. Few producers would wish to deny themselves the lighting effects which are so potent a means of creating the right atmosphere for these ghostly dramas. Yeats showed the way himself in *Purgatory*; impossible to ignore the hint and refrain from trying out the method on the dance plays too. Similarly, though musicians playing live music must remain the ideal, the plays can be effective with recorded, off-stage music, and there is a strong case for choosing artificial, electronic sounds on occasion; for the dance of the goddess in *The Only Jealousy of Emer*, for instance. Once we admit these variations, it would be arbitrary to deny the arts of television a place in the production of Yeats's plays. The screen can provide us, at the very least, with illustrations of what the plays have it in them to be, and that is what readers need if they are to turn into audiences. At a time, too, when dramatic criticism is more theatrically orientated than it was in Yeats's own day, critics cannot afford to do without concrete illustrations, and the video tape is an ideal means of supplying them. So it is good to know that attempts are being made to build up collections of Yeats recordings. In the University of London, for instance, recordings are available of the Yeats Theatre Company's productions of *At the Hawk's Well* and *The Cat and the Moon*; Richard Cave's *The King of the Great Clock Tower* and *Calvary*, my own *The Dreaming of the Bones*.[14]

The problem involved in the act of transfer from stage to screen can illuminate the essential nature of the plays, for the viewers, as certainly for those who do the adapting. To record a student production of *A Full Moon in March*, for instance, was to realise to the full how thoroughly Yeats had followed Maeterlinck's advice to 'send the actors farther off'. In the love scene between the Queen and the Swineherd where, if anywhere, we might have expected the closeups the camera always yearns for, it was blocked: the characters' faces cannot be got at; the Swineherd's is a mask, the Queen's hidden behind a veil: no lingering on intimate personal detail was possible. In that instance, the essential nature of the play may have been high-lighted at the cost of its effectiveness as television drama. But it is not beyond imagining that television could find its own equivalent for stage devices of distancing and impersonality; perhaps we should look forward to adaptations capable of standing in their own right, and of realising Yeats's vision in the most modern medium.

It seems to me that it must be so, that the vitality of the Yeatsian theatre can only increase in this climate which is now so favourable to it. Eliot's prophecy begins to look a very accurate one: 'I do not know where our debt to him as a dramatist ends—and in time it will not end until the drama itself ends'.

[14] Recordings by the University of London Audio Visual Centre are available for hire or sale to educational institutions.

9 ∽ O'Casey

O'Casey was Yeats's first heir. He took over the idea of total theatre, carried it from Dublin to London and turned himself into the flying wasp[1] whose task was to sting the English theatre into modernity. The history of his later drama is a history of his struggle to naturalise techniques derived from Yeats in the realism-bound theatre of his adopted country. He had continually to explain or defend his experimental methods to the uncomprehending critics of the day. When James Agate berated him for causing confusion by mixing fantasy and realism he replied: 'I do so, Sir, because, first, a change is needed in the theatre, and, secondly, because life is like that—a blend of fantasy and realism'.[2] On another occasion he said still more militantly: 'I am out to destroy the accepted naturalistic presentation of character; to get back to the poetic significance of drama'.[3]

He was the coloniser of the Yeatsian theatre and in a way the populariser too, for although his experimental drama did not achieve popularity in his own time, being too far ahead of it, he gave a massive demonstration in the thirties and forties of how the Yeatsian dance drama could be opened up into popular forms and serve many purposes, including social satire, without necessarily losing the 'interior' dimension. He suffered from a sense of neglect and his later plays were not generally understood, often, no doubt, because they were badly performed. But he did, after all, break into the West End theatre with two audaciously innovative plays, *The Silver Tassie* (Apollo, 11 October 1929) and *Within the Gates* (Royalty, 7 February 1934), and the other plays, even the most fantastic, did usually find some enterprising company like the People's Theatre, Newcastle, to perform them: his influence seeped into the English theatre in this way and helped to create the climate in which a whole crop of later plays in musical/balletic mode could flourish. Some of them, like *Oh What a Lovely War* (1965), followed very closely his method of

---

[1] *The Flying Wasp* (1934) was the title O'Casey gave to his collection of essays on the English Theatre and its critics: it included stinging attacks on Agate.

[2] Letter to *The Sunday Times*, 18 February 1934. Reprinted in *The Letters of Sean O'Casey, 1910–1941*, ed. D. Krause (1975), pp. 499–502.

[3] Interview in *The Sunday Times*, 21 October 1934.

handling disturbing social subjects through popular songs, music-hall routines and other unexpectedly frivolous techniques. John Arden and Peter Nichols are among the many post-war writers who have continued along O'Casey's line. Arden has explicitly acknowledged him as an influence. When asked about the European playwrights who had been important to him, he named first, when he turned to those writing in English, 'The Irish people—Synge, O'Casey, Yeats to an extent'.[4]

O'Casey also stands unmistakably behind Beckett who has paid him the rare tribute of a public expression of admiration and who showed how deep his feeling for O'Casey's farce was in the review he wrote (in 1934) of *The End of the Beginning* and *A Pound on Demand* (I shall say more of this in discussing Beckett).

O'Casey, then, has an important place among the playwrights who fashioned the Irish drama of Europe and it is natural to discuss his plays in that context even though his own European affiliations were very different from theirs. He was indeed alone among them in his indifference to the French theatre and to Maeterlinck. Insofar as there was any direct continental influence on his drama, it came from the German expressionists, especially Toller whom he admired as writer and social crusader: his own experiments in scenic distortions do sometimes call to mind plays like *Masses and Men*. But it seems unlikely that O'Casey could have had more than a very limited sympathy with German expressionism which leans so heavily to the abstract and is not notable for its humour. Probably expressionist techniques came to him more importantly through the plays of the Irish American, Eugene O'Neill; that was an influence he did acknowledge, as when he said in his note on *Within the Gates* that the idea for the front curtain was derived from *Mourning Becomes Electra*.

I suggest, however, that by far the most important single influence on his dramatic technique was that of Yeats. Despite the bitterness O'Casey felt over the rejection of *The Silver Tassie* he never lost his admiration for Yeats the poet: 'Masked pompously he was, in style and manner, but under all was the poet immortal who will be remembered for ever.'[5] The spirit of Yeats, the 'silvery shadow of Ireland', as he

[4] Interview with John Arden in *The Playwrights Speak*, ed. W. Wager (1969), p. 208. O'Casey returned the compliment, for he singled out *Serjeant Musgrave's Dance* (1960) as 'far and away the finest play of the present day' ('The Bald Primaqueera' in *Blasts and Benedictions*, ed. R. Ayling (1967), p. 73).

[5] Sean O'Casey, *Autobiographies* (1963), ii, 232.

called him, haunts O'Casey's *Autobiographies* and other writings.
'You're speaking the solemn truth Mr Yeats; go on, son of my heart,
go on', he will shout delightedly, when he finds Yeats expressing his
own views on theatre, or, 'Come on, Yeats—sing out your song!'
Or he may give Yeats the last word, as when he closed an article he
wrote for the New York production of *Cock-a-Doodle Dandy* with a
quotation from *The Dreaming of the Bones* and thereby acknowledged
obliquely the inspiration Yeats's lyric provided for his own dancing
Cock:

> So, to end this explanation, I leave the play in the hands of actors,
> director, designer, and in yours, dear playgoers, turning my last
> words into a quotation from the poet Yeats:
> 'Lift up the head / And clap the wings / Red Cock, and crow!'
> *(Blasts and Benedictions*, p. 145)

In his own theatrical practice he moved steadily closer to Yeats. From
the solidly 'real' world of the Paycock and Fluther, he turned to a
more ethereal landscape where the feel of ordinary life remains, but
pressure from the interior intermittently breaks up the conventional
shape of reality and imposes more fantastic and revealing patterns.
As he said about *Within the Gates*, these plays are 'written round life
not from outside looking in, but from inside looking out' (*Blasts and
Benedictions*, p. 114). O'Casey was sceptical about the notion of a
'theatre of the inexpressible'. He wrote sardonically (in 1942) about
the 'monastic awe for silence on the stage' and 'the sacred postulate
that the more poignant emotions are too deep for words' (*Blasts and
Benedictions*, p. 18).[6] His characters sometimes seem trapped in their
own marvellous volubility as O'Casey once imagined himself caught
and doomed to listen to his own voice for ever! 'Words for ever
sounding, pounding, expounding, and astounding my poor afflicted
ears'. But increasingly in the plays written after he had left Dublin, he
found himself, like Yeats, exploring regions which did defy expression
in words and his later technique was devised to bring in mysterious
dimensions of reality through a new synthesis of words and music,
dance and visual image. In the so different context of his rich, diffuse
drama, he achieves moments of supernatural intensity which are
strikingly in the Yeatsian spirit. Such is the scene in *Red Roses for Me*

---

[6] It was the strong, silent character of the realistic drama he had in mind:
'Kill him in the plays of Alfred Sutro, and he will appear, strong and silent as
ever, in the plays of John Galsworthy' (*Blasts and Benedictions*, p. 18).

when by a trick of light Ayamonn's head, seemingly separated from his body, gleams in the darkness 'like the severed head of Dunn-Bo', or the final scene of The *Drums of Father Ned* when the spirit of the always invisible Father Ned invades the stage in a distant drum roll (with the kind of precision Yeats applied to scene, O'Casey directed that the drum roll should be 'the kind used by Haydn' in his Symphony No. 103 in E Flat Major).

As W. A. Armstrong has suggested, the full meaning of O'Casey's plays for dancers 'is sometimes to be sought in O'Casey's reactions to Yeatsian ideals'.[7] There can certainly be no doubt that the image of the red cock in *The Dreaming of the Bones*, crowing the daylight in, gets a new lease of life in the fantastic, Dionysiac cock that prances across the stage in *Cock-a-Doodle Dandy* (People's Theatre, Newcastle-on-Tyne, 10 December 1949): a supremely characteristic transference, this, from the delicate Yeatsian mould to O'Casey's bold, comic form.

The closeness between the two playwrights has been obscured by the excessive attention given to the rift that developed between them over Yeats's rejection of *The Silver Tassie*. It was certainly an irony that Yeats should have failed to recognise the importance of the first play in which O'Casey broke totally with the realistic convention of *Juno and the Paycock* (1925) and moved into the more direct and musical mode which he himself had pioneered. But indeed their relationship as playwrights was attended with ironies, for if Yeats could not grasp the value of *The Silver Tassie*, neither did O'Casey at first appreciate Yeats's dance plays, which were later to play a vital part in shaping his own dramatic technique. He saw *At the Hawk's Well* in 1924 in a performance in Yeats's Merrion Square drawing-room and it seemed to him very alien. He was oppressed by the fashionable exclusiveness of the occasion, his feeling that the audience were only there for social reasons, 'because Yeats was Yeats', as he put it. He tried to imagine his own rumbustious character, Fluther, bursting in among the dress suits, looking for someone to fight him: 'Any two o' yous, any three o' yous; your own selection'. But it couldn't be done: Fluther was 'lost to, and separate from, these elegant ones here in Yeats's drawing room'. 'It wasn't even the ghost of the theatre', he said, with perhaps unconscious irony (*Autobiographies*, ii, 233).

It seemed as though the Yeatsian seed had fallen on barren ground, but in fact just the opposite was true, as later events proved and as

[7] 'Sean O'Casey, W. B. Yeats and the Dance of Life' in R. Ayling (ed.), *Modern Judgements* (1969), p. 131.

O'Casey acknowledged himself, both directly and indirectly by allusion and quotation. It would have been surprising had it been otherwise, for O'Casey was ideally formed by temperament and by his early theatre-going experience to respond ardently to Yeats's concept of total theatre. He had been familiar from boyhood with the melo-dramas of Dion Boucicault which used music and song (including the old Irish airs) and spectacular tableaux to work on the audience's feelings and add a richer dimension to the words; the text is often no more than a scenario for what might now be called a 'multi-media show'. There are many passing allusions to Boucicault in O'Casey's writings: he will tell, for instance, of seeing scenes from *Conn the Shaughraun* [*sic*] along with a minstrel show where his brother was playing the bones; or he will speak of the 'folk poetry' in Boucicault's style.

He himself was full of music—the music of the singing voice, that is, for he came late to orchestral and classical music, as he modestly records. Even in his earliest plays, his characters, like himself, took naturally to song, but in the later ones the singing is part of a complex, total theatre technique for varying the mood and hinting the theme. The plays often take their tone from a dominant song and sometimes their titles, as *The Silver Tassie* does, and *Red Roses for Me*. Eileen O'Casey says indeed that the ballad of the silver tassie was the germ of the whole play, and she interestingly describes how O'Casey used to sing when considering ideas for a new play: 'I imagine that by lilting folk-airs he probably got an unconscious rhythm into the whole of his work'.[8]

O'Casey wrote a foreword to a volume of his selected plays in 1954 and by then he had become fully aware how closely he was working in the musical mode of Yeats. He says:

In a number of his plays, Yeats, the poet, brings in music from flute, zither, drum, and gong—elegant sounds, and beautiful too. I, too, have tried to bring in the music of the flute, the fiddle, and the drum; not in the actual instruments, not through them, but by an occasional song, and by the lilt in the dialogue; by weaving into the emotional action of the plays the shrill or plaintive notes of the flute and the reckless rally that the drums of life so often give.

(*Blasts and Benedictions*, p. 86)

He could have made an even fuller acknowledgement, for by this

[8] *Sean* (1971), p. 147.

time all kinds of instruments as well as songs had been heard on O'Casey's stage, from popular favourites of his own—accordion, melodeon, ukelele—to those so much used by Yeats, especially the flute and the drum. The ukelele has an important role in *The Silver Tassie*: a drum beat sounds notes of warning in *Within the Gates*: every act of *Red Roses for Me* (Olympia, Dublin, 15 March 1943) ends with music, and the strains of the melodeon are heard at the tragic close; distant drums and a fife are heard in *Cock-a-Doodle Dandy*, and the accordion is played by the Cock's lusty young Messenger; there is a great medley of instruments in *Purple Dust*, and one of the latest plays of all takes its title from the unseen drums that are heard off-stage throughout.

In his visual sensitivity too O'Casey was well fitted to take over the Yeatsian method. Despite acute eye trouble, he had an intense and very precise visual imagination; like Yeats, he had wanted as a young man to be an artist and his mind was bursting with fantastic pictorial images, which often erupt in his letters as lively sketches. 'I am getting to love the Art of painting more and more', he told Lady Gregory in 1929 (*Letters*, p. 319), and in all his talk and correspondence of later years he increasingly dwells on pictures he admires or owns.

I have suggested that he took over from Boucicault the melodramatic technique of 'transformations' but he applied them in a modern way, for he was as quick as Yeats to see how the strange world of the interior could be expressed through the subtle treatment of stage scene. Yeats's own settings made a great impact on his imagination, to judge from a letter of 1924 to Lady Gregory in which he runs together his thoughts of actual people and Yeats's directions for the scene of *The Shadowy Waters*: 'I have been thinking of Synge, Hugh Lane, Robert Gregory—standing on the galley deck in *The Shadowy Waters*, 'blue and dim, with sails and dresses of green and ornaments of copper' (*Letters*, p. 119).

Along with Yeats, O'Casey was one of the first to recognise the genius of Gordon Craig. Craig's passion for light in the theatre must have had a special appeal, for in his later plays light is one of his chief means of creating stage images of the mind's fantasies. O'Casey's colours, in tune with his bold comic imagination, are more consistently astringent and strident than Yeats's: brilliant yellows, greens and reds mix and clash with blacks and purples, and they are always symbolic, sometimes crudely, as in *The Star Turns Red* (Unity, 12 March 1940), more often subtly and suggestively as in *Within the Gates,* where, as he explained to George Jean Nathan, he had 'tried to give a symbolism' in the seasonal colouring of the four scenes (*Letters,* p. 775). He was at home with popular forms—ballad singing, folk dance, melodrama, music hall—and was as clear as Yeats or Arthur Symons that the theatrical vocabulary of the future should be based on them: indeed he continually reaffirmed Symons' doctrine of the popular arts in his own more vehement style:

> What these Literary & Art controlling posers want is to be chained together & made to look at Punch & Judy Shows, visit Circuses, stare at Revues, & do years of hard labour dancing Jazz. Then there might possibly be a glimpse of God for them.
>
> (*Letters,* p. 373)

In ways they could hardly have envisaged he fulfilled many of the prophecies of the symbolists. Their favourite image, the mirror, becomes in his hands a comic distorting glass, for life, he once said, would crack any ordinary mirror from top to bottom 'as reality cracked the mirror of the Lady of Shalott'. His mirror was to be a 'huge magnifying glass, showing ourselves as we never saw ourselves before'. In the late plays, as the stage direction explicitly requires in *The Silver Tassie,* the stage was to be 'a little distorted from its original appearance', producing an effect of caricature, but caricature of the kind that is more lifelike than life itself.

He has his own style of mask and marionette. His marionette effects he manages to invest with much comic vitality even when they are being used to indicate a rigid or narrow view of life. This is true, I suppose (though I have not seen the play in performance), of the two Chair Attendants in *Within the Gates,* a Laurel and Hardy pair, one young and thin, one old and stocky, one limping on the right leg, the other on the left; both 'in the last lap of physical decay'. They see themselves as the puppets the symmetrical limping suggests: 'It's our destiny', one of them says, with the defeatism which O'Casey hated, as the threat of unemployment draws nearer.

Masks figure on O'Casey's stage, though he rarely used the full mask, preferring the 'mask-like look' which Yeats reserved for his Musicians. The mask is not, oddly enough, a source of comedy for O'Casey but is associated with the fixity of grief or death: when she loses her son, Dame Hatherleigh's face is 'mask-like in its lines of resignation', and the young singer in *Red Roses for Me* has a face 'pale and mask-like in its expression of resignation to the world and all around him'.

Perhaps the impact made by Yeats on his imagination shows most obviously in O'Casey's adoption of dance as a vital element in his own technique. From *The Silver Tassie* onwards most of the major plays contain a dance which often has the same function as Yeats's dances, namely to reveal the psychic forces at work behind the forms of the external world. In two of the plays, *Oak Leaves and Lavender* (Lyric, 13 May 1947) and *Cock-a-Doodle Dandy,* the debt to Yeats is especially clear, for the dancers are supernatural beings, thin ghosts of the past in one, and in the other a fantastic bird, 'the joyful, active spirit of life as it weaves a way through the Irish scene' (*Blasts and Benedictions,* p. 144). The first play which demands to be thought of as a dance play is *Within the Gates* (Royalty, 7 February 1934) with its insistent musicality and its extraordinary climax when the heroine dances herself to death in Hyde Park, urged on by the Nietzschean Dreamer to assert her will against the defeatism of the Down and Outs: 'Sing them silent; dance them still, and laugh them into an open shame!' But even in *The Silver Tassie,* where the mode, except in one act, is more naturalistic, a complex pattern of contrasts between free and fettered movements runs through the whole play and comes to a bitter climax with the boisterous waltz in which all join at the end except the wrecks of the war, the paralysed man who was once a footballer and the blinded man whose function must now be to push the wheelchair of his crippled comrade. In the Royal Shakespeare Company's production of the play in 1969, the departure of the two from the dance of life—blind man pushing paralysed man—was exceptionally moving, its bleak realism modified by the stylisation which suggested they might, like Yeats's Lame and Blind Beggars, patch up a whole life by complementing each other's deficiencies.

It was bitter for O'Casey when the Abbey refused *The Silver Tassie,* but it looked at first as though the move to London would profit him as a playwright (as it certainly profited the English theatre). In the light of his plays' later history, however, it is clear that the omens attending the first production of *The Silver Tassie* (Apollo, 11 October 1929) were misleadingly auspicious. He came into a theatre dominated by realism except in the sphere of light entertainment and rigidly compartmentalised—one set of responses for musical comedy, quite another for 'straight' drama. O'Casey was a heretic intent on ignoring

boundaries and on correcting the deficiencies of the genteel and con-
formist theatre he saw in 1929: 'Not a stone flung through any amiable
window of thought'. He was ready now, as he told Eileen O'Casey at
that time, to 'break from his present style of writing and try one that
would employ music as well as words'.[9] And musical comedy was the
one thing on the English stage that impressed him; of all he saw when
he first explored the London theatre, he remembered only 'the extraordinary beautiful slide and slip, shimmering with colour', of the
chorus in *Rose Marie* (*Autobiographies*, ii, 261).

He had an outstanding piece of luck at the start of his audacious,
one-man campaign for a theatre of all the arts when he attracted the
interest of that remarkable impresario, C. B. Cochran. He was
another heretic for whom 'entertainment' meant anything from
Shakespeare to prize fights; so A. P. Herbert observed in verses
celebrating his fifty years in the theatre:

> Reinhardt and Hackenschmidt were one to you;
> Carpentier, Bernhardt, Duse did your will;
> Helen of Troy and Jessie of Revue,
> Barrie and Pirandello filled a bill.[10]

Here was an eclecticism exactly to O'Casey's taste: he told Lady
Gregory in 1928 (*Letters*, p. 320), when plans for the production were
just beginning, how impressed he was by Cochran's knowledge of art
and drama as well as of the world of light entertainment: 'He has
produced himself a scene called "Dance, Little Lady, Dance" in his
latest Revue, which is a marvel of Expressionism. And he has some
lovely pictures by Cezanne, Renoir, V. Gogh, Degas & John.'

Cochran backed *The Silver Tassie*, and Shaw wrote to him after
seeing the production: 'The Highbrows *should* have produced it; you,
the Unpretentious Showman, DID, as you have done so many other
noble and rash things on your Sundays'.[11] The praise was justified,
for Cochran brought together in the Apollo production some brilliant
and unusual talent; Augustus John designed the set for the Great War
scene in the second act and Martin Shaw 'conducted' the chanting into
which the dialogue of the soldiers continually ran. Though few people
at the time perceived it (Shaw being a notable exception), O'Casey

[9] *Sean*, p. 68.
[10] 'Fifty Years'. Verses from *Punch* reprinted as an epigraph to C. B. Cochran,
Cock-a-Doodle-Doo, 1941.
[11] Letter of 23 November 1929 in S. Heppner, '*Cockie*', 1969, p. 158.

employed his new technique throughout the action. Dance, movement, tableau and music convey, often with painfully incongruous 'lightness', the horror of the war; the play ends when Harry no longer tries to 'sing his song' and the pathetic tinkle of his ukelele is overwhelmed by the boisterous strains of 'Over the Waves', leaving Mrs Moran to make her sublimely inadequate comment: 'It's a terrible pity Harry was too weak to stay an' sing his song, for there's nothing I love more than the ukelele's tinkle, tinkle in the night-time'.

But it was in the second act that the revolutionary nature of O'Casey's new technique was made manifest. When the curtain went up, the first audience saw a great and terrible picture called, to borrow a phrase from the stage directions, 'In the war zone'. Before a word was spoken, they were being given the play's subject, the war, and O'Casey's sad, angry, compassionate comment upon it. Augustus John's set was cumbersome, Eileen O'Casey says, but overpowering as a realisation of O'Casey's vision of war. In the wrecked landscape, littered with shell holes, heaps of rubbish, and all the paraphernalia of war, including the gun to which a soldier is tied as a punishment, there stand out with symbolic force from the monastery ruins, two objects; the white faced, black robed Virgin in the stained glass window, lit from within so as to be: 'vividly apparent', and a life-size crucifix, so battered by shells that the Christ leans forward 'with the released arm outstretched towards the figure of the Virgin'. And at the centre of the composition where the span of the monastery arch should be, there is instead the howitzer with its 'long, sinister barrel', to which the soldiers pray at the end of the act before going into battle; by then it has become the mightiest object on the stage.

The visionary impression created by the scene is reinforced by the musical treatment of the dialogue; there are continuous modulations from speech to song and passages of biblical intoning from a shell-shocked soldier; the delivery of the poignant songs of the First World War is dream-like. 'Most of the second Act is sung', O'Casey told Lady Gregory. Martin Shaw who conducted this near-recitative used Gregorian chant which rose to a sombre climax in the blasphemous litany to the gun: 'We believe in God and we believe in thee'.

The final moment when the soldiers move into battle gains unusual power from O'Casey's totally unexpected use of silence: the outbreak of violence is suggested by lighting in a way that Craig would surely have approved. The scene darkens and intermittent light represents the firing of the gun: 'Only flashes are seen; no noise is heard'. In the

Royal Shakespeare Company's production of the play in 1969 the rhythmically mechanical movements of the soldiers in the deadly silence gave an impression of nightmarish automation more dreadful, it seemed, than any noisy outburst of realistic gunfire could have been.

Even those who were bewildered by the first production of *The Silver Tassie* were impressed by its theatrical originality, especially perhaps by its visual effects. Looking back in 1945, C. B. Cochran said it was 'without exception the finest symbolic scene I can recall on the London stage'.[12] It was unfortunate for O'Casey that John did not go forward with him, nor indeed did Cochran. O'Casey had to find other backers and designers and never again enjoyed such a triumphant stage realisation of his vision.[13] But that did not deter him from his experiment in total theatre: he continued to compose stage pictures, as he composed music and dances, for a theatre that could not yet come into being.

The next play, *Within the Gates*, needed equally dynamic direction but did not receive it: according to O'Casey, it was 'hearsed within an atrocious production' when first given in London. Heavy demands were certainly made on the inventiveness of the director and the skill of the performers by this piece in which a huge and daunting topic, the Depression, was handled in terms of dance, song, and farcical exaggerations. O'Casey originally envisaged it as a film (first called *The Green Gates*) and traces of that approach show in such suggestions to the stage producer as, 'Picture: the Guardsmen, one at each side, looking over the bushes. On Rostrum, first the Dreamer, then the Bishop. . .' (*Letters*, p. 489). Everything the audience saw was to suggest the cyclical nature of life: he tried 'to knit the wild themes and wandering dialogue into a design of Morning, Noon, Evening, and Night, blending these in with the seasons, changing the outlook of the scenes by changing the colour of flower and tree, blending these again with the moods of the scenes' (*Autobiographies*, ii, 352). This would be much to ask of the scene designer even now; it was far beyond reach in O'Casey's theatre, as it turned out.

So too with the music. O'Casey himself felt later on that the musical structure was rather too intricate and especially that there was too

[12] *Showman Looks On* (1945), p. 226.

[13] In the last volume of his autobiography, he complained about the productions of his plays: 'Apart from the Irish Players in their heyday, and the production of *The Silver Tassie*, all were bad, a few worse than others, and one worst of all.' *Autobiographies*, ii, 655.

much singing. For anyone reading the play, certain musical motifs emerge boldly and could easily be imagined as theatrically effective. There is the slow beat of the muffled drum which announces the approach of the Down and Outs singing their desolate signature tune, 'We've but a sigh for a song, and a deep sigh for a drum-beat!' and, in conflict with that funereal sound, the dance music which calls the characters to life. Elsewhere the musical effects do sometimes seem over-complicated and were apparently found so at the time of the first production. O'Casey himself was unhappy with Herbert Hughes's elaborate arrangements of the simple airs he had planned: they did not make singing easier for actors who were in any case unused to making the rapid transitions from speech to song that were required. By this time, in fact, his aspirations and problems were coming closely to resemble those of Yeats; he had to find composers who could marry words and music, and actors who could sing. Should he make it easier for the actors in *Within the Gates* by introducing an instrumental accompaniment, he asked Cochran, adding: 'I have no fear of characters breaking into song, accompanied with music, during the performance of the play;—in fact, I think there should be more of it in the newer drama' (*Letters*, p. 461). Cochran drily pointed out that it was hard enough to find a good actress without expecting her to sing as well.

In *Within the Gates* O'Casey made an ambitious attempt to use dance in a more complex way, relating it both to the external world of Hyde Park and the Depression, and to the inner world of the characters' dreams and visions. The first time the Young Woman dances the emphasis is social: she is the 'innocent prostitute' defying the public forces of defeatism which are the target of O'Casey's satire in the play. The defeatists range from the Atheist and the Bishop's Sister—in different ways both afraid of life—to the chorus of Down and Outs who represent the defeated unemployed. Saros Cowasjee has suggested that the germ of the play is contained in Toller's poem about the power of dance—'Only in dance do you break your fetters, / Only in dance do you shout with the stars'.[14] But O'Casey's intention is more complex, for the chief conflict of the play is a private one, fought between the Dreamer and the Bishop for the soul of the Young Woman. There is no obvious right and wrong here. O'Casey saw the Bishop as 'good-natured, well-intentioned, religious and sincere' but nevertheless one whom life had passed by. He can help the Young Woman only

[14] *Sean O'Casey* (1963), p. 146.

at the moment of death, with encouraging talk of Christ and the immortal life of the soul. The Dreamer is the man for the *present*; a Nietzschean character, 'symbol of a noble restlessness and discontent . . . of ruthlessness to get near to the things that matter'. He too is lacking in full sympathy; all he can do for the Young Woman is urge her not to give in to the pressures of society but dance while she can and live from one crowded hour of glorious life to the next. The Young Woman's dancing is an embodiment of the Dreamer's creed, and O'Casey indicates the creed's inadequacy by making her first dance bitter and unhappy. She taunts the Bishop—'Faith in God, old purple buttons, faith in God! Be merry, man, for a minute. . .'—and dances to the tune of 'Little Brown Jug', accompanied by the two crippled Chair Attendants. That servile and unctuous pair are deeply unsympathetic characters; their grotesque accompaniment—'Sling aht woe, 'ug joy instead, / For we will be a long time dead!'—undermines the value of the dance and emphasises its sense of feverish insecurity.

With the second dance the emphasis tilts towards private, inner experience. The Young Woman, dying of consumption, does as she has sworn she would, dance to the end: 'I'll go the last few steps of the way rejoicing; I'll go, go game, and I'll die dancing!' It is still a gesture against demoralising social pessimism, but more important now, it represents an affirmation of spiritual vitality in the girl herself. Now she dances to the song of the Dreamer, as if a deeper vision were being projected in the dance—perhaps that part of his vision which she accepts, as she also accepts part of the Bishop's. We are to perceive some subtle movement of mind here, so O'Casey indicates in his stage direction: the music she dances to is faint 'as if the tune was heard only in the minds of the Dreamer and the Young Woman'.

This faint music of the interior is heard increasingly in the later plays. I will conclude with a few illustrations of how O'Casey adapts the Yeatsian total theatre technique to the transformations of reality which are his special interest—those changes that come about in solid 'real' materials as the mind shapes them to its individual purposes and communicates them to other minds. The fantasies of the 'multiple mind' (to use his own phrase) are something he excels in depicting, though in the latest plays he finds increasingly subtle means of modulating from the communal to the private vision.

Red Roses for Me (Olympia, Dublin, 15 March 1943) shows him taking over an old, popular form—in this case the spectacular transformation scene of pantomime and melodrama—and making it, in Yeats's phrase, 'subtle and modern'. In the third act the idealistic hero, Ayamonn, on the eve of the workers' strike which he is leading, is confronted with a group of the Dublin poor, women flower sellers and unemployed men, dispiritedly lounging on a bridge over the Liffey. The stage direction tells us that the place is known as the Bridge of Vision, and this is the clue to the experience O'Casey aims to involve us in. First he constructs an elaborately coloured picture as a stage image of the 'multiple mind'. Dull and dark colours predominate, brown parapets, black dresses, drab-coloured baskets and the black figure of Nelson on his red pillar. A touch of contrast comes into the picture when the Rector and the Inspector pass by, the one with a green scarf enlivening his professional black and the other brilliant in blue and silver uniform; the colours are taken up into the metamorphosis which Ayamonn's vision brings about. First the atmosphere is insidiously changed by music; the old man, Brennan, sings to his melodeon in a husky baritone, the mood becomes more emotional and Ayamonn is inspired to declare his prophetic message; 'We will that all of us shall live a greater life'. The glowing words cause the stage scene literally to glow. The materials remain the same but under the play of coloured light they show their hidden aspect; it is a group of living statues we see now in sumptuous colours, green, bronze and silver. 'Something funny musta happened', says one of the loungers, 'for, 'clare to God, I never noticed her shinin' that way before'. We may laugh, but we are meant to be feeling something of the awe that spreads among the people as they see themselves in a new light, feel a new dignity: 'Our city's in th' grip o' God'.

It is only this one scene which moves away from the rational, realistic convention, and the break is not total, for the transformation can easily enough be accounted for; the sun has emerged from behind the clouds. But what we actually see when the change begins is something more mysterious than that. The stage is cast into darkness so that only certain objects stand out in startling perspective, and then, most strangely, Ayamonn's head appears 'set in a streak of sunlight, looking like the severed head of Dunn-Bo speaking out of the darkness'. The Yeatsian image of the severed head has been re-created in a context that is more external and worldly and yet manages to suggest the remoteness and strangeness of the interior, for an unearthly quality comes in when Ayamonn and the youngest flower seller dance a gavotte to music from an unknown source, a flute mysteriously played 'by someone, somewhere'. As they move round the stage to the pure flute notes, she in a golden pool of light, he in a violet-coloured shadow, the daylight world recedes and we do seem to be looking into a deep of the mind, where the transforming vision originated.

That ethereal music is not heard in *Purple Dust* (People's Theatre, Newcastle-on-Tyne, 16 December 1943), the play from which my next illustration comes. The sounds are more robust here, in tune with the general boisterousness of this satire on the two English business men who take over a Tudor mansion in the West of Ireland to indulge their pastoral fantasy. The play shows O'Casey's skill in adapting the technique derived from Yeats to a more extrovert and comically satirical drama: it also shows how visionary 'moments' could still be achieved, even in so farcical a context.

Music and dance make a second language in *Purple Dust*: the conflict between the Englishmen and the Irish workmen who resent their attempts to settle in the ancient Irish house, is fought out very largely in musical terms. The note is struck at the start, when Stoke and Poges come dancing on with their Irish mistresses, all dressed in smocks decorated with stylised animals, carrying dainty rakes and hoes garlanded with ribbons and singing a ludicrous pastoral number: 'Rural scenes are now our joy: / Farmer's boy, / Milkmaid coy, / Each like a newly-painted toy, / In the bosky countrie!' It is an absurdly self-conscious imitation of the unselfconscious absurdities of Christmas pantomime and of musical comedies like *The Arcadians* with their prettily dressed 'rustic' choruses. That takes it a very long way from the prototype folk play from which all these rituals ultimately derive:[15] the point is not an academic one for it is the Englishmen's affected cultivation of old traditions that especially enrages the Irishmen. They fight back with genuine folk song and dance, as when, in contrast to the musical comedy 'country dance', a true Irish reel is introduced; the leading spirit among the Irish workmen, O'Killigain, encourages Stoke's young Irish mistress to abandon herself in the dance to an air lilted by the workmen standing round; the reel becomes a wild ritual, ending with lines which might have come straight out of *The Cat and the Moon*. 'Bow to your partner', says O'Killigain, and when she does so, 'Bow, bow to the bards'. The ritual is destroyed at that point, for

[15] I am indebted to Pauline Smith of the University of Sheffield for the information that folk plays have been recorded in which smocks decorated with animals are worn and garlanded hoes and rakes used.

he takes the opportunity to give her 'a sharp skelp on the behind'; it is a no-nonsense start to a love affair that in the end takes her from her English lover. The Englishmen are defeated, one might say, by Irish airs. O'Killigain captures Avril's imagination with the lilting strains of songs like 'Rory O'More' which represent, as they are presented in the play, the life of true feeling. Stoke and Poges cannot compete, since they find it so hard to distinguish the true from the imitation.

Scenic, musical and sound effects combine to express the absurdity of their pastoral dream. A fantastic soundscape develops, with rural noises coming in on cue with exaggerated insistence. The cock crows, the cuckoo responds and the sequence works up to a surrealistic symphony of birds shrilling, dogs barking, cattle lowing, sheep bleating, pigs grunting and hens cackling. 'Damn that cock and cuckoo!' says Poges, giving the game away completely.

The tone is light-hearted, but serious notes sound increasingly in the last act when the house is threatened by flood waters from the rising river. Astonishingly late in so farcical a context, O'Casey then contrives a 'moment' of supernatural intensity (whether it could work as he intended is very much a question for the stage designer, as so often in these late plays). A Figure suddenly appears, dressed from head to foot in black oilskins; he has come to warn them that the river has broken its banks, so there is a rational explanation for his presence, but O'Casey's stage direction makes it impossible to take him so prosaically. The scene was to be spectral, an effect he aimed at by darkening the stage and having one flickering light focused on the 'gleaming' black oilskins and on the blue mask which is all there is for a face. The Figure, he says, should seem 'like the spirit of the turbulent waters of the rising river'. It is also as if some inkling of the truth of things had risen up at last in the mind of the more sensitive Englishman, for as the waters tumble into the room and the refrain of the departing Irish, 'Far away O!' recedes, Poges is left in totally changed mood, brooding: 'My comfort's gone, and my house of pride is straining towards a fall'.

The strange apparition provides a Yeatsian moment, highlighted, unusually for O'Casey, by the use of a full mask. Yeatsian echoes are stronger still in *Oak Leaves and Lavender*, a play which was in part at least a tribute to England at a time of peril in the Second World War; although it has its share of farce and exaggeration (some striking scenic distortions are called for), the sense of historical actuality is much stronger than in *Purple Dust*.

Yet it is in this more time-bound war play that O'Casey takes a further step into the timeless zone of the interior and comes closer than ever to Yeats in doing so. The topical, 'real-life' action is entirely enclosed in a ghostly framework. Lighting, music and movement combine to convey a twilight effect closer to the dreamy monotones of the Yeatsian, or even the Maeterlinckian interior style than any one could have imagined O'Casey capable of in the days of *Juno and the Paycock*. In a misty light figures in powdered wigs and 'mistily' grey eighteenth-century costumes dance to the faint strains of a minuet into the room where the whole scene is set. All their movements are slow and stiff as if in a dream where it is hard to move at all; the piano accompaniment too is slow and 'somewhat staccato, as if the player found it hard to press down the notes': when the dancers speak, their voices are faint and uninflected. Everything is muted and attenuated except for the brilliant colouring and clear bell-like voice of the mysterious being who presides over the dance, the Young Son of Time. He seems a force outside the history in which the modern characters (and perhaps the dancers) are trapped.

A curious impression develops of many possible dimensions of existence. One of the dancers speaks of 'the deep silences of where we always are', yet there they are in the room, moving, talking and some-how able to sense the terrible events approaching the modern characters who live there. A sound is heard from the street outside, the tender and musical cry of a girl selling lavender. Where does it originate? We can have no idea: it is not a cry of the 'present' time and yet to the dancers of the time gone by it seems equally strange and unfamiliar; 'from another world', one of them says. We are forced to wonder whether it comes from some region beyond the veil which we are permitted dimly to perceive at the beginning and end of the 'real' action.

None of the flesh and blood stage characters perceives the dancers until the final scene when the house has become a factory and its owner, Dame Hatherleigh, has lost her son in the war. Then the bereaved mother, in the sensitivity of her grief, apprehends the presences around her. The stage returns to its misty grey, and the dancers are revealed, grouped in the pattern of the dance as though they had been there all the time. Only the Young Son of Time is missing: Dame Hatherleigh stands where he did, wearing the black and silver (though not the youthful green) of his costume; as if she had been drawn into a space he was keeping for her. In this time of death she seems to become more aware of life. A dancer dwells fearfully on 'the wistful look of eternal life' and Dame Hatherleigh reflects aloud, as if answering her: 'Only the rottenness and ruin must die. Great things we did and said; things graceful, and things that had a charm, live on to dance before the eyes of men admiring'.

She is almost one of the grey figures now: her voice is 'toneless' and she senses that 'the dancers are very close', though she is still on this side of the threshold. At the end, when she sinks down by the clock as if taking leave of time, she calls, 'Wait a moment for me, friends, for I am one of you, and will join you when I find my son'. Her voice becomes 'a little more wakeful' at this point, an ambiguous stage direction which suggests that the dance may not be a dream but a glimpse into some larger reality to which we are not normally awake. The stage scene affirms this view, for as she falls silent, it comes back to its ghostly life. The dancers move once more through the minuet, the music becoming fuller when they curtsey to one another, and the Lavender Seller's voice is heard musically extolling the sweetness of lavender from a dimension which can never be identified.

This is Yeatsian territory indeed, as O'Casey seems to be reminding us through an important detail of his dance. Like the unhappy pair in *The Dreaming of the Bones*, these dancers, though always together, can never touch each other. For those who know Yeats's play, the echo brings out the greater optimism in O'Casey's view of life in time. For though the dancers' faintness and stiffness suggest a running down (in historical terms, England losing contact with her past greatness), there is communion and continuity too; the graceful dance, with its 'fair deeds' endures and can still be appreciated by the dancers' descendants. 'Fear not, sweet lady', says one of the Gentleman Dancers, 'Our hands still mingle, though they do not touch. Fear not, sweet lass, for shadows are immortal.'

Finally, *Cock-a-Doodle Dandy* (People's Theatre, Newcastle-on-Tyne, 10 December 1949). This was O'Casey's favourite among his own plays and of them all it shows most clearly the impact made by Yeats's dance plays on his imagination.

It is the closest to being an out and out dance play itself, for it is dominated by a dancer, the Cock in his brilliant colours of black, yellow and green, with his crimson crest and flaps and his 'look of a cynical jester'. He starts the action off by dancing round the stage house to the tune of an off-stage accordion, and whenever he appears or his cheeky crow is heard, cracks open up in the façade presented to the world by the respectable bourgeoisie of Nyadnanave, the parish under the puritanical rule of Father Domineer.

For much of the time the stage is the Cock's domain and under his aegis the characters are mesmerised into revealing their minds, both the prudish distortions of view forced on them by their clerical mentor and also their hidden affinities with the Dionysiac visitant. The Cock is a jester, as O'Casey says, who performs practical jokes like a comic turn from a Crazy Show. He tricks them into confusing him with their sacred icon, the 'silken glossified tall-hat' which is bandied about, shot at and battered until every scrap of dignity has been removed from it. This comic craziness, however, highlights a more serious kind. Life at Nyadnanave is dark where it need not be: a shadow is cast by the illusions which encourage the incurably ill girl to go uselessly to Lourdes and the priest to exert such tyranny; he causes a man's death and the final rejection of home and family by the young woman whom he tries to bully into conforming to his 'crazy' sexual creed. In this darker sphere, the actor—or perhaps it should be dancer—playing the Cock has to suggest a super-subtle force, terrifyingly demonic to some, sympathetic and suggestive to others. He can be led on by the young Messenger on the end of a ribbon, perfectly docile and friendly: 'Just a gay bird, that's all. A bit unruly at times, but conthrollable be th' right persons . . .'. He can also be uncontrollable, able at will, it seems, to summon up thunder and lightning and to release Father Domineer's parishioners from their inhibitions with a suddenness and violence which is comical but should also seem truly disturbing.

The 'interior' effect is not limited to a single moment in this play. The characters struggle to maintain an impervious façade, but under the power of the Cock it is peppered with shots that open up startling views into the haunted abysses of their minds. Scene and sound take on the shapes of their fantasies: Michael has only to imagine his young wife's secret longings and the stage makes them real:

MICHAEL   Up there in that room (*he points to the window above the porch*) she often dances be herself, but dancin' in her mind with hefty lads, plum'd with youth, an' spurred with looser thoughts of love. (*As he speaks, the sounds of a gentle waltz are heard, played by harp, lute or violin, or by all three, the sounds coming, apparently, from the room whose window is above the porch. Bitterly*) There,

d'ye hear that, man! Mockin' me. She'll hurt her soul,
if she isn't careful.

Under the lustful but timid eye of Michael and Sailor Mahan the pretty
girls sprout horns, the whisky bottle glows a devilish red and the top
hat becomes a focal point of wild confusion.

The fantasies explode in a physical outburst which is the most
Dionysiac of all O'Casey's dances. It is unsentimental, in fact impersonal (the young women dance frenziedly with older men they
have no real affection for) and aggressively sexual—the cock-like
crest in the girl's hat rises higher as she dances. The dancing has a
manic quality: it should not be possible to dismiss as simply absurd
Father Domineer's rage when he interrupts them, shouting: 'Stop that
devil's dance! . . . Th' empire of Satan's pushin' out its foundations
everywhere, an' I find yous dancin', *ubique ululanti cockalorum ochone,
ululo!*' We should feel the power of the dance to do just what the
priest suspects it will, destroy the desire for prayer or for work,
weaken clerical authority, create a revolution.

The Cock who inspires such dances should have acquired by the
end of the play, in his own mischievous style, something of the
numinous quality of Yeats's Hawk Woman. Like her, he is dumb except
for his bird cry, like her he seduces and terrorises with a dance, like
her he irresistibly opens up the deep interior. There can be no doubt
about the Yeatsian inspiration behind this play. O'Casey himself
makes it very clear by having his Messenger introduce the cock with a
quotation from *The Dreaming of the Bones:*

Go on, comrade, lift up th' head an' clap th' wings, black cock,
an' crow!

By the slight misquotation which inserts the word 'comrade', O'Casey
allies himself with the popular movements in the arts which he saw no
incongruity in crossing with the Yeatsian strain. *Cock-a-Doodle Dandy*,
it seems to me, is a triumphant demonstration of his ability to effect
this new synthesis which has proved so attractive to subsequent
playwrights, notably John Arden. Of course, like all the plays in the
Yeatsian mode which use total theatre techniques to reveal the fantastic
processes of the interior, O'Casey's plays depend to a very great
degree on the ability not just of performers, but of scene designers,
musicians and choreographers and they present difficulties which
Yeats's do not, being on such a big scale and demanding all the

facilities of a proscenium set for the elaborate, artfully lit 'pictures' which are a crucial element in the whole effect. So far he has not had much luck in this country (though in France it is another matter). We cannot really know how these late plays work until we have a chance to see them properly staged: let us hope that in the context of today's theatre there will be new productions sufficiently bold and adventurous to realise the vision which was so far ahead of its time.

Many lines of the European imagination meet in Beckett, but as playwright he is above all the heir of Yeats and the Irish/French drama whose courses I have been tracing. He strides from Dublin into France like the modern man of Synge's imagining whose role it would be to 'take Ireland into Europe'. In himself he seems the epitome of that union. With almost uncanny appropriateness he takes his place among those Irish predecessors who felt so strongly the lure of France, sometimes even to the extent of turning themselves into Frenchmen; Wilde writing *Salomé* in French, bilingual Synge, one foot in Aran, the other in Paris, Yeats so receptive to the flow of experience and ideas from European art and drama. Beckett seems to sum all this up: an Irishman who lives in France, writes with equal facility in French and English, regularly translates himself from one to the other and always keeps in his English an Irish lilt, whether his characters are called Rooney and grope their way down a road near Dublin or Estragon and Vladimir who might be travelling on any road in Europe.

Modernism arrives in the popular theatre with Beckett. 'Popular' may seem an unlikely word, but must be the appropriate one for plays which, for all their strangeness, have become known all over the world, and are continually being revived by the professional as well as the amateur theatre: it was hardly fortuitous that the repertoire of the National Theatre for its opening season in its new South Bank home should include *Happy Days*: Beckett now occupies a position in the English theatre where it is natural to turn to his plays for such great occasions; they have become our 'modern classics'. And yet he has drawn these international audiences for a theatre which is intensely inward, the complete fulfilment of Yeats's idea of a drama of 'most interior being'. Such a drama was confined to corners of Dublin and of London in Yeats's day; it is a measure of Beckett's virtuoso skill and also of his humaneness that he has been able to give it this great extension into the public domain and in doing so change the course of modern theatre, for nothing has been the same since *Waiting for Godot*.

Beckett's theatre has always startled and impressed by its bareness, his 'void' effect, but the final impression the plays leave is not bare but rich; they spark off such a host of associations, images, echoes, it seems

one would never come to the end of them. In the intricate web he
weaves the Irish strands are strong. It would be a futile labour to pull
apart and try to identify the separate threads, but it is possible to
distinguish shades of colour and perhaps in so doing illuminate the
subtle synthesis.

We do not have to strain to catch in Beckett's theatre echoes from
the drama I have been discussing. He himself has drawn attention to
his feeling for his Irish inheritance. He has spoken of the plays he
saw at the Abbey Theatre—'the Yeats *Sophocles*, most of Synge,
O'Casey's three'[1]—and made very clear the value he sets on them.
When asked by Cyril Cusack for a contribution to a centenary
programme on Shaw,[2] he replied:

> I wouldn't suggest that G.B.S. is not a great playwright, whatever
> that is when it's at home. What I would do is give the whole
> unupsettable apple-cart for a sup of the Hawk's Well, or the
> Saints', or a whiff of Juno, to go no further.

The plays themselves tell us of this allegiance. It is easy to hear
behind Hamm's stories or Winnie's romancing the tale-telling of the
Douls, behind the knockabout turn of Hamm and Clov, O'Casey's
sad, sardonic and farcical double acts—the blind and paralysed pair in
The Silver Tassie, the neatly afflicted Chair Attendants in *Within the
Gates*—as behind them those other blind and lame beggars of *The
Cat and the Moon*.

To think of the importance blindness has on Beckett's stage is
inevitably to be reminded of *The Sightless*. There is not a direct
connection here: Beckett is unfamiliar with Maeterlinck's drama, except
for *Pelléas and Mélisande* which he thinks of as a work totally new in
its time. But their plays do show some curious affinities, enough to
suggest that Beckett may have absorbed something of the Maeterlinck
spirit through the theatre into which it was so widely diffused. At
times he might even seem to be caricaturing it, in the silent frustrations
of the mime plays, *Act Without Words* 1 and 2 (1958 and 1960), for
instance, or in *Breath* (1972) where we see a rubbish heap, hear a cry
and a drawing in of breath accompanied by an increase of light, then

---

[1] Letter to J. Knowlson, 17 December 1970, in *Samuel Beckett: an Exhibition
held at Reading University Library May to July 1971*, catalogue by J. Knowlson
(1971).

[2] In Shaw Centenary programme, Gaiety Theatre, Dublin, 1956. Quoted in
Beckett Exhibition catalogue, op. cit., p. 23.

an exhalation of breath and decrease of light; finally a cry which suggests that the cycle is about to begin again. A mocking, microscopic version of a world such as Maeterlinck imagined, where 'the problem of existence is answered only by the enigma of annihilation'.

It is only in the dumb plays that Beckett comes quite so close to writing allegory in the grim vein of *The Sightless*. Humour usually prevents it elsewhere, though the other plays have moments which hint at similar preoccupations. One characteristic he and Maeterlinck share is a habit of focusing intensely on some small, cryptic fact, often to do with colour; Hamm's 'nearly white' toy dog, Krapp's 'black, hard, solid rubber ball', the blue line which the blind man in *The Sightless* speaks of seeing under his eyelids when the sun shines. The suggestion of some underlying metaphysical pattern in these and other odd little details has attracted a similar kind of exegesis to the two oeuvres. History amusingly repeated itself, indeed, when the dog in *Endgame* (1958) was seized on by commentators as an anagram for God, for just so had the dog in *The Sightless* been taken—and then too the critic had needed to be reminded that the anagram did not work in the original French!

These are likenesses on the fringe, but the affinity between the playwrights can be felt at the very heart of their drama, above all in the audacious attacks they make on the central mysteries. Their characters are always on the extreme edge of things, 'hemmed in', as one of Maeterlinck's blind says of the vast invisible sea that lies around those lost ones. Beckett goes very far into the region imagined by Maeterlinck in *The Blue Bird* as the 'land of the unborn'. He claims, as we know, to have a painfully real memory of life before birth.[3] And certainly he captures for the theatre remarkable impressions of such a limbo—a waiting-place between modes of being, where, as in *Endgame*, death comes so alive that it is next door to birth. The old progenitors fade out in the dustbins, but a child waits outside to get into the room and the relationship of Hamm and Clov has not ended but only taken an ambiguous new turn when Clov positions himself by the narrow door, jauntily dressed for the outdoors.

Unsettling intuitions of some other order of existence are experienced in this limbo and often take the Maeterlinckian form of half memories or a haunting sense of *déjà vu*. A large part of the experience of

[3] 'I have a clear memory of my own fetal existence. It was an existence where no voice, no possible movement could free me from the agony and darkness I was subjected to.' Interview with John Gruen, *Vogue* (London), February 1970.

Estragon and Vladimir cannot be brought over the threshold of consciousness. Vladimir questions Estragon anxiously and lovingly about his nightly misery—'Who beat you? Tell me.'—and like Mélisande shrinking from Golaud's so similar questioning—'Who was it that hurt you?'—Estragon can only turn away with an evasive 'Another day done with'. The line between memory and dream is blurred. 'You dreamt it', says Estragon of Vladimir's 'yesterday' which for the audience is still to come, the moment when they nearly hang themselves from the tree.

Of course in Beckett's world we are able to laugh at these lapses and assertions of memory ('What *is* that unforgettable line?', says Winnie), as at everything else, including the eccentricities of his afflicted characters. Blindness, for instance, is almost as prominent on his stage as on Maeterlinck's and carries many similar associations with perception and insight: Hamm and Pozzo when blind strike vatic notes and indulge in apocalyptic brooding, like the statuesque figures in *The Sightless*. But Beckett's wise-cracking pair are not statuesque: their thorough immersion in the comic element prevents us from taking them too seriously as Tiresias figures, much though they might like us to. They are not allowed to stand on their dignity or make too sustained a bid for pathos. In place of the blind people solemnly feeling for each other's cold hands to locate themselves, comes Hamm feeling his way into the dead centre of his room with much incidental clowning and irritating Clov with his pernickety 'I feel a little too far'. The absurd pomposity of Pozzo invites laughter even after he has been stricken blind and acquired some new insights. 'The blind have no notion of time. The things of time are hidden from them too', he says, and we listen seriously, but Vladimir still comes in to undercut him with 'Well just fancy that! I could have sworn it was just the opposite'. Krapp is, of all Beckett's characters, the nearest to the Maeterlinckian prototype, the old man sitting motionless in the lamplight who has to interest us simply by being himself. He has some of that pathos, but he is a clown too, slipping regularly on banana skins and sharing bad jokes with the earlier selves on the tapes.

And yet in the end, of course, this nearly blind character 'sees'— brings his life into a new perspective where the value of love is recognised for the first time. Laughter does not preclude vision on Beckett's stage; on the contrary, the wittiest characters often experience the most profound revelations. One such that they share with Maeterlinck is the intuition that an invisible eye is upon them. At such moments they approach very close to the Old Man in *Interior* who reflects 'We too are watched', and compares human feeling with the indifference of the universe: 'We have pity but no one has pity on us!' So Vladimir looks at the sleeping Estragon and broods:

> At me too someone is looking, of me too someone is saying, he is sleeping, he knows nothing, let him sleep on.

Beckett's characters, of course, separate themselves decisively from Maeterlinck's by their self-conscious theatricality. Clov turns his telescope on the audience and Winnie seems to recognise that she might be on a stage when she expresses her anxious sense of being overlooked:

> WINNIE Strange feeling that someone is looking at me. I am clear, then dim, then gone, then dim again, then clear again, and so on, back and forth, in and out of someone's eye.

Still, like Maeterlinck's Old Man, she is only half conscious that her audience is really there in the flesh. It is an invisible eye she conjures up with something of the supernatural quality of the 'eye' that threatens Maeterlinck's characters; like the deadly red eye gleaming from the Queen's tower in *The Death of Tintagiles*.

It is clear that Beckett has provided the most complete answer to Maeterlinck's question, 'Is a static theatre possible?' With a panache which seems almost like saying 'Look, no hands', he devises endlessly ingenious ways of immobilising his characters and depriving them of sensory variety in order to concentrate on the fine shades of their inner life. The methods of total theatre are indispensable to the technique: Beckett is at home with this paradox, and here again he writes out of the centre of the theatrical tradition that first flowered with Maeterlinck. He has some similar tastes in painting and music; a Netherlands painter, Bram van Velde, ranks high among his favourite artists; his sense that van Velde's 'art of poverty' was the only one for our time[4] is closely akin to Maeterlinck's conviction that drama should concern itself with 'the treasure of the humble'. Beckett composes his stage scene in a way that recalls the Belgian symbolists praised by Maeterlinck for their quietude, their ability to enhance our consciousness of life by placing on their canvas such simple details as 'an open

---

[4] See the passage on 'the ultimate penury' in 'Bram Van Velde', *Proust and Three Dialogues* (1965), p. 122.

door at the end of a passage, a face or hand at rest'. His canvases are mostly in shades of grey, white and black; the notable absence of vivid, 'external' colours perhaps reflects what is said to be a common experience, the dreaming mind's lack of colour sense. It brings to mind an early critic's remark that Maeterlinck's preference for moonlight and shadows, cold blues and greens produced the effect of a 'curious subconsciousness rather than full, everyday consciousness'.[5] It is common for audiences to be uneasily affected by the ubiquitous greyness of the closed room in *Endgame*: so too, one would guess, by the sealed-in grey look of the room in *Ghost Trio*: though both door and window can be opened in that play, what is seen outside is still grey, a shadowy corridor and driving rain. The deprivation, however, is one which stimulates the inner eye. Little ordinary things acquire enormous significance: a tree stands for the whole of nature in *Waiting for Godot* (proving nature most unnatural!): the kitchen door in *Endgame* becomes an obsessive focal point for the audience, an opening to the unknown; Clov's difficulty in leaving the room through that aperture is of the same order as the fearsome effort called for in *Pelléas and Mélisande* to open the castle door and let the day begin. And the simple act of opening door and window in *Ghost Trio* creates a shock effect of astonishing power.

Like a painter too, Beckett expresses himself through spatial arrangements, drawing suggestive, often deeply troubling effects from unexpected or asymmetrical relationships; the unnaturally high windows in *Endgame,* the awkward posing of Mouth and Auditor in *Not I* (1973) which forces us into her position of dissociation. In the two television plays, *Ghost Trio* and . . . *but the clouds* (both 1977), the figure of the actor moved silently and ritualistically within an austerely defined space like an element in a picture come to life; in the latter piece an enigmatic figure-grouping like an art object became a point of reference which one had to try to 'read' as if it were some cryptic composition of Bosch or Francis Bacon.

The lack of bold colour on Beckett's stage and screen is more than compensated for by his ingenious and subtle use of light. Here again he is very much in tune with Maeterlinck, whose world is dominated by imagery of light and darkness. Beckett has become increasingly bold in his free play with darkness, 'wasting' vast areas of the stage in order to emphasise an illuminated area; Krapp at his table under the single light, the characters in the urns forced into view by the spotlight,

[5] M. Clark, *Maurice Maeterlinck* (1915), p. 240.

the composite shade in *Footfalls* (1976) trembling in and out of the dark, the ring of light in . . . *but the clouds* which the actor must move through in order to reach his sanctum of the dark where a much-desired face appears to him.

In his love of music and passionate sense of the value of silence, Beckett is again close to Maeterlinck. In his study of Proust he endorsed the view of the Proustian narrator, for whom music was 'the ideal and immaterial statement' of a unique beauty, in a memorable summary: the 'red phrase' which haunts the novel, appearing 'like a Mantegna archangel clothed in scarlet', proclaimed, said Beckett, an 'invisible reality that damns the life of the body on earth as a pensum'. For Beckett too music is a means of aiming at that 'invisible reality'. To the music of Beethoven's 'Ghost Trio' the character in that play senses the approach of distant and seemingly longed-for presences and we too seem to move nearer to revelation of the secret life behind the hidden face. From the start the plays attracted composers. *Krapp's Last Tape* (1959) was rapidly turned into an opera by Mihalovici (produced in 1961)—a new kind of opera, for the conventional form was anathema to Beckett as to the symbolists before him (a 'hideous corruption of this most immaterial of all the arts', he says in *Proust*).[6] His own miniature radio opera, *Words and Music* (1964), for which music was written first by John Beckett and then by Humphrey Searle,[7] dramatises the 'corruption' of opera and leads into a final harmony of a most Maeterlinckian kind, for Words and Music, in pure concert at last, end by celebrating the virtue of silence:

> Then down a little way
> Through the trash
> Towards where
> All dark no begging
> No giving no words
> No sense no need
> Through the scum
> Down a little way
> To whence one glimpse
> Of that wellhead.

[6] For all these quotations see *Proust and Three Dialogues*, pp. 92–3.
[7] For the production recorded by the University of London Audio Visual Centre in 1975, with Patrick Magee as Words; produced by Katharine Worth and directed by David Clark.

Here Words needs Music to help him out of his sterile fluency, but words also of course create their own music on Beckett's stage. The musical phrasing of his dialogue, with its changes of rhythm, long pauses and silences, can produce hypnotic, ritualistic effects strikingly like the murmurings of the blind characters in *The Sightless*:

ESTRAGON   All the dead voices.
VLADIMIR   They make a noise like wings.
ESTRAGON   Like leaves.
VLADIMIR   Like sand.
ESTRAGON   Like leaves.
                    Silence . . .

In these incantations the dream deepens, we go further into the nebulous region where it is hard to distinguish between the dead and the living. That passage is highly finished, performed with conscious musicality, but of course Beckett excels also in suggesting stumbling, hesitating words, coming mysteriously, not expected or planned. It would be misleading to talk of 'inarticulacies' where his witty people are concerned, but although they are so good at finding just the right word, Beckett manages to get them into Maeterlinckian positions all the same, through their bad memories, their inconsistencies, their difficulty, as in *Words and Music*, in finding the right tone, and through the undermining of their words by silent visual contradictions, as in the most famous of all, the 'Let's go' of Estragon and Vladimir, never to be followed by their going.

We cannot but think of Beckett as Maeterlinckian in these musical orchestrations of little words, laconic phrases, pauses and silences. So too in his extraordinary ability to give dramatic life to seemingly deadly negatives, go so far into the 'blank' experience of death and birth, make silence and immobility so active, draw from blindness and darkness such strange light.

But of course within the sombre Maeterlinckian outlines there is a drama of quite another sort, richly humorous, dense with human interest, less 'passive', to use Yeats's term. Where Maeterlinck's emphasis was on the fragility and helplessness of human life, Beckett's is on its resourcefulness and resilience—and its humour. Winnie sunk in the earth can still keep her head above ground with her jokes, and death itself is cut down to size in *Endgame* when Hamm and Clov go into their knockabout turns and Clov comes out with laughter-raising lines like 'If I don't kill that rat he'll die'. The echoes we hear now are

Irish, the gallows humour of Synge, O'Casey's gusty farce with its black undertones. As with everything he touches, Beckett takes that humour to its furthest limit: hanging is a harsh conversational joke in *The Playboy of the Western World*: in *Waiting for Godot* it provides the climactic situation when Estragon and Vladimir try to hang themselves from the tree and are let down by the rope:

ESTRAGON   You say we have to come back tomorrow?
VLADIMIR   Yes.
ESTRAGON   Then we can bring a good bit of rope.
VLADIMIR   Yes.
            Silence
ESTRAGON   Didi.
VLADIMIR   Yes.
ESTRAGON   I can't go on like this.
VLADIMIR   That's what you think.

The scene is serious all right—I think especially of the German production Beckett directed at the Royal Court Theatre in 1976 which was heavy with moonlit sadness and the sense of mind at the end of its tether. But in the cool 'That's what you think' we sense an irresistible energy as well, an energy that changes things, anything—even the brute fact of death—by changing the angle of vision, insinuating its wry, droll view which is so friendly to life.

Energy was what Yeats thought missing from Maeterlinck and admired so much in Synge. It was Synge above all, as we saw, who showed Yeats the way out of the more passive symbolist world, and it is Synge who can be sensed in the background of Beckett's drama[8] especially when his characters are engaged in their energetic creation of a dynamic universe out of unpromising dead-looking materials. *The Well of the Saints* was one of the plays that came naturally to Beckett's mind, to drive out the unwanted image of Shaw. No wonder, for the blind, physically unprepossessing Douls are unmistakable prototypes for all those characters with sore feet, kidney trouble, poor sight, failing memory and mobility who dominate Beckett's stage, marvellously opening it up by the force of their imagination.

Again, as ever, Beckett gives us the situation in its most intense and condensed form. Loneliness in Synge's drama is modified by its

---

[8] Critics who have felt this include Alec Reid, 'Comedy in Synge and Beckett', *Yeats Studies*, 2 (1972); J. Knowlson, 'Beckett and John Millington Synge', *Gambit*, 28 (1976).

setting in a real world. On Beckett's stage the isolation is complete; ordinary life is always outside, somewhere else; the Pyrenees might be there, but all that is uncertain, only what is inside is known: the boy of *Endgame* will have to get into Hamm's room where the pattern of the story is being fabricated, to have a chance of life. Beckett's is the modernist version of Synge's lonely fantasising, though his instrument is essentially the same, the speaking voice, uttering a stream of non-stop sound. It is a voice with many similar notes, telling tales, mixing memory and fiction, wheedling, lyricising, mimicking, creating roles, sometimes forcing language into unnatural shapes, as Mr Rooney in *All that Fall* (1957) tells Maddy she does:

MR ROONEY   Do you know, Maddy, sometimes one would think you were struggling with a dead language.

MRS ROONEY   Yes indeed, Dan, I know full well what you mean, I often have that feeling, it is unspeakably excruciating.

MR ROONEY   I confess I have it sometimes myself, when I happen to overhear what I am saying.

MRS ROONEY   Well, you know, it will be dead in time, just like our own poor dear Gaelic, there is that to be said.

This is a joke that would have appealed to Synge (with his sardonic views on the life expectancy of Gaelic) and looks like a sly aside to his memory.

It was inevitable that Beckett should be the first major artist to recognise the possibilities of radio. He exploits to the full the listener's dependence on the voice to shape the dramatic illusion through the sounds it makes and the stories it tells. We hear Henry in *Embers* (1959) 'producing' himself, weaving in and out of fiction and fact (as they might seem) until we can no longer distinguish one from the other.[9] Does the doctor called Holloway who appears in the 'story' with his black bag and his reluctance to get too involved with his patient belong to life or the invented world? We cannot tell; all we know is the importance of the incident to the narrator; he cannot get it out of his mind; perhaps has to disguise it in fictional form before he

[9] In the stereo version recorded by the University of London Audio Visual Centre in 1975 we attempted to indicate the movement of mind by locating passages in different 'zones' of sound. Patrick Magee was Henry in this recording and Elvi Hale was Ada; it was produced by Katharine Worth and directed by David Clark.

can tolerate the tale of the two old men by the dying embers and somehow do what he feels he has to do, relate it to the other story of his father, whose spirit haunts the entire piece. Nothing exists until Henry has found words or sounds for it: we are never sure how real his wife, Ada, is, for she makes no sound as she sits down by him on the beach, and she can never get the full intonations of life into her voice; it remains throughout rather flat and remote. Similarly the child, Addie, is made unreal by the separation of her voice; she is always heard at a distance in a kind of sound inset.

In his use of sound effects in the radio plays, Beckett's affinity with another of his Irish predecessors, O'Casey, becomes very apparent. The most overtly Irish of his plays, *All that Fall*, contains a sound sequence thoroughly in the style of the scene in *Purple Dust* when the Englishmen's sham pastoral is mocked by a cacophony of farmyard sounds—cocks crowing, dogs barking, cattle lowing and so on. A similar set of rural sounds comes up on cue in *All that Fall*, though here, characteristically, it is all much more pointed and self-conscious. Mrs Rooney pauses to give the sound effects man more time:

> The wind—(*brief wind*)—scarcely stirs the leaves and the birds— (*brief chirp*)—are tired singing. The cows—(*brief moo*)—and sheep —(*brief baa*)—ruminate in silence. The dogs—(*brief bark*) are hushed and the hens—(*brief cackle*)—sprawl torpid in the dust. We are alone. There is no one to ask.
> *Silence*

Sounds natural are not really so, we are reminded. The spurt of effort lapses till, with another effort, Mr Rooney, 'clearing his throat, narrative tone', launches us on a new sequence, protecting the pair of them from silence, creating a world to live in.

Rather sadly, O'Casey never came to know Beckett properly and was antagonistic to what he took to be his pessimism:

> Beckett? I have nothing to do with Beckett. He isn't in me; nor am I in him. I am not waiting for Godot to bring me life; I am out after life myself, even at the age I've reached.[10]

Splendidly characteristic lines, but he was wrong all the same, for he is certainly in Beckett even if he thought Beckett wasn't in him. Beckett himself is in no doubt about this, to judge from his inclusion of *Juno*

[10] 'Not Waiting for Godot', in *Encore: A Quarterly Review for Students of the Theatre* (Easter 1956), reprinted in *Blasts and Benedictions*, p. 51.

and the Paycock in the rare tribute to which I referred earlier. He showed his sympathy with O'Casey in a practical way by withdrawing his mime plays from the Dublin Festival of 1958 when *The Drums of Father Ned* was banned from performance there. And he reveals his understanding and feeling for O'Casey's comedy in the review he wrote in 1934 of the two one-act farces, *The End of the Beginning* and *A Pound on Demand*. O'Casey is, says Beckett, a 'master of knockabout' who 'discerns the principle of disintegration in even the most complacent solidities and activates it to their explosion': so that we end with 'the triumph of the principle of knockabout in situation, in all its elements and on all its planes, from the furniture to the higher centres'.[11]

As this suggests, Beckett and O'Casey share a very similar sense of fun. Beckett is equally fascinated by the special relationship with intractable matter enjoyed by clowns, loves the release of knockabout and often draws from the same music-hall and musical comedy repertoire. Articles of clothing—boots and hats in *Godot*, handbag and umbrella in *Happy Days*—figure on his stage with the same absurd seriousness as on O'Casey's. Like the top hat in *Cock-a-Doodle Dandy*, which leads the characters such a dance, the hats in *Godot* acquire a life of their own; are solemnly passed round, knocked off, jumped on. Beckett's stage abounds with grotesquely afflicted pseudo-couples who are blood brothers to O'Casey's Barrys and Darrys and limping Chair Attendants, and sometimes indeed, seem to speak for all of them, as in the darkly droll scene when Clov pushes Nagg back into his bin. 'Sit on him!', says Hamm:

CLOV   I can't sit;
HAMM   True. And I can't stand.
CLOV   So it is.
HAMM   Every man his speciality.

And yet, despite all these likenesses, Beckett's characters are a long way from the largely unselfconscious dramatising of Synge's and O'Casey's. For always, in the very act of building up a drama, Hamm, Winnie and the rest are scrutinising it, puzzling about its source, registering the bewilderment, amusement or torment they undergo in the process of playmaking. Much of the interest in *Cascando* (1964) is centred on the vain attempts the Opener makes to keep remote from the story it is his function to open; he ends by being drawn in but never

[11] 'The Essential and the Incidental', *The Bookman*, 86 (1934), p. 111.

ceases to be perplexed by the power he has to open music as well as words—'Is that mine too?'. The whole of *Words and Music* is a struggle between Words and Music to express themselves and Croak to get them to express him. In *Embers* the focus is always on the mysterious relationship between the willed and unwilled sounds, between those that stay in place and those that get out of hand, like Addie's uncontrollable paroxysms or the sucking sound of the sea.

In his sardonic self-consciousness, as in so many other ways, Beckett is supremely Yeats's heir. His is above all a drama of 'moments' ('an action . . . taken out of all other actions') or 'briefs', to use his own word. Beckett indeed has done more than anyone to acclimatise the theatre to the idea of such a drama. At a time when audiences were still geared to the three or even four act play, he gave them the two acts of *Waiting for Godot* followed by one act *Endgame* (cut down from the two of an early draft) and by the many ruthlessly concentrated short plays, where, if there is a division, it is only a means to intensification, as in *Happy Days* and *Play*. The plays have become increasingly condensed and so intense that it seemed entirely natural for *Not I* to be performed on its own at the Royal Court in 1975, though it lasted less than half an hour. Perhaps audiences are still resistant to the idea of paying for so short an evening, but Beckett must certainly have made them more ready to do so, and in that way have created an atmosphere helpful to all experimental drama; the fringe theatre has taken full advantage of the new taste. There is more hope for Yeats's dance plays too if the professional theatre no longer regards a programme of one-acters as a recipe for disaster. What we should like to see, indeed, would be some mixed bills of Beckett and Yeats; *Purgatory* and *Play*, for instance go together as naturally as Estragon and Vladimir or the Blind and the Lame Beggars.

Beckett's are ghost plays too in Yeats's sense of a ghost as a clinging presence, an emanation from some obscure region of consciousness or a mysterious continuation of mind outside the body: 'An earthbound shell, fading and whimpering in the places it loved'. 'Fading' and 'whimpering' are words that might have been chosen with *Play* in mind, and its urn-dwellers who fade in and out as the light moves over them, whimpering hysterically: '. . . Is anyone listening to me? Is anyone looking at me? Is anyone bothering about me at all?' The merciless interrogator, the spotlight, has a Yeatsian ancestry in *Purgatory*, known to be one of Beckett's favourite plays. Like the light at the window of Yeats's ghostly house it is a palpable force in the action, stirring the trapped characters into an obsessive replay of their past drama, a 'dreaming back', in the Yeatsian phrase it is so natural to use of Beckett's characters also. The mood of *Play* is very different, of course. The production at the Royal Court in 1976 brought out with special vivacity its droll comedy; the first time round was extraordinarily funny. Repeated, the self-same lines and comic noises like the hiccough, took on new seriousness, as they had to—it was a remarkable change of mood—but through it all, the sense of witty control remained: a great part of the pleasure was just this delicate balance between the impression of obsessed unawareness and humorous self-consciousness. In later plays the balance has changed a little. The Old Man in *That Time* (1976) is totally caught up in his memories, unable to joke much, though the tone of his reflections, as always, is lightened with humour. In *Footfalls* the 'dreaming back' is a truly ghostly process, nearer still to *Purgatory*, for it makes such a powerful impression of the invisible world engulfing the visible, we must wonder at times if there is any corporal life in it at all. And in the television plays, *Ghost Trio* and . . . *but the clouds*, for the first time there are ghostly manifestations; the face of a child, enigmatically smiling in the shadowy corridor of *Ghost Trio*: a woman's face materialising in . . . *but the clouds*, her mouth forming words, though the narrator's voice has to supply the sounds. 'Shades', the sub-title of the plays, was in every way the right one.

In all these plays of shades and 'presences', lighting is used with exquisite precision to undermine our confidence in the evidence of our senses. At the end of an evening that began with *Play* and *That Time*, the intense darkness of the stage in *Footfalls*, with the narrow dimly lit strip in the foreground was difficult to keep in steady focus. Was that glimmering outline up in the darkness, the ghostly face of the mother, a 'semblance' passing like a moon through rack, or the moon itself? The girl pacing the strip always wheeling on the seventh step, how real is she? Though so spectral looking, in her ritualistic pacing, her trailing gown of 'pale grey tatters', she is present for us as the mother to whom she calls is not. We hear the mother only as a voice, in a dialogue with the dead which suggests a sad replay of a traumatic experience, the long illness, the laborious nursing:

M   Would you like me to inject you again?
V   Yes, but it is too soon.
   . . .

M . . . Sponge you down? (*Pause*) Moisten your poor lips? (*Pause*)
   Pray with you? (*Pause*) For you? (*Pause*)
V Yes, but it is too soon.

A whole history encapsulated here, preliminary to the movement into a stranger dimension when the mother's voice takes over the stage and she becomes our viewpoint on the daughter, telling us how as a young girl she already had the need to walk: 'I must hear the feet, however faint they fall'. The mother's voice suggests that somehow in her silence, her ritualistic pacing, May is trying to accomplish something, tell how it was, how 'it all' was. And this is what happens in the final sequence, brought in as each is by a chime whose echoes slowly die away, like the footfalls and the light (Beckett originally suggested a gong for this musical effect, which would have accentuated still further the closeness to the use of music, light and silence in Yeats's dance plays).[12]

The final sequence is an event in some other dimension, as Billie Whitelaw, who created the part, suggested in the long-drawn-out emphasis she gave to the word, 'sequel'. 'A little later', she says, 'when she was quite forgotten'—then corrects herself, 'as though she had never been'—'she' began to walk, at nightfall. Who is that 'she', the image of the mother (that painful memory) or, as the visual pattern strongly hints, the daughter herself, so like the semblance she describes, in her pale grey tatters? To be there is difficult; she seems to be seeking ways to project herself and the pain she is supporting. It is a comical and unsettling moment when this remote being confronts the audience directly, forcing them to collaborate as readers of fiction who will be able to help on the process by which characters acquire life. So the story is re-cast, with May as narrator and the shadowy mother given a presence as Mrs Winter going to evensong with her daughter, Amy. That story too ends with the daughter's sense of not being fully there: 'I saw nothing, heard nothing, of any kind. I was not there'. She has never been anywhere but where we see her, pacing her strip, calling out to her mother and 'creating' her by speaking in her person:

Will you never have done . . . revolving it all? (*Pause*) It? (*Pause*)
It all. (*Pause*) In your poor mind. (*Pause*) It all. (*Pause*) It all.

The voices are inextricably intertwined at this point, all the suffering

[12] A gong was one of the instruments Yeats used in the dance plays and also to announce curtain rise at the Abbey Theatre.

of those two and of the unnamed person[13] referred to in the recurring phrase 'his poor arm' is concentrated in that pacing figure revolving it all in a long 'shudder of the mind'.

Moments of intense life, transcendent moments of insight and realisation, Beckett arrives at these by a process which is completely of the stage, stagey. Through an attack on our senses, the play of light and dark, the strangeness of his scenic arrangements, he compels us to concentrate on fine shades like those traced in *Footfalls*, moving us all the time to subtler modes of perception, a more imaginative view of things. The experience is all the more impressive because the characters through whom we receive it are drawn from such ordinary environments, have so much that is prosaic about them, seem at first view such a world away from the romantic dreamers and dancers of Yeats. His ability to sustain this piquant tension between the colloquial and the poetic and mysterious is obviously a chief reason for Beckett's appeal to audiences of all kinds.

Yet for all their greater worldliness, his characters have the same capacity as Yeats's for romantic transformations. Confined as they are within the so-narrow limits of their stage or screen set, with so few and humdrum properties to call on, they nevertheless force whatever medium they are in to express their limitless longings. It is no accident that a line from *At the Hawk's Well* is quoted in that play which is the testament of the ordinary, *Happy Days*. For Winnie is an indefatigable romancer; nothing can deter her; even sunk up to her neck in earth, she can summon up her will to go 'romancing through a romping lifetime', calling upon the spirit of Yeats to assist her:

> That is what I find so wonderful, a part remains, of one's classics, to help one through the day. (*Pause*) Oh yes, many mercies, many mercies. (*Pause*) And now? (*Pause*) And now, Willie? (*Long pause*) I call to the eye of the mind. . .

What does she call to the eye of the mind? Something very different from the supernatural being invoked by Yeats's musicians. It is a commonplace pair she sees, Mr and Mrs Shower or Cooker, passing by and making coarse comments on her plight. '. . . Getting on . . . in life. . . Seen worse shoulders', he says, 'in my time'. That is a hard nugget for the romantic imagination to work on, but Winnie can manage it; it is the measure of her seriousness as a dreamer that she

[13] The context suggests Christ and at one stage in Beckett's drafts 'his' was written 'His'.

faces so many unpalatable facts, builds up her dream without evasions, using what she is provided with, her small set of properties—the bag with its seemingly inexhaustible contents, the parasol, the revolver—and coping with stage aids she would rather do without, like the hard bright light which refuses her any concealment. With what she can muster up within the narrow space she is confined to and the minimal help she gets from Willie with the dialogue, she constructs a play that is flexible, lively, full of light and shade, comedy and romantic feeling.

Her resilience is the most striking feature of the whole play, it seems to me. When the parasol catches fire and leaves her, she knows she will be able to get it back tomorrow; she likes to have the revolver within reach, but we should never expect her to use it. By the second act, indeed, she no longer could, having lost the use of her arms, but though she is more run down, even melancholy, at that stage of attrition, the revolver remains an unused thought. Admittedly when Willie makes his huge effort to crawl up her mound at the end, he is, as has often been observed, moving towards the revolver as well as to her; the stage direction 'dressed to kill' is an equivocal joke, reminding us perhaps that Willie might be more tempted to end it all. But as long as Winnie is bossing, goading and charming him, we don't really expect that to happen. With those few words he gives her from time to time, with her memories, her store of poetry, she keeps alive the romance of their love, succeeding even so far gone as they both are—such a 'sight'—in bringing him back to her as he was—almost—on their wedding day. So her evocations work and, like the great evocation of *At the Hawk's Well*, lead into a moment of transcendence when at last, enraptured by Willie's barely audible endearment 'Win', she is able to sing her song, the song we have been waiting all the play to hear, to the tune of that potent waltz rhythm from *The Merry Widow:*

> Though I say not
> What I may not
> Let you hear,
> Yet the swaying
> Dance is saying,
> Love me dear!

Absurd, pathetic, in a way mechanical, irritating—as Beckett hints in his direction, a 'musical-box tune'—and yet in that situation, what a wonder. From the woman lodged up to the neck in earth comes the potent sound of the waltz rhythm and all its associations of youthful vitality, gaiety and ardour. This most static of plays is also, paradoxically, almost a dance play; through the rhythm, music, the words of a song we arrive, in Yeatsian mode, at a revelation of a profound deep of the mind.

Beckett's 'interior' has many Yeatsian features. *Waiting for Godot* especially recalls *At the Hawk's Well,* one of Beckett's favourite plays. The ironic repetition of the 'luck' motif in Yeats's play is echoed in the bizarre figure who bears the name Lucky in Beckett's and who performs the dance of the Net, Hard Stool or Scapegoat's Agony, that grim parody of man's freedom of movement. 'The wind in the reeds' is one of the sounds Estragon and Vladimir hear (an affectionate Yeatsian allusion here)[14] and above all there is the situation of waiting by the bare tree for the events that will always elude them—both Vladimir who gets as far as speaking with Godot's messenger and Estragon who always sleeps when he appears, like the Old Man mesmerised by the Hawk Woman's unmoistened eye.

In other plays equally strong echoes occur. Hamm and Clov too wait for an end which we cannot imagine, and Hamm has in full measure the faculty Yeats's characters so often possess for knowing what he has to do without knowing why. He shares with the Old Man at the well a sense of being at a distance from what is happening to him; indeed he could be speaking for that character who so regularly misses the water of life when he muses to Clov, 'Absent, always. It all happened without me. I don't know what's happened. (*Pause*) Do you know what's happened?'. Certain sounds from Yeats's stage come up again on Beckett's. There is the sea—an ubiquitous sucking sound in all the pauses of *Embers*—and the beat of horse hooves in the same play, summoned up by Henry as an element in Addie's story, but also as a monstrous beast, like Yeats's unicorn: 'A ten-ton mammoth back from the dead, shoe it with steel and have it tramp the world down!'. The feverish pulse in the brain suggested by the hoof-beats in *Purgatory* comes up in a new form in the obsessive drip complained of by Hamm, who has been hearing it in his head 'ever since the fontanelles', and by Henry who makes it real for us too as a weird sound effect, a violent drip and then silence.

That long-standing concern of Yeats to achieve a right relationship

[14] Yeats's collection of early poems, *The Wind among the Reeds*, was published in 1899. Another poem, 'The Tower', which ends 'Among the deepening shades' provides the title and some quotation for . . . *but the clouds* . . .

between words and music is close to Beckett's heart too. His music drama derives from Yeats, as he seems to hint in the name *Words and Music*, which is so close to the title Yeats gave his collection of late poems, *Words for Music Perhaps*. Beckett's is also a drama of masks. He does not put his characters into physical masks; that would separate them too sharply, we might guess, from the context of ordinary life, which he always wants in. But they often have a mask-like look, with faces that are shaded or eroded. The faces in *Play* are 'so lost to age and aspect as to seem almost part of urns'; the women in *Come and Go* (1967) wear hats that almost conceal their faces, so again they are lost to age and aspect: a clown's shock of hair covers the face in *Ghost Trio* till the startling moment when it is revealed in the mirror and again at the end, looking out with a smile which seems to reflect the mysterious smile of the child in the corridor. And in several plays, close-up techniques create a startling mask-like impression. The camera slowly moves in to leave the face of Joe at the end of *Eh Joe* (1967) a tragic clown's mask with a gash of mouth and pits of eyes; the steady light on the mouth in *Not I* and the old man's face in *That Time* throw up the isolated features into high relief that takes them away from the appearance of ordinary humanity.

Above all Beckett is close to Yeats in his achievement of a remarkable 'double' effect: the self-conscious and unconscious elements in his drama are kept in a delicate state of equilibrium so that the incessant activity of the conscious, scrutinising, probing self leaves untouched the integrity of the spontaneous, intuitive, irrational self. Along with this goes the striking doubleness which makes the drama seem at once real and dream-like, the reflection of an outer and an inner world, an engagement of recognisable personalities and at the same time something more impersonal, as if these pseudo-couples were interlocking elements of a complex psychic organisation. As in Yeats's world, everything depends on the pull between opposites—life drifting between a fool and a blind man to its end—and on the ability of the opposites to complement one another; Clov climbing ladders and looking out of windows on behalf of blind Hamm, Hamm keeping him going with endless orders. The characters tend to fall into groupings like Yeats's blind and lame beggars, though Beckett's inseparable pairs characteristically have names. They may be forgetful or unsure of them—Vladimir and Estragon are happier using the homely nicknames Didi and Gogo, May turns into Amy—but anonymity is reserved for the dumb characters or used to make some point about temperament. The characters in *Play*, for instance, are known only as M, W1 and W2, presumably because they are so far from having a full sense of each other as persons; they have chosen to exist in this stereotype world. And even here names creep in with the minor characters like Erskine the butler. In the late plays which move so far towards ghostly insubstantiality, the characters are still rooted to the earth by their names except when they have no voices of their own, like the marionette figures in *Ghost Trio* and . . . *but the clouds*.

I have been stressing likenesses and have shown, I hope, that they are indeed real. Beckett's affinity with Yeats, with Synge and O'Casey and—although there is no direct influence here—with Maeterlinck, stands out from the page and asserts itself in production. To feel the closeness of these relationships we need only imagine a programme made up, say, of *Interior*, *At the Hawk's Well* and *Endgame*, or *Purgatory* and *Play*, *Purple Dust* and *All that Fall* or *The Sightless*, *The Well of the Saints* and *Waiting for Godot*. But of course Beckett works within this 'modern tradition' as a great original, and as I suggested in my introduction it is he who has launched the Irish drama in Europe into the centre of world theatre. There are many reasons for his fuller appeal—fuller, at least, than any Maeterlinck or Yeats has yet commanded—and I have been trying to keep these in mind throughout the comparison.

His humour is entirely his own and a great source of his universal appeal. Not separate from that, but crucially bound up with it is the sense of spiritual achievement coming out of the strange and painful experiences his characters endure. Always there is a movement, however faint or obscure, towards a closer truth, a clearer perspective, and it is this, I feel sure, that has given him his special position in the modern movement. For he goes as far as anyone and further than most, into a modern universe which is terribly empty and accidental looking, without losing the sense that man's aspiration to truth is serious; it is not what it might sometimes seem (and often seems to his characters) simply one of nature's crueller jokes.

Especially from *Krapp's Last Tape* onwards, the emphasis is on characters under fearful pressure to see it all, say it all. 'It all' is the dominant phrase of *Footfalls*. From the tissue of his memories Krapp selects, with effort and melancholy, one moment of value, the moment with the girl in the boat, which makes clear to him that his life was worth having and that he would, despite all, despite even his own scepticism, be glad to live it all again:

Be again on Croghan on a Sunday morning, in the haze, with the bitch, stop and listen to the bells (*Pause*) And so on. (*Pause*) Be again, be again. (*Pause*) All that old misery. (*Pause*) Once wasn't enough for you. (*Pause*) Lie down across her.

It is melancholy here because knowledge comes so long after the experience. In *Happy Days* on the other hand Winnie is seen from the start facing the truth, suffering under the relentless stage light that allows no concealment, but surviving it; she sees the 'sight' she and Willie have become, is sensitive to the absurdity of her romantic dreams, but is still able to sustain them and so lift up both herself and Willie from the negations and passivity that threaten them continually. Her achievement is more obvious: elsewhere we often have to be given help in strange ways to allow us to see the minute movements of mind towards better condition. The characters in *Play*, for instance, must strike us the first time round as unlikely to do what they feel is asked of them 'tell the truth—at last'. First we hear the gabbled drama of their triangular affair; it is all comedy then, and they are fit subjects for mocking treatment, being so self-centred, hard and shallow. Then comes the 'change' when they have been broken down, become aware of the pressure on them from the 'invisible inquisitor' to see the story differently; now they can recognise the others' point of view, feel twinges of pity for them, entertain visions of a more civilised relationship. At this point the whole process is repeated, word for word, and of course this makes a strong impression of circularity; for some critics it suggests that they are trapped in the circle, the hell of other people, which Sartre laid out in *Huis Clos*. But it does not have to be taken in this way. Certainly the repetition is alarming and throws doubt on their capacity to proceed beyond the stage of development they have reached, when they are cut off for the second time at exactly the same place. We know, however, that they must need time, for we ourselves have needed it to grasp the change that has been made so far. It is certain that we do not appreciate it the first time round because no doubt we are still laughing then. It is only the second time that we are able to see it differently, find moving and serious what was at first more like a cruel joke; we too have become more refined in our perception. That is not a depressing but an exhilarating experience, and though we may remain doubtful about the fate of the characters, the change we have experienced is a promise.

Always something positive comes out of the negative. The pressures are terrible: those inquisitory rays of light 'ferreting around'; the sense of solitariness. Mouth's account of her helpless sense of disintegration in *Not I* is almost unbearably real; by being made to concentrate so intensively on that one illuminated feature, the mouth, we are drawn into the symptoms she describes, the buzzing in the head, the 'whole body like gone', the brain begging the mouth to stop talking. Yet even in this most desperate gabble the drive to positive values persists. She knows that something is asked of her, 'something she had to tell . . . could that be it? . . . something that would tell . . . how it was . . . how she . . . what? . . . had been? . . .'. We are not deceived by her depreciation of her own drive to truth—'. . . some flaw in her make-up . . . incapable of deceit . . .'—nor by her dour comment on the lack of love in her life—'spared that'. Throughout her anguished evocation of her life we are aware that truth and love are the dominant values, felt by her to be there somehow if only she could grasp them. She is right, for she has an Auditor who is compassionate though helpless. His gestures, which express both the pity and the helplessness, become more muted by the end; ambiguity here, but it is open to us to feel that she may be approaching the moment of release when she no longer, in Beckett's phrase, vehemently refuses 'to relinquish third person'. Her last shriek of 'what . . . who? . . . no! . . . she! . . . SHE' does indicate a point of high tension (capitals are used for the first time for the final SHE); beyond this it may be breakdown or it may be the beginning of a new integration. In accepting the truth as her own, she may move closer also to the love that haunts her and that comes up in the kindly image of the April morning in a field with which the play ends: '. . . God is love . . . tender mercies . . . new every morning . . . back on the field . . . April morning . . . face in the grass . . . nothing but the larks . . . pick it up'.

These late plays bring us very close to the 'door', in Yeatsian phrase. Life is almost extinguished; the characters in *Not I*, *That Time* and *Footfalls* and in the still more abstract *Ghost Trio* and . . . *but the clouds* are attenuated and solitary beyond anything even in Beckett's own drama; they are *in extremis*. Yet in each play there is a strong sense of something forming, flowering into shape, something never perceived till now or only just becoming attainable. Although Mouth is a long way from her release, still it is with the healing vision of the April field that the play ends. In *That Time* we are a stage further on: the old white face with its long, flaring white hair that floats in the darkness of the stage has to struggle to breathe; it is the sound of his panting that we hear at each pause. But he does not have to struggle like Mouth to tell his story: he is a listener, not a teller; what he hears is his own life as a tale brought to him by his own voice; it comes at him from three separate quarters of the stage, with an extraordinary effect of belonging to him and yet having cut free. There is a suggestion of fragmentation here; there must be, says Beckett, a perceptible shift in the source of the voice. Physically we feel this as our ear follows the voice from one quarter to another and we detect it in the content too at the beginning, for each location has its own special theme; in one there is a focus on the child—'. . . was the ruin still there where none ever came where you hid as a child . . .'—in the other two on the lovers sitting in cornfields and on the old man slipping into galleries and libraries to get out of the rain. But the voice is one voice, and as the play continues it comes to seem less broken up than circular; it weaves round the white face a melodious chain of sound, the pattern he has created in his life. It is in some ways a melancholy pattern, but only in the way of life's ordinary changes, the trams disappearing, the railway colonnade crumbling away, ways back into the past closing up—'was your mother ah for God's sake all gone long ago all dust the lot you the last huddled up on the slab in the old green greatcoat with your arms round you whose else . . .'. But it is bound together by personality, above all by humour and by the continual creative activity of measuring and weighing the words to bring up all those 'times' good and bad and restore their life. A continuity appears; from the solitary child peopling the stone where it sits with imaginary playmates to the old man 'at the big round table with a bevy of old ones poring on the page and not a sound'. Everything is seen with such precision: there is an overwhelming impression of complete truthfulness, which gives great force to the moments of ecstasy that occur from time to time; the lovers on the stone in the sun—'in a daze no sound not a word'—and the mysterious moment in the picture gallery when a face appears reflected in the glass of a romantic picture —'. . . some young prince or princess of the blood black with age . . .'. And finally, the mystic moment of revelation in the library when the solid world crumbles, '. . . when you opened your eyes from floor to ceiling nothing only dust and not a sound . . .'. But in the silence something is said which he is listening to as the play ends; it is perhaps his quietus: 'come and gone was that it something like that come and gone come and gone no one come and gone in no time gone in no time'.

Like the feathery shape Cuchulain sees waiting for him after his death, the pattern of sound in *That Time* seems in the end a triumphant 'weaving' of a life, an achievement. Though memory contains so much that is painful, confused, anxious, yet the relentless flood of time has been subdued, turned into 'that time', the jewels of memory. And in *Footfalls* too from the tenuous being of daughter and mother, something immensely s'rong survives. The dim figure, continually fading and renewing, imprisoned in the strip where she walks like a ghost, nevertheless sustains 'it all', the mother and her suffering and all that is implied in the phrase 'his poor arm'. The creature who feels herself 'not there', who changes her name and puts herself in a new story as if to make herself more real, ends by drawing us with her into a benediction, creating an extraordinary moment of communion in the theatre.

The status Beckett has achieved in the modern theatre is not hard to account for. He has looked so far into the darkness of the interior by the light of his humorous, quizzical mind, made the stage a place where the most deadly negatives—absence, darkness, death, things which are not—are transformed and transcended. It is especially pleasing to end a study of the Irish drama of Europe with Beckett because he is the guarantee that the story has not ended. He has given it a powerful extension into the future, by direct influence on individual playwrights (Pinter notably, in the English theatre) and more generally by the immense attractiveness of the forms he offers for a modernist exploration of the interior. Beckett's bare stage, where the actors create a play which is also a mystery by playing with the idea of creating a play, has become one of the great modern models; the place to start from, as the productions of a hundred 'fringe' or amateur groups testify. In that way, as well as in its more celebrated germinations, his drama proclaims itself a sturdy seed of the future.

People hunger for 'a ritual expression of the true driving forces of our time', Peter Brook says. Like Yeats and Maeterlinck, Beckett identifies these 'driving forces' in the deep of the mind and by probing into that deep, casts into subtle, modern forms the questions that trouble us about the mystery of life. He does it with a colloquial verve and humour (and a reserve of scepticism) which make him seem a most trustworthy guide in that labyrinthine region. Audiences all over the world have endorsed this view: in the quantity of translations and productions of his work, Beckett is acquiring the status of a modern Shakespeare. I began by saying that the tale of the Irish drama of the interior was a tale of Europe; with Beckett as the theme, it would be more appropriate to say 'the world'. There can be no doubt now that the Irish drama of Europe has a future and it seems fitting to close by repeating those words of Eliot which can be applied to Beckett as to Yeats: 'I do not know where our debt to him as a dramatist ends—and in time it will not end until the drama itself ends'.

Note on Editions

Except where otherwise indicated, the following editions have been used for quotation from the main authors discussed:

Beckett, S. *Waiting for Godot*, 1965
Endgame, 1964
All That Fall, 1957
Krapp's Last Tape and *Embers*, 1965
Happy Days, 1966
Play, Words and Music and *Cascando*, 1968
Not I, 1973
That Time and *Footfalls*, 1976
Ends and Odds (*Ghost Trio* and . . . *but the clouds*), 1977

Maeterlinck, M.
The standard French text at the time of the English translations was:
Théâtre, 4 vols, Brussels, 1891–1910
As I discuss the plays primarily in relation to the English and Irish theatre, I have quoted from English translations which are now out of print, though usually obtainable from libraries, viz.:
The Intruder, 1892
Pelleas and Melisanda (sic), and *The Sightless*, n.d.
Three Plays (*Alladine and Palomides, Interior* and *The Death of Tintagiles*), 1911
The Blue Bird, 1911

O'Casey, S. *Collected Plays*, 1963–
The Drums of Father Ned, 1960

Synge, J. M. *Collected Works* (general editor R. Skelton), vols iii and iv, ed. A. Saddlemyer, 1968

Wilde, O. *Collected Works*, 1948

Yeats, W. B. *Collected Plays*, 1952
The Variorum edition of the Plays of W. B. Yeats, ed. R. K. Alspach (New York 1966). Plays not included in *Collected Plays* above, e.g. *Where There is Nothing*.

Quotation is also made from the following other writings of main authors:

Beckett, S. *Proust and Three Dialogues*, 1965
Maeterlinck, M. *The Treasure of the Humble*, 1897
O'Casey, S. *Blasts and Benedictions*, ed. R. Ayling 1967
Autobiographies, 2 vols, 1963

	The Letters of Sean O'Casey 1910–1941, vol. i, ed. D. Krause, 1975
Synge, J. M.	*Collected Works*, vol. ii (Prose), ed. A. Price, 1966
Wilde, O.	*The Letters of Oscar Wilde*, ed. R. Hart-Davis, 1962
	The Artist as Critic: Critical Writings of Oscar Wilde, ed. R. Ellmann, New York 1970
Yeats, W. B.	*Letters*, ed. A. Wade, 1954
	Autobiographies, 1955
	Essays and Introductions, 1961
	Explorations, 1962
	Memoirs, ed. D. Donoghue, 1972
	Uncollected Prose by W. B. Yeats, i (First Reviews and Articles 1886–1896), ed. J. P. Frayne, 1970; ii (Reviews, Articles and Other Miscellaneous Prose 1897–1939), ed. J. P. Frayne and C. Johnson, 1975

Select Book List

Because of the wide scope of this study, I have been obliged to include in this book list only those works which have a special bearing on the subject or which I have had occasion to consult most frequently. Place of publication is London except where otherwise indicated.

Allan, M., *My Life and Dancing*, 1908
Andrieu, J.-M., *Maeterlinck*, Paris, 1962
Ayling, R. (ed.), *Sean O'Casey: Modern Judgements*, 1969
Bablet, D., *Edward Gordon Craig*, 1966 (first published in French, 1962; translated by D. Woodward)
Beerbohm, M., *Around Theatres*, 1953 (first published in 2 vols, 1924)
Bradford, C. B., *W. B. Yeats at Work*, Carbondale, 1965
Bridge, U. (ed.), *W. B. Yeats and T. Sturge Moore: Their Correspondence 1901–1937*, 1953
Bushrui, S. B., *Yeats's Verse-Plays: The Revisions 1900–1910*, 1965
Clark, M., *Maurice Maeterlinck*, 1915
Clarke, A., *The Celtic Twilight and the Nineties*, Dublin, 1969
Cowasjee, S., *Sean O'Casey: the Man behind the Plays*, 1963
Crawford, V. M. M., *Studies in Foreign Literature*, 1899
Craig, E. G., *On the Art of the Theatre*, 1911
—, *Index to the Story of my Days*, 1957
Eliot, T. S., *Selected Essays*, 1932
—, *On Poetry and Poets*, 1957
Ellis-Fermor, U., *The Irish Dramatic Movement*, 1939 (rev. edn 1954)
Ellman, R., *Yeats: the Man and the Masks*, 1948 (rev. edn 1951)
—, *The Identity of Yeats*, 1954
Fay, G., *The Abbey Theatre*, 1958
Fay, W. G. and Carswell, C., *The Fays of the Abbey Theatre*, 1935
Gordon, D. J., *W. B. Yeats: Images of a Poet*, 1961
Gray, T., *Dance Drama*, 1926
Greene, D. H. and Stephens, E. M., *J. M. Synge 1871–1909*, 1959
Grene, N., *Synge: A Critical Study of the Plays*, 1975
Halls, W. D., *Maeterlinck*, 1960
Heppner, S., *'Cockie'*, 1969
Hone, J. M., *W. B. Yeats, 1865–1939*, 1942 (rev. edn 1962)
Jeffares, A. N. and Knowland, A. S., *A Commentary on the Collected Plays of W. B. Yeats*, 1975
Jullian, P., *Dreamers of Decadence*, 1971 (originally published as *Esthètes et Magiciens*, 1969)

Kermode, F., *Romantic Image*, 1957
—, *Modern Essays*, 1971
Knowlson, J. (ed.) *Journal of Beckett Studies*; Winter 1976
—, Catalogue for *Samuel Beckett: an Exhibition held at Reading University Library May to July 1971*, 1971
Krause, D. *Sean O'Casey: the Man and his Work*, 1960
Marshall, N., *The Other Theatre*, 1947
Montague, C. E., *Dramatic Values*, 1941
O'Casey, E., *Sean*, 1971
O'Driscoll, R. and Reynolds, L. (eds.), *Yeats and the Theatre* (Yeats Studies), Toronto, 1975
Roose-Evans, J., *Experimental Theatre*, 1971
Skelton, R., *The Writings of J. M. Synge*, 1971
Skene, R., *The Cuchulain Plays of W. B. Yeats*, 1974
Symons, A., *The Symbolist Movement in Literature*, 1899
     Plays, Acting and Music, 1903
     Studies in Prose and Verse, 1904
     Studies in Seven Arts, 1906
Worth, K. (ed.), *Beckett the Shape Changer*, 1975
Yeats, J. B., *Letters to his Son W. B. Yeats and Others*, 1944

Index